Hands-On Photoshop 4

for Macintosh and Windows

Clay Andres

A Subsidiary of
Henry Holt and Co., Inc.

First Edition—1997

Printed in the United States of America.

Library of Congress Cataloging-in-Publication Data

ISBN 1-55828-538-5

10 9 8 7 6 5 4 3 2 1

MIS:Press books are available at special discounts for bulk purchases for sales promotions, premiums, fund-raising, or educational use. Special editions or book excerpts can also be created to specification.

For details contact: Special Sales Director
                         MIS:Press
                         a subsidiary of Henry Holt and Company, Inc.
                         115 West 18th Street
                         New York, New York 10011

Associate Publisher: *Paul Farrell*

Managing Editor: *Shari Chappell*   **Production Editor:** *Gay Nichols*
Development Editor: *Rebekah Young*   **Technical Editor:** *Jonathan Lipkin*
Copy Edit Manager: *Karen Tongish*   **Copy Editor:** *Gwynne Jackson*

Acknowledgments

I am grateful to many people for their help on this project. The team of people who worked directly on the book with me includes: my editor at MIS:Press, Rebekah Young, patient and supportive; agent, Brian Gill at Studio B, who got the project rolling; technical editor, Jonathan Lipkin, precise and encouraging; my brother, Tom Andres, who supplied many of the photographs and in numerous formats without complaint; and my wife, Katharine Andres, who has the final word.

I'd also like to thank members of the Adobe Photoshop team, Sonya Schaefer, PR coordinator, and Kevin Connor, product manger, for their timely help despite their own demanding product launch schedule.

For the screen shots on nearly every page of the book, I used two different programs: ScreenShot, a shareware utility from the Beale Street Group, and Captivate Select, part of a commercial package of utilities from Mainstay. It turns out to be especially tricky to capture some of Photoshop's cursors in action. Keeping both of these control panels loaded allowed me to get them all. I'd like to thank Stephen Espy at the Beale Street Group and Lance Merker at Mainstay for donating copies of these programs to me.

I've also had the use of a QuickTake 150 digital camera and Color StyleWriter 2500 printer lent to me by Keri Walker at Apple Computer.

Dedication

To my children, Timothy, Guthrie, and Wells, with pride and love.

Contents

SECTION II Painting Tools 43

CHAPTER 3 45

CHAPTER 4 59

INTRODUCTION

What makes Photoshop Photoshop?

How did Photoshop become the undisputed leader of a huge market that barely existed before its introduction? It's not enough that Photoshop is to desktop imaging what PageMaker is to desktop publishing. Being there first doesn't guarantee success. After all, you aren't still using VisiCalc for your spreadsheets.

Perhaps it is Photoshop's unique and powerful feature set that has kept it preeminent. This is pure marketing hype. Photoshop is certainly feature-rich, but there are many programs that do similar things and even go beyond Photoshop's capabilities in some areas.

It doesn't hurt that Photoshop was first and that it is extremely powerful, but I think that Photoshop's popularity is primarily due to its look and feel. Photoshop looks good and makes users feel that anything is possible. You don't even have to be a professional designer or computer expert to feel empowered by using Photoshop.

Photoshop is the most elegantly designed software program available, and even as new features are added, it becomes more elegant. Adobe's designers and engineers have managed to avoid the industry's dread contagion—*featuritis.* Photoshop is not a "kitchen sink" collection of every feature a product manager might wish for. Instead, existing features are refined and strengthened with each new version. New features are integrated into the existing interface, or the interface is subtly redesigned to accommodate them.

This is not to say that Photoshop's array of tools, palettes, and commands isn't somewhat intimidating to the first-time user. Yet Photoshop 4 is no more difficult to use than Photoshop 1.0. In fact, in many ways, it's easier.

You may not become an all-star compositor the first week you have Photoshop, but it's possible to learn some of the basics and do useful work without getting stuck in places you haven't read about, yet. It's possible to feel comfortable with Photoshop right away and then learn about new features as you need to use them.

The capacity to use what you know and learn as you go makes Photoshop a friend to all users, regardless of experience. It's part of the essence of Photoshop.

Photoshop Essence

no surprises here. There are some changes from previous versions worth noting. The Mode menu is now a subitem of the Image menu, and Layer and View menus have been added. The Layer menu includes the powerful new Transform commands, and the View menu has been moved out from under the Windows menu to emphasize new viewing options. There are also many new Filters and other new menu items which will be discussed in greater detail later. Photoshop 4's menu bar appears in Figure 1.2.

File   Edit   Image   Layer   Select   Filter   View   Window

Figure 1.2 Photoshop 4's Menu Bar.

A few of the commands contained in the menus are also available from Photoshop's palettes. This is for convenience and does not change the operation of these particular commands.

In brief, the File and Edit menus are typical of all such program menus.

- The Image menu contains commands that pertain to the entire image, like image size and tonal adjustments.
- The Layers menu allows manipulation of individual image layers and duplicates some of the commands found in the Layers palette.
- The Select menu allows you to manipulate image selections you have made.
- The Filter menu contains all Photoshop and third-party filters.
- The View menu allows you to adjust the image magnification and display rulers and grids.
- The Window menu lets you show/hide all palettes and activate any open image window.

THE TOOLBOX

The toolbox has continually evolved to include new tools and improve the logic of their arrangement. Version 4's Toolbox is divided into selection, painting, editing, and viewing subsections. The function of each tool is discussed in detail in later chapters. There are twenty primary image manipulation tools, plus color and mode selection tools in the Toolbox.

To select a tool:

- Move the pointer over a tool and click the mouse button to select. The tool is highlighted and ready for use.
- Type a shortcut key to select a tool without using the mouse. Shortcut keys are shown in Figure 1.3.

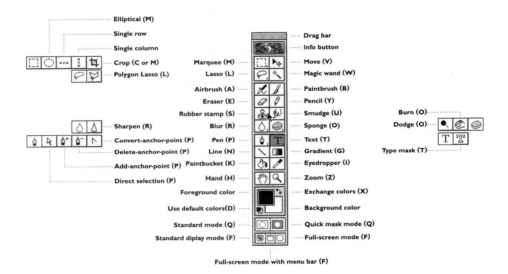

Figure 1.3 The Photoshop Toolbox with tools logically arranged by function. The small triangles on some tools indicate hidden tools. Typing an assigned shortcut key selects a tool, but not all tools have shortcut keys.

Not all tools have shortcut keys assigned. There is no way to change key assignments in Photoshop 4.0.

Small triangles on tool icons indicate the presence of hidden tools. These are groups of related tools or tool options.

To select hidden tools:

- Move the pointer over a tool. Hold down the mouse button and an additional palette of tools pops up. While continuing to hold down the mouse button, move the mouse so that the pointer is over one of the previously hidden tools. When you release the mouse button, the hidden tool is selected and highlighted in the Toolbox.
- Move the pointer over a tool and **Option-Click** (Macintosh) or **Alt-Click** (Windows) to cycle through the tools in that square.
- A few hidden tools have shortcut keys and may be selected without the mouse by typing the assigned key. Hidden tools can also be selected by typing the shortcut key of the primary tool. This cycles through the tools that share a square on the Toolbox.

The Toolbox may be moved around on your desktop by moving the drag bar. Photoshop remembers where you leave the Toolbox or can be set to display it in the default position. The Toolbox cannot be resized, but it can be hidden/closed.

To hide/show the Toolbox:

- From the Window menu, select the **Hide Tools** command. The Toolbox is hidden and the command toggles to the Show Tools command. Select this command to redisplay the Toolbox.
- Click on the **Tab** key once to hide the Toolbox and again to show the Toolbox. Pressing the Tab key hides/shows all palettes, as well.

AN OVERVIEW OF TOOLS

Here is a brief description of the function of each of Photoshop's tools. More detailed descriptions of how to use the tools is included in later chapters.

Selection Tools

The **Rectangular Marquee** makes rectangular selections.

The **Elliptical Marquee** makes elliptical selections.

The **Single Row** and **Column tools** make selections either one pixel wide or tall.

The **Crop tool** is used to trim images.

The **Move tool** is used to move selections, layers, and guides.

The **Lasso tool** makes freeform selections.

The **Polygon Lasso tool** makes freeform, straight-edged selections.

The **Magic Wand tool** makes selections by color.

Painting Tools

The **Airbrush tool** paints like an airbrush.

The **Paintbrush tool** paints brush strokes.

The **Eraser tool** reverts pixels to the background color or to a saved image.

The **Pencil tool** draws hard-edged strokes.

The **Rubber stamp tool** is used for cloning images.

The **Smudge tool** spreads colors from one area into another.

The **Blur tool** decreases contrast in adjacent pixels giving the effect of softening hard edges.

The **Sharpen tool** increases contrast in adjacent pixels giving the effect of hardening soft edges.

The **Sponge tool** increases/decreases color saturation.

The **Burn tool** darkens the image area.

The **Dodge tool** lightens the image area.

Editing Tools

The **Pen tool** draws paths.

The **Direct-Selection tool** selects and edits paths.

The **Add-Anchor-Point tool** adds anchor points to paths.

The **Delete-Anchor-Point tool** deletes anchor points from paths.

The **Convert-Anchor-Point tool** converts between straight and curved path segments.

The **Type tool** is used to enter text.

The **Type Mask tool** enters text as selection borders.

The **Line tool** draws straight lines.

The **Gradient tool** creates graded fills.

The **Paint bucket tool** fills areas with color.

The **Eyedropper tool** samples colors in an image.

Window Tools

The **Hand tool** moves the image within its window.

The **Zoom tool** magnifies and reduces the image display.

Mode Buttons

The **Foreground/Background Buttons** allow you to change, swap, or revert to default color settings.

The **Standard/Quick Mask Mode Buttons** turn the quick mask on and off.

The **Three Screen Mode Buttons** allow swapping among normal display, full-screen image with menu bar, or full-screen image without menu bar.

A Word About Tools and Pointers

In Photoshop, each tool has its own distinctive pointer, so changing the tool changes the pointer. This is helpful. You can't forget what tool you're using, because the pointer identifies it for you. The brush tool's paintbrush and the pencil tool's little pencil become familiar very quickly. On a simple level, this works well. But for detailed work where precision is more important than a pretty icon, it's cumbersome. Each tool has a different "hot spot," the actual point at which pixels are affected by the tool, and it's not always immediately obvious. So Photoshop provides an alternate set of pointers for its most demanding users.

To Use Precise Pointers, select **Preferences** from the File menu. Choose **Display and Cursor preferences** either from the menu or from the dropdown menu in the dialog box. You can set precise cursors for all Painting tools and all other tools by clicking on the radio buttons in the dialog box. This replaces the default iconic cursors with icons that show the brush size or the exact position of the tool on your image.

IMAGE WINDOW

Every time you open a new or existing image, a new image window is opened. Windows automatically open to fit the exact size of the image up to the size of your monitor. Even though only one image can be actively edited, you can open as many images as you wish with Photoshop.

To activate an image window:

- Click on an image window to bring it to the top and make it active.
- From the Windows menu, select an image window from the bottom section of the menu list to make it active. This will work even if an image window is completely buried under other windows.

Each image is contained in an image window that can be moved around within the work area or resized like any window.

To move an image window, move the pointer over the drag bar along the top of the image window. Hold down the mouse button and drag the window to the desired location.

To resize an image window, move the pointer to the lower right corner of the image window. Hold down the mouse button on the resize box (Macintosh) or resize corner (Windows) and drag in or out as desired.

Photoshop displays image-specific information in the lower left corner of the image window, including the view magnification and image file size (see Chapter 2).

PALETTES

Palettes have become popular with many programs, because they give you instant access to commands and information that might otherwise require digging deep through a hierarchy of menus and dialogs. Palettes allow you to execute multiple commands without going to the menu bar multiple times. They also update dynamically, so that you can keep track of the changes you're making and check the state of various options at a glance. Figure 1.4 shows a palette group window.

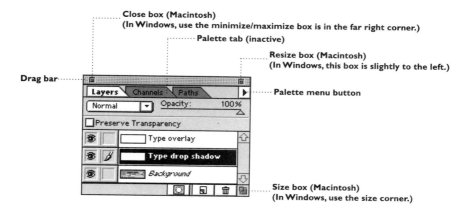

Figure 1.4 A palette group window showing palette tabs and other features common to all palette windows.

Palettes have become ubiquitous, and while they are not unique to Photoshop, Photoshop's palettes are uniquely flexible and are a key feature of its elegance and ease of use.

There are four default palette groups: Navigator/Info/Options, Color/Swatches/Brushes, Actions, and Layers/Channels/Paths (specific functions of the individual palettes are discussed in Section V). The default palette groups have multiple functions (except the Actions palette) as indicated by Palette tabs.

It's a subtle distinction, but what you see in three out of four cases is a palette group containing multiple palettes. Click on the palette tab to activate the palette within the group window. For instance, the Layers/Channels/Paths group contains three palettes (note the that there are three tabs to match). Clicking on a different tab brings that palette to the front. The active tab within a group is shown in white, while inactive ones are gray.

The beauty of this system of groups and palettes is that you can customize palette groups to suit your preferences. Drag a tab outside the group window and Photoshop creates a new window with the palette you've selected. Drag a tab into a group window, and it becomes part of the group. You can rearrange all the palette and group windows this way.

There are several other properties that all palette windows share.

To reposition palette windows on screen, position the pointer in the gray bar at the top of a palette window. Click and hold down the mouse button while you drag, and the palette will follow to a new position. Adobe palettes and windows have *magnetic properties*: if you position a palette close to another window or to the edge of your display, the palette will snap into place. This makes it easy to line up your windows with pleasing regularity.

Photoshop remembers the position of palettes when you quit and opens them in the place you left them. If you like Photoshop's default positions with palettes in a neat column, select **File, Preferences, General** and click on the **Reset Palette Locations to Default** button.

To hide/show palettes:

- The Window menu lists all windows, open and closed, including palette tab headings arranged by window. This should be obvious, but not all programs do it the same way. With the Window menu pulled down, click on a **Hide** command to hide a palette and on a **Show** command to show a palette. The commands toggle between Show and Hide depending on the state of the palettes. Note that only one palette per window can be showing (see Figure 1.5).

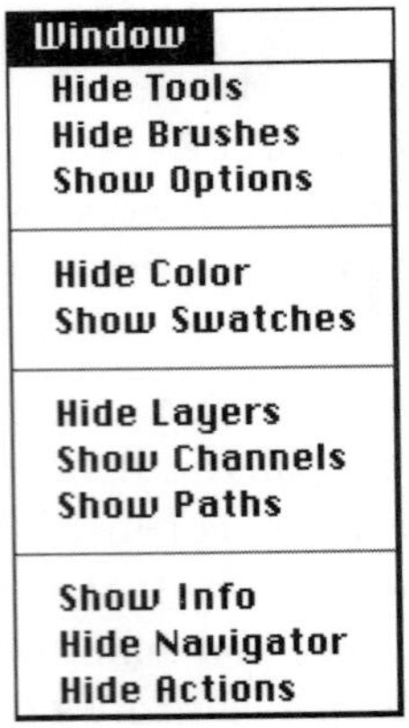

```
┌──────────────────────┐
│ Window               │
├──────────────────────┤
│ Hide Tools           │
│ Hide Brushes         │
│ Show Options         │
│                      │
│ Hide Color           │
│ Show Swatches        │
│                      │
│ Hide Layers          │
│ Show Channels        │
│ Show Paths           │
│                      │
│ Show Info            │
│ Hide Navigator       │
│ Hide Actions         │
└──────────────────────┘
```

Figure 1.5 The Window menu commands toggle between Hide and Show, dependin on the state of the palettes and Toolbox. (Image windows are also listed in this menu, but none are open here.)

- Click on the palette window's close box. This is the click box in the upper-left corner of the window on Macs and in the upper-right corner in Windows. You'll have to use the Window menu, as described above, to reopen the window.

To collapse/expand palettes:

- In the upper-right corner of each palette is a Resize box. (Windows palettes have two boxes in the right corner. Don't use the one with the "x" to collapse and expand.) Position the pointer over the Resize box and click the mouse button. The palette collapses so that only the tabs are showing. This provides additional work space if you need it, while keeping the palettes within easy reach. Click on the Resize box again to expand.

To display palette menus:

- On the upper-right side of every palette window, not quite in the corner, is a right-pointing triangle. Move the pointer over this triangle and hold down the mouse button. A menu pops up from which you can select palette-specific commands (see Figure 1.6). Specific commands will be discussed later in the book.

Figure 1.6 The new Navigator palette showing the palette menu expanded for selection.

To change palette window size:

- Most palettes have a size box (Macintosh) or sizing corner (Windows) in the lower-right corner of the window. (The Color, Options, and Info palettes cannot be resized.) Drag the box or corner to change the window height and width. (The Brushes palette adjusts for height only.) Click on the **Resize** box to revert to the default palette size.

CONTEXT-SENSITIVE MENUS

One feature of Photoshop that is not apparent upon first glance is context-sensitive menus. These provide immediate access to commands that pertain to the position of the pointer in the work area. These are shortcuts and do not add any additional functionality.

For instance, the context-sensitive menu for the color bar in the color palette allows you to change the color gamut displayed. You could also use the palette options menu, select the color bar command, and select a color display option from the dialog box.

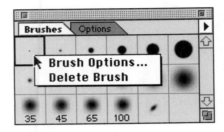

Figure 1.7 The brushes palette contains this context-sensitive menu; control-click (Macintosh) or right-mouse click (Windows).

To use context-sensitive menus, position the pointer over an image, thumbnail, layer, channel, palette, or path name in a palette. Press **Control** and hold down the mouse button (Macintosh) or the right mouse button (Windows). A menu pops up at the pointer. Slide the mouse over a command and release the mouse button to select it.

POP-UP HELP

Photoshop 4 has added a feature that is especially useful for new and casual users of Photoshop: pop-up help cues.

To use pop-up help, move the pointer over any tool or palette window. Wait two seconds and a label pops up indicating the name of the tool (see Figure 1.8).

Figure 1.8 When you let the pointer linger for more than a second over a tool, a label pops up to identify the tool.

Lesson 1:
A First Look At Photoshop

This lesson highlights a few of Photoshop's most commonly used features. If it seems like a tour of a foreign country where you don't speak the language, don't worry. Follow along, and there will be more about each of these features in later chapters.

In the lesson, you will...

- Open an existing photograph
- Crop it
- Adjust the image levels

- Add text
- Rotate a layer
- Merge two layers
- Use the Emboss filter
- Save your new image

1. Launch Photoshop. (You should know how to do this without help.) This starts Photoshop with its default settings and opens the Toolbox and palettes. It does not open an image.

2. Select the **Open** command from the File menu. All sample files are located on the *Hands-On Photoshop 4* CD in the Lessons folder. Open this folder and the Lesson01 folder within it. Select the file called **GEORGEP1.PSD**. This is a scanned photograph of George Seldes, with his cat, Peepers.

3. Select the **Crop** tool from the toolbox. This is one of the hidden tools located under the rectangular marquee tool. Either **Option-Click** (Macintosh) or **Alt-Click** (Windows) on the rectangular marquee until the crop tool is selected. You can also hold down the mouse button and drag to select the **Crop** tool or type a **c** to activate the **Crop** tool (Figure 1.9).

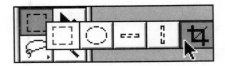

Figure 1.9 The Crop tool is hidden under the Marquee tool.

We're going to make this image a little smaller.

4. Make a selection. The pointer is now the shape of the crop tool (see Figure 1.10). Drag from the left side above George's head, across to the right side below George's hand. (The **Crop** tool makes selections the same way the rectangular Marquee tool does.) Don't worry about precision, because it's easy to adjust the selection.

Figure 1.10 The Crop tool makes selections similarly to the Marquee tool, but it lets you work with the selection differently. Notice the eight handles on each side and corner for adjusting the selection.

The pointer now changes shape according to its position and context. Put the pointer inside the selection and it becomes a standard arrowhead. Hold down the mouse button and move the selection rectangle around without changing its shape.

You'll notice that the selection rectangle has eight handles. Move the pointer over a handle and it turns into a double-headed arrow. Click on a corner handle to move the corner point in any direction. Click on a side handle to move the side in two directions.

When you move the pointer outside the image completely, it turns into a curved pointer. By clicking and moving the mouse, you can rotate the crop area in any direction in real time. When you execute the crop (as you will in the next step), the rectangle is rotated back to 90°, which has the effect of rotating the image and cropping at the same time. Try this out, because it's amusing, but leave George on the level when you're done. We wouldn't want Peepers to fall out of his lap. You can use the **Edit Undo** command to undo any inadvertent rotations.

5. When you've got your selection rectangle where you want it, execute the **Crop** command from the Image menu. (It's the only one that isn't grayed out.) This will resize the image to match the borders of the selection rectangle.

Now we'll liven up the color and contrast of this photograph.

6. Select the **Auto Levels** command from the Image Adjust submenu (a dropdown menu appears when you move the mouse over the Adjust command). Photoshop has a wealth of tools for improving (or otherwise adjusting) image quality. The simplest and most direct way for our purposes is to use Photoshop's automatic adjustment capability. This automatically adjusts the color levels so that they are more evenly distributed (see Figure 1.11). Color levels are discussed in more detail in Chapter 21.

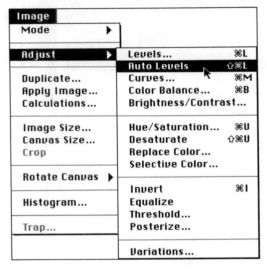

Figure 1.11 Select the **Auto Levels** command from the Image, Adjust submenu. This command has no options and can also be accessed from the Levels dialog.

7. Select the **Type** tool (t). With the Type tool selected, click on the image in the upper-left corner. This brings up the Type Tool dialog.

8. Specify the type. Select a font from the dropdown menu. I chose ITC Legacy Serif Medium, because I like the way it looks; traditional without being old-fashioned and highly readable. You may not have this font installed, so pick any typeface you like. Sixteen points should be about

the right size for most typefaces. Under the Alignment heading, click the centered radio button to select it. Make sure that the Anti-aliased box is checked. This makes type look smoother in Photoshop. Figure 1.12 shows the Type Tool dialog box.

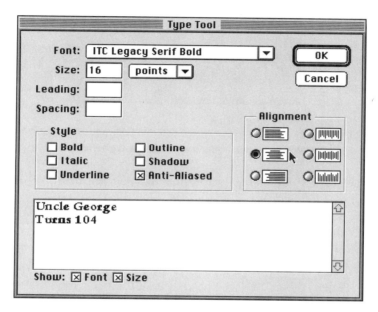

Figure 1.12 The Type dialog with font and alignment specified and text entered. Note that the check box at the bottom allows you to view text in the specified font, but it doesn't show alignment.

9. Type **Uncle George Turns 104**. Put a carriage return between **George** and **Turns** so that the text fits the space better. Click the **OK** button.

10. Position the text with the Move tool. The text is placed in a new layer at the point you clicked. We haven't talked about layers yet, but they are fundamental to editing in Photoshop. We'll be doing a little work with layers here, and a full description follows in Chapter 15.

    Select the Move tool. This allows you to move the active layer around without disturbing other layers. Hold down the mouse button and position the text in the upper-left corner of the image. Figure 1.13 shows text being proportioned with the Move tool.

Figure 1.13 Since Photoshop creates a new layer for the text, you can move the whole layer around without disturbing the background photograph.

11. Follow steps 9 and 10 again to enter the text **Photoshop Turns 4.0** in the upper-right corner of the image. Use the same type specifications, but click the **Left Align** radio button and do not enter a carriage return within the text. Don't worry about positioning the text yet.

12. Rotate the text layer using the Transform submenu. Take a look at the Layers palette. If it's not visible, choose **Show Layers** from the Windows menu. There should be three layers listed: the background layer with the photograph; Layer 1, which contains the first text string, and Layer 2, which contains the current text string. All the layers are visible, as indicated by the eye icon next to the layer name, and Layer 2 is highlighted, indicating that it is the active layer. If Layer 2 isn't highlighted, click on the words **Layer 2** in the Layers Palette to make it active (see Figure 1.14).

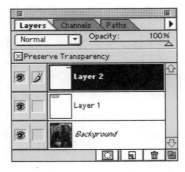

Figure 1.14 The Layer palette showing the background layer and two text layers, the second one active. You can work on the active layer without affecting any other layers.

From the Layer menu, choose the **Rotate 90° CW** command from the Transform submenu. This rotates the entire layer in a clockwise direction. But since the only thing in the active layer is the text string, only it is affected. Now you may position the text using the Move tool, so that it is well-spaced in the upper right-hand corner of the image.

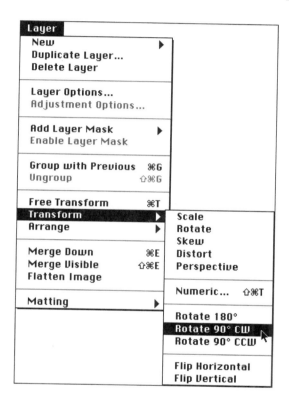

Figure 1.15 The Layer Transform submenu contains many commands for manipulating a single layer. This is one of the nicest new features of Photoshop 4.

13. Merge the two text layers with the **Merge Down** command. Still in the Layers palette, move the pointer over the right pointing arrow toward the upper right corner of the palette window. Hold down the mouse button and select the **Merge Down** command from the dropdown menu (Figure 1.16). Your two text layers are now merged into one.

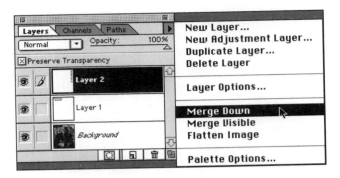

Figure 1.16 The new Merge Down command in the Palette options dropdown menu makes it simple to combine layers.

Open the palette options dropdown menu again and select the **Layer Options** command (see Figure 1.17). In the Options dialog, change the layer name to Text layer.

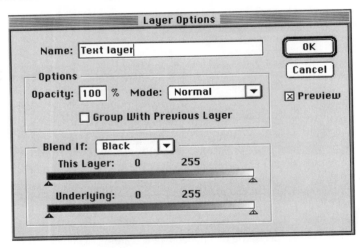

Figure 1.17 The Layer Options dialog lets you change a layer's name.

14. Use the Emboss filter to highlight the text.

With your newly-named Text layer still active, select the **Emboss** filter from the Filter Stylize submenu (see Figure 1.18). There are several options, and you can try them out to see what they do. Photoshop will show you the preview. For our purposes, the default setting will work fine.

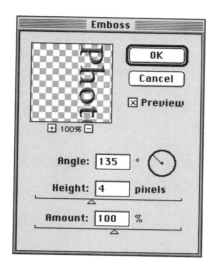

Figure 1.18 The Emboss filter is one of many new filters that used to be sold as Aldus Gallery Effects, but are now part of Photoshop.

15. Save the file. Without too much effort, we have related Uncle George and Photoshop in a single image (Figure 1.19).

Figure 1.19 The finished image; cropped, cleaned up a bit, with a caption added.

Now it's time to save your work. Choose **Save As** from the File menu. You should know how to use a standard file dialog to choose a location and name for your file. You can also set the format for the file from the Format dropdown menu. But since this image has multiple layers, Photoshop format is the only option available.

Photoshop Theory and Practice

In this chapter…

- Two kinds of computer images
- About painting programs and pixels
- About drawing programs and vectors
- The source of color—color models
- The size of color—color modes
- Resolution, image size, file size, and scratch files

Photoshop is a powerful tool, in part because it is founded on principles of color, light, and the technologies and science of projection and printing. Some of Photoshop's features may seem esoteric if you have no idea of the principles behind them. Here is an introduction to some of the more important features.

TWO KINDS OF COMPUTER IMAGES

There are two ways to create computer images:

- pixel-based "painting" programs like Adobe Photoshop and Fractal Design Painter.
- vector-based "drawing" programs like Adobe Illustrator and Macromedia FreeHand.

While the actual programs continue to add features that blur this distinction, the basis of the two program types remain distinct—painting programs operate at the pixel level, while drawing programs operate on vectors or objects. One way to distinguish between the two program types is the presence or absence of an eraser tool. Erasers are used by painting programs to wipe out large areas of information—collections of bits. With drawing programs, you can just select an object and delete it, without the help of any tool except the delete key.

ABOUT PAINTING PROGRAMS AND PIXELS

Digital images, displayed on a monitor or printed, are composed of dots or pixels. This is usually expressed as dots or pixels per inch or millimeter, and is distinct from continuous-tone analog images like photographs, where the emulsion, and therefore the image, is spread continuously across the surface. Anything that has ever been drawn or painted using traditional media is an analog image and must be converted to a digital, pixel-based image to be used by a computer.

Painting programs like Photoshop work by changing the pixels that make up a digital image. Photoshop is capable of working at very high resolutions that mask the fact that an image is composed of discrete pixels. But when you work at lower resolutions or magnify an image, the pixels are revealed, as shown in Figure 2.1.

Figure 2.1 George Washington as painted by Gilbert Stuart. On the left, as digitized at high resolution and, on the right, as viewed at low resolution in Photoshop. Both images are composed of pixels, but the second reveals the square pixels that make up the image.

Working at the pixel level means that you can edit an image dot-by-dot or apply commands to a group of pixels or every pixel at once. This is what makes painting programs so powerful and gives them the ability to create textures, manipulate images, and work in a photo-realistic manner. In Figure 2.2, some image manipulation is shown.

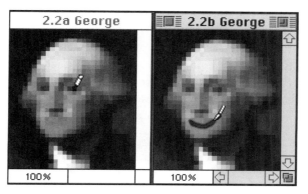

Figure 2.2 Photoshop allows you to edit single pixels. On the left, the pencil tool is editing at its narrowest setting, giving George a black eye. On the right, with a moderate stroke the Paintbrush tool is improving George's smile for the campaign trail.

ABOUT DRAWING PROGRAMS AND VECTORS

Vector-based programs such as Adobe Illustrator use algorithms rather than pixels to create images—the mathematical relationships of end-points, the geometries created, and the sequencing of events. Issues of resolution and pixels do not affect these algorithms, which means that images created with drawing programs look the same no matter what you use for viewing or printing—they are resolution-independent.

When you draw an object in a vector-based program, you indicate to the computer its size and shape and attributes pertaining to stroke and fill, like thickness, color, and pattern. If you want to edit, click to select the entire object.

Contrast this with Photoshop, where each brush stroke affects the pixels that came before it, and you can build up shapes and textures as you would with traditional painting tools. You have to lasso the pixels to select a shape, and your selection may or may not corral a few extra pixels while missing others.

Vectors and objects have the advantage of remaining discrete from one another. If you draw one shape on top of another it doesn't matter. You can always go back and edit the hidden shape; you may not see it, but it remains a part of the algorithmic image. In a sense, vector-based graphics are like malleable paper cut-outs that can be endlessly shuffled, overlaid, resized and rearranged.

Most people find the metaphors and tools of painting programs easier to learn than those of drawing programs. This has been true since MacPaint and MacDraw, the grandparents of graphics programs, were first available in 1984. But drawing features, like keeping parts of images intact for later editing, are so useful, that Photoshop has added several over the years, including the implementation and refinement of drawing paths and layers. Figure 2.3 demonstrates the difference between painting and drawing programs.

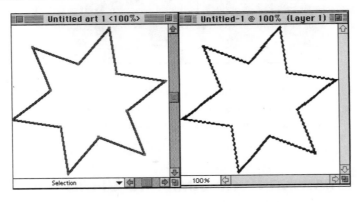

Figure 2.3 A simple star as object in Adobe Illustrator on the left, and a painted star as pixels in Photoshop on the right. In Illustrator, not only can you adjust the attributes of stroke and fill, but you can change the shape at any point. In Photoshop, you can change the attributes of the pixels within the selection and apply various filters and effects to them, but you'll have to redraw to change the shape.

THE SOURCE OF COLOR—COLOR MODELS

Reproducing color on the screen and in print requires opposite approaches. One is produced by projecting light onto or through a surface (additive), while the other stamps inks or pigments onto a surface (subtractive).

Projected Light Sums to White

If red, yellow, and blue are the primary colors, why does mixing red, yellow, and blue paint yield an unappetizing brown? As everyone knows, this model works well in a perfect world, but since paint pigment can only approximate precise spectral colors, in practice the whole thing turns to mud. Even mixing red, yellow, and blue light sources doesn't produce the closest approximation of the full color spectrum. Instead, red, green, and blue are the primary colors of visible light. This RGB color model has been used for every color TV and monitor ever sold.

When R, G, and B are added together in equal intensities, we perceive white light—*additive color* (see Figure 2.4). In the absence of all light, we perceive black. Changing the intensities produces the full color spectrum.

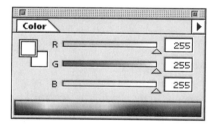

Figure 2.4 The RGB color palette. The colors converge to white as their values are increased.

In the digital realm of computers, the full spectrum can only be approximated by mixing 256 values each of red, green, and blue to yield 16.8 million colors (actually 256^3 or $2^{24}=16,777,216$ distinct color values). This is known as 24-bit color and is thought to yield as many colors as the eye is capable of discerning. Eight-bit systems can only display 256 colors, which, unless you confine your work to grayscale images, can be a serious limitation when working with Photoshop.

Reflected Light Diminishes to Black

The RGB model works well with direct lights, but it fails with print media where reflected light determines color. The application of inks or pigments on the printed surface actually subtracts from the amount of light reflected—*subtractive color*. As more ink is applied, the perceived color converges toward black. In this case, the secondary colors of cyan, magenta, and yellow (CMY) are used.

But we live in an imperfect world, and CMY inks yield an impure pure black and muddy grays. So the standard printing model has added black (K) ink (see Figure 2.5).

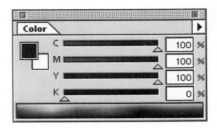

Figure 2.5 The CMYK color palette. The colors converge to black as their values are increased, even without adding any black.

The CMYK color model has become the standard of the printing industry where it is known as four-color or process-color printing. It requires the use of four printing plates (one for each color of ink); these are known as color separations. It's important to know a little about the technology of printing, because it will affect the way you use Photoshop. It's also important to know that the RGB and CMYK color models differ substantially in their abilities to reproduce color. What you see on the screen is not necessarily what you get back from the printer, and we'll discuss ways of dealing with this in later chapters.

Perceived Color—Hue, Saturation, and Brightness

Human perception discerns color in terms of hue, saturation, and brightness (HSB). Rather than describing colors as a blend of primary or secondary colors, these three attributes are used (see Figure 2.6).

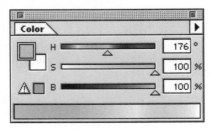

Figure 2.6 The HSB color palette. The hue value determines the color and that it is measured in degrees around the standard color wheel.

- Hue—the wavelength of light is described as hue and is often identified as a color name, such as red, orange, yellow, and so forth. The value of hue is determined by the location on a color wheel and is expressed in degrees, from 0° to 360°.

- Saturation—also known as chroma, saturation is the intensity of a color, or its purity. Saturation is a measure of gray in proportion to hue, from 0% to 100%. As saturation decreases, the color becomes less intense, appearing to fade to white.

- Brightness—a description of how bright or dark the color appears, in terms of how much light is reflected back to the eye or is transmitted through the pixels on screen. Another word for brightness is value. As brightness decreases, the color becomes darker or appears to fade to black.

The HSB color model is useful for viewing and evaluating the color in an image.

THE SIZE OF COLOR—COLOR MODES

In addition to the several color models discussed, Photoshop provides several color modes. And while the models are accessed from the Color palette, the modes are accessed from the Image Mode submenu. You'll notice that in the menu, RGB and CMYK are available as modes. The difference is that in the palette, you can view the value of any color using the different models. The Mode command (see Figure 2.7) actually changes the way the entire image is stored, and this affects the physical size of the image file.

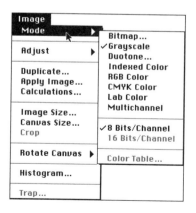

Figure 2.7 The Mode submenu of the Images menu. Photoshop will convert between any of its modes, but converting back and forth between modes may cause a loss in image quality.

Measuring the Size of Information

All digital processing is done with bits—the smallest unit of measurement for computing. Bits are small and simple, the electronic representation of a switch—either on or off. But if you string a bunch of bits together, then you can do binary arithmetic, which is basically adding and subtracting, but in base 2.

Eight bits together make a byte. A byte can represent 2^8 or 256 values. This is why you will see so many ranges in Photoshop go from 0 to 255, because that's exactly eight bits of information. As was already mentioned, 24-bit color images contain eight bits per pixel for each of the three components, red, green, and blue.

File sizes are often expressed in thousands of bytes—*kilobytes*. You'll usually see this abbreviated with the letter *k*, which is not to be confused with the K in CMYK.

Disk drives are usually measured in millions of bytes, or *megabytes*, abbreviated *mb* or *meg*. As drives have gotten bigger, the need to express their size in billions of bytes, or *gigabytes*, has arisen. This is abbreviated as *gig* or *Gb*.

While a long word processing document might be tens of kilobytes, Photoshop documents quickly become one or two orders of magnitude larger than that. This is because it takes 24 bits for every pixel, and at 200 pixels per inch, a standard 4"x 5" photograph is 20 square inches, or 800,000 pixels, or 1.92 mb of information. Now you can begin to understand why Photoshop likes to have lots of random access memory (RAM) and plenty of fast hard disk space to work with.

Bitmap Mode—1-Bit Images

All digital images are assembled from a map of bits—a *bitmap*. A simple bitmap has no color depth and is therefore composed only of black or white pixels. Bitmaps are true black-and-white images. Very few computers have black-and-white displays any more. They are either grayscale or a limited number of colors. However, bitmap images are still very important in printing.

If you only have one color of ink to print with and the printer can only print in a single intensity, even a grayscale image isn't going to do you any good. This is a classic problem and gave rise many years ago to halftone technology. Instead of changing the ink color, halftones change the dot size or density. By adjusting dot density, the illusion of gray is achieved. The most obvious example of this is newspaper photographs, which use a relatively coarse halftone dot density or screen. But you can see the halftone dots in most printed images.

Bitmap files have the advantage of being relatively small. With only one bit of information per pixel, an entire dimension of information is unnecessary. Not all of Photoshop's tools can be used on a bitmap image. After all, it's simply not possible to create a gradient in a black-and-white image. In a case like this, you can edit in grayscale mode and convert the final image to bitmap to create the effect of a gradient.

Grayscale, Duotone, and Indexed Color Mode—8-Bit Images

By representing each image pixel with 8 bits instead of 1, computers are capable of displaying 256 true shades of gray. This does not require changing dot sizes to achieve photorealistic gray. To the eye, 256 shades is enough to create the image of a completely smooth gradation from black (0) to white (255).

As you might expect, 8-bit image files are 8 times larger than bitmap files. Photoshop uses a single channel (more about channels in Chapter 17) to display 8-bit images.

However, grayscale images need not be printed using black ink. Any single color of ink can be used. If you want to see what this effect is going to look like on screen, you need to use Photoshop's Duotone mode to create a monotone image. The problem with montone images, whether they are grayscale or any other color, is that printing presses are only capable of reproducing about 50 shades of gray. By using multiple inks, duotones, tritones, or quadtones to print an 8-bit grayscale image, you can achieve more realistic and sometimes very striking results.

It's also possible to produce color images with a single 8-bit channel. This is useful when the final output is a computer monitor as for many multimedia animations and most Web-based work. Indexed color images use a lookup table of 256 colors and then match colors in the image to the table as closely as possible. You can also build a custom lookup table for use with multiple images.

RGB Mode—24-Bit Color Images

RGB mode uses three channels of 8 bits each to achieve 24-bit photorealistic color. RGB image files are three times larger than grayscale images. This is Photoshop's default color mode and is probably where you will end up doing most of your work.

When you work in RGB mode, the Channels palette shows four channels: one for each color and a composite channel. This allows you to edit all channels at once, or each color individually.

CMYK Mode—32-Bit Color Images

Before you get all excited about having four 8-bit channels of color to play with, realize that the purpose of the CMYK mode is to create color separations for printing. CMYK presses are not capable of reproducing 16.8 million colors, so you gain nothing in terms of artistic flexibility by using this most resource-intensive mode.

In general, it's best to edit in RGB mode and convert to CMYK before making color separations for printing. You will lose fidelity by going back and forth between the two modes, since the color values have to be recalculated each time.

Note that Photoshop also includes a Lab Color mode, but its use is fairly limited and is more important to the internal workings of Photoshop than to this book.

RESOLUTION, IMAGE SIZE, FILE SIZE, AND SCRATCH FILES

As already mentioned, every document window displays information about the image file in the lower left corner of the window. The default display shows the image magnification in percent and two values for the file size. The first value is the nominal size for the flattened image with no extra layers—the size of the image as it would be sent to a printer. The second value shows the size the image would be if it were saved with all its layer and channel information.

If you click and hold down the arrow to the right of the file sizes, you can choose to view scratch file sizes. (Photoshop creates scratch files on your hard disk to manipulate images—see Figure 2.8.) This option lets you see the amount of scratch space on disk that Photoshop needs to manipulate the current image with and without its layer and channel information. To be fair, Photoshop only needs to use scratch space on disk if it uses up its allotment of RAM. But since file manipulation requires about three times the file size in RAM, this can get used up quickly.

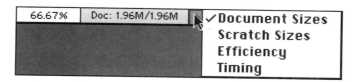

Figure 2.8 The lower-left corner of an image window showing document information. Every image window displays this information, which is updated as you edit the image.

These file statistics may seem a bit esoteric at this point in your Photoshop experience, but the point is, you're using a lot of disk space. And as the resolution of your image increases, the size of the image and the amount of space Photoshop needs to work with your image increases by the square of the resolution.

To view dimensions, channel, and resolution information, position the pointer over the file information box of the image window (the lower left corner). Press the **Option** key (Macintosh) or **Alt** key (Windows) and hold down the mouse button. Another box pops up displaying the image dimensions, the number of channels, and the resolution, as shown in Figure 2.9.

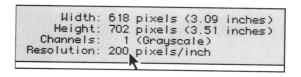

Figure 2.9 You can get information about an image directly from the image window.

The good news is that Photoshop is fairly efficient when it needs to save information on disks, which are slower, rather than in RAM. Also, RAM is as inexpensive as it has ever been. So it's worth buying as much RAM as you can get if you're going to be doing 24-bit color work.

Lesson 2: Looking at Images

Open the file **SEURAT.PSD** from the Lessons folder on the CD-ROM. Behold an exercise in pixel manipulation; Georges Seurat's masterpiece of 1884, *Sunday Afternoon on the Island of La Grande Jatte* (Figure 2.10). Seurat lived and painted during a period of experimentation with light and color. As a pointillist, he believed that juxtaposed points of opposite hues would make the eye perceive the combined color with more vivid clarity.

Figure 2.10 La Grande Jatte, by Georges Seurat. When pixels first became popular.

This early work led to theories of color whose influences can be seen in Photoshop's color palettes. Use the Color Palette Options menu to examine the RGB and HSB color palettes.

We can also see an 8-bit equivalent palette of the colors Seurat used and even borrow them for our own work.

- Select **Indexed Color** from the Image Mode submenu (Figure 2.11) and click **OK** to the Flatten Layers? alert. In the dialog box, select **Adaptive** and set Options Dither to **None**. The other defaults are fine. This will reduce the image to 256 colors.

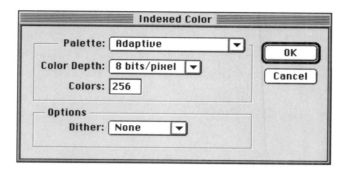

Figure 2.11 The Indexed Color dialog box allows you to index the spread of colors in the image to a palette of 256 colors.

Before you click OK, take a look at the Swatches palette shown in Figure 2.12. If it isn't showing, either select **Show Swatches** from the Windows menu or click on the **Swatches** tab in the palette window. Now click **OK** and watch the swatches change. You've got a nice approximation of the Impressionist color palette of the 19th century. If you wish, you can save this palette using the Palette Options menu command and load it for use with another image.

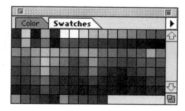

Figure 2.12 The Swatches palette changes to reflect the current color selection—in this case, the 256 most commonly used shades from La Grande Jatte.

Unfortunately, you won't be able to examine Seurat's dot-like brush strokes, because the resolution of this image is too low and the brush strokes have already been blended into larger dots by Photoshop. But if you were to go to the Art Institute of Chicago and look at the painting, you could probably measure the brush strokes and see just what resolution Seurat used in dots per inch.

If you've seen any pointillist paintings, you realize that when you stand back, the dots merge, the eye perceives the intended blend of color, and the form is revealed. The same is true when working with Photoshop resolutions.

You can magnify or expand the view to reveal or hide the pixels. You can also change the resolution of the output to suit the media and viewing environment.

With inspiration from Seurat, we'll try out some of Photoshop's tools for color and resolution and see how they affect the physical file.

Resolution and File Size

- Take a look at the lower-left corner of the image window for La Grande Jatte. You can see that the image size is 202k (see Figure 2.13). Not very much for a painting that is 7' tall by 10' wide, but that's all it takes for this little 72 dpi reproduction. Perhaps by increasing the resolution, we'll reveal the brush strokes of the original.

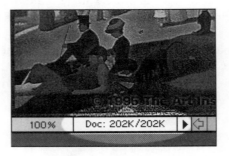

Figure 2.13 The file information corner of the image window. The print file size is 202k, and since there are no additional layers defined, the saved file size is the same size.

 Photoshop has its own built in compression scheme that compresses files slightly when they are saved in Photoshop's native file format.

N O T E

- Open the Image Size dialog box from the Image menu (see Figure 2.14). Select the **Resolution** field and change it to 300 pixels/inch. Don't click on the OK button, yet. At the top of the dialog box you see the new image size and the old, "3.42M (was 202K)." When the significance of this huge file size increase sinks in, go ahead and click **OK**.

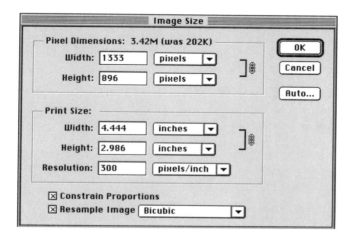

Figure 2.14 The Image Size dialog box indicating the new file size after increasing the image resolution to 300 dpi. Notice the link between resolution, image size, and file size.

When you change the image resolution, Photoshop changes the display, in this case seemingly enlarging the image to fill beyond the boundaries of your screen.

- Choose the **Print Size** command from the View menu. Voilá, the image is back to its original size, and surprisingly, it doesn't look as if anything has changed from the original. Increasing the resolution didn't make this image look any sharper, because Photoshop had no information to work from. We've increased the number of dots and the file size, but gained nothing in terms of image quality.

- Choose **Revert** from the File menu to go back to the 72 dpi image. Oops, now the image is displayed very small. What's Photoshop doing? When you change the resolution of an image, Photoshop maintains the image magnification based on the size of the pixel. With more pixels, the image fills more of the screen, and with fewer pixels, less.

You need to keep in mind the differences among:

- resolution—the number of dots/pixels per linear measure,
- image size—the printed dimensions of the image, and
- file size—the amount of space on disk a file occupies.

These three variables are distinct and interdependent. Photoshop allows you to change one without changing the others, but there are consequences. In our example, we changed the resolution, which affected file size but not image size or quality.

Before you start fiddling with resolution and sizes, know why you are doing it. Our goal was to achieve a higher quality image of the same image size; our only solution was to start with higher quality input.

Painting Tools

In this section…

- Painting Terminology
- Brushes
- Options palette
- Using the Painting Tools

Painting Terminology

In this chapter…

- Anti-aliasing
- Foreground and background colors
- Blending modes

There are a couple of terms that come up repeatedly in discussing many of the tools and commands you will use in Photoshop. These terms and the concepts they refer to are not unique to Photoshop, but we will discuss how Photoshop uses them.

ANTI-ALIASING

In Chapter 2, you had a look at the discrete bits that make up an image and saw that as the resolution increased or magnification decreased, bits became smooth lines—like standing back to view a painting or looking close to see the brush strokes. The blending of the edges of a line, shape, selection, or piece of type in relation to its background is called *anti-aliasing*. All of Photoshop's image creation tools and many commands include anti-aliasing options

Anti-aliasing is used to make jagged lines appear smooth, overcoming the limitations of resolution. You should consider anti-aliasing most of the work you do in Photoshop, unless you have a specific reason not to. For instance, the screen shots in this book are not anti-aliased, but most of the other images are. See Figures 3.1 and 3.2.

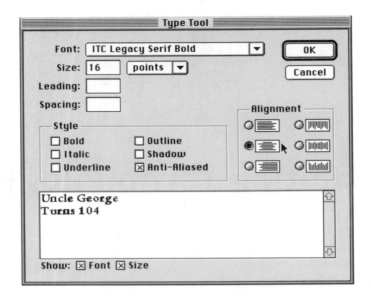

Figure 3.1 When we created type in Lesson 1, we checked the Anti-aliased box as indicated in this screen shot. Many of Photoshop's tools and commands can turn anti-aliasing on.

Figure 3.2 Here, in magnified view, are the results of adding type without anti-aliasing on the top, and with anti-aliasing on the bottom. The magnification reveals the true nature of anti-aliasing. It gives the appearance of smoothness by adding gradations of gray or color around the edges.

FOREGROUND AND BACKGROUND COLORS

With Photoshop, foreground and background each have two separate meanings.

- There are foreground and background colors that can be chosen from the Color Picker dialog or the Colors or Swatches palettes. The current colors are indicated in the Color Control area of the Toolbox. The foreground color is used by painting tools when you paint on an image. The background color is used by the Eraser tool, the gradient fill tool, and when the brush options are set to fade to the background color. It is also the color used to fill a void left when a selection is cut or moved.

- Images also have a foreground and background, which is why we can speak of a brush stroke being anti-aliased into its background. As a default, Photoshop 4 labels the first layer of an image Background. Anything visible on a layer in front of the background is in the foreground.

Despite the two uses for these terms, it's usually evident whether one means the foreground/background of an image or the foreground/background colors. For one thing, images can be ambiguous in the use of figure and ground, while Photoshop always has an unambiguous foreground and background color assigned—unless you assign the same color to both. See Figure 3.3 for an example.

Figure 3.3 Ambiguous figure-ground relationships are possible, as in this image, but there is no ambiguity about the assigned foreground and background colors.

Using the Foreground/Background Color Control Box

The Color Control box is located in the Toolbox (see Figure 3.4) and displays the current foreground and background colors. It also allows you to change these colors.

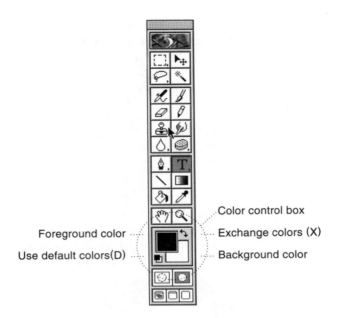

Foreground color ····
Use default colors(D) ····

···Color control box
···Exchange colors (X)
···Background color

Figure 3.4 The color control section of the Toolbox.

Changing the Foreground/Background Color

There are several ways to change the color selection. This variety of methods facilitates numerous working styles and gives greater flexibility for working with images.

- Move the pointer over the foreground or background color in the Color Control box. Click to bring up Photoshop's color picker. Select a color, click **OK**, and the color is changed and will be used until it is changed again.
- Click on a color in the Swatches or Color palette to change the foreground color.
- **Option-click** (Macintosh) or **Alt-click** (Windows) in the Swatches or Color palette to change the background color.
- Select the Eyedropper tool (i) in the Toolbox. The Eyedropper tool can be used to sample colors from open images, as shown in Figure 3.5.

Move the pointer to a color in your image and click to change the foreground color. To change the background color, **Option-click** (Macintosh) or **Alt-click** (Windows).

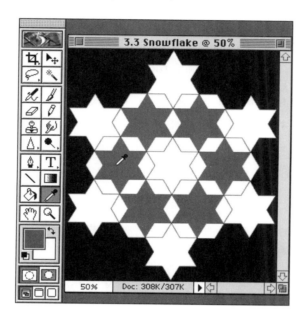

Figure 3.5 Sampling the color of this gray star using the eyedropper tool changes the foreground color to the same gray.

 By holding down the **Option** key (Macintosh) or **Alt** key (Windows), the pointer becomes an eyedropper ready to take a quick color sample. This can be used when the Airbrush, Paintbrush, Pencil, Text, Line, Gradient, or Paintbucket tools are selected.

To swap foreground and background colors, click on the **Exchange colors** icon (x) in the Color Control Box. Click again to swap back.

To return to Photoshop's default colors, click on the **Default colors** icon in the Color Control Box, and the colors are returned to their defaults.

Note that Photoshop saves the foreground/background colors when you quit and restores them when you restart.

USING BLENDING (PAINTING) MODES

Blending modes (also known as painting modes) are differentiated by the effect of the overlying brush stroke on the underlying pixels. Each mode affects pixels in a unique way. As you read this, keep in mind that each color is the numerical representation of its RGB values.

Blend modes are selected from the **Modes** dropdown menu within the Options palette. These modes affect all painting and drawing tools, layers, and some commands, like Fill and Stroke.

To understand how these modes work, you need to think of three different colors involved in the process:

- **Blend color** is the foreground color and therefore the color you are painting with.
- **Base color** is the color already in the image you are painting on top of. (There may be many base colors, but remember, only one color per pixel.)
- **Result color** is what you get after you apply a blend color to a base color.

The whole point of modes is that the same two blend and base colors produce different results depending on the mode selected.

- **Normal mode** is about what you'd expect; the blend color is the result color, with some variation for opacity.

 Normal mode is called threshold when working with bitmap images.

NOTE

- **Dissolve mode** results in a random application of normal mode. In other words, some of the base pixels are replaced with the blend color and others are not. The result is a "scatter" pattern.
- **Behind mode** paints only on the transparent part of a layer. It gives the effect of painting under the base color.
- **Clear mode** makes pixels transparent. It works only in a layer and when using the line tool, paintbucket tool, Fill or Stroke commands. This is new to version 4.

- **Multiply mode** mathematically multiplies the value of the blend color and the base color to yield a result color that is darker than either. Multiplying by black always yields black, while multiplying by white leaves the base color unchanged. Unlike normal mode, successive strokes yield darker and darker results, as if the paint were building up on the image.

- **Screen mode** is the inverse of multiply, so that the result color is always lighter than the base color. Screening with black makes no change, while screening with white yields white.

- **Overlay mode** either multiplies or screens depending on the base color. This has the effect of changing the base color to the blend color while maintaining highlights and shadows.

- **Soft light mode** treats the blend color like a diffused light source, so that colors more than 50% gray darken the base color while colors under 50% gray lighten it.

- **Hard light mode** works similarly to Soft light, but treats the blend color like a focused light source. This can be useful for emphasizing highlights or shadows.

- **Color dodge** and **Color burn modes** are new to Version 4. Using these modes is like dodging or burning with color. Dodge brightens the base color, while burn darkens it.

- **Darken mode** examines both the base and blend colors and uses the darker as the result color.

- **Lighten mode** is the inverse of Darken mode; the lighter color becomes the result.

- **Difference mode** uses the brightness value of the blend and base colors, subtracts the dimmer from the brighter, and calculates the result.

- **Exclusion mode** is new to Version 4 and is similar to Difference mode with a softer result.

- **Hue mode** uses the hue value of the blend color, while maintaining the saturation (intensity) and luminosity (a measure of brightness) of the base color.

- **Saturation mode** changes the saturation of the base color, while maintaining hue and luminosity.

- **Color mode** changes hue and saturation, but not luminosity. This preserves gray levels and is useful for colorizing monotone images.

- **Luminosity mode** changes the luminosity while leaving hue and saturation unchanged (the inverse of Color mode).

Lesson 3: Painting Concepts

In this lesson, you will see the difference between aliased and anti-aliased objects, foreground and background images and colors, and we'll try out a few of Photoshop's blend modes. We will not be creating masterpieces—just fooling around for now, so that our later work can approach that of the masters.

ANTI-ALIASING

Many of Photoshop's tools have an anti-aliasing option. But what do you call objects that aren't anti-aliased—not anti-aliased, un-anti-aliased, or just plain aliased? We'll use the latter.

Start by opening a new blank document, **File, New**. For this exercise, the document can be any size. If you want it to be the same size as the example, enter these numbers from Figure 3.6 in the New File dialog:

Width: 6 inches
Height: 4 inches
Resolution: 72 dpi

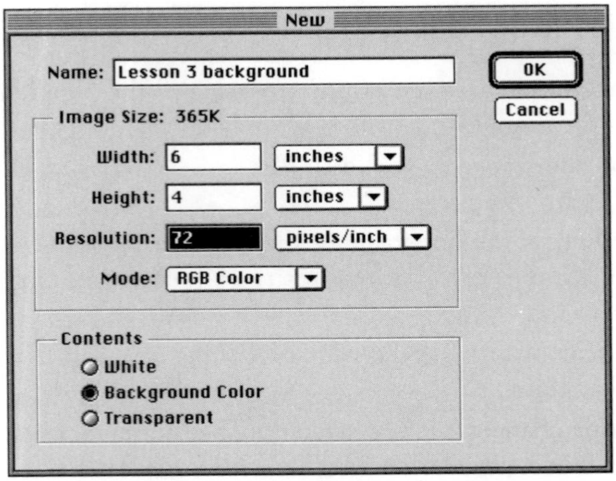

Figure 3.6 New File dialog indicating the specifications for this lesson's image.

Enter some aliased type.

1. Select the **Type** tool (t) from the Toolbox.

2. Click inside the image window. The type will need to be approximately in the middle of the image window, but we can position this later.

3. In the Type Tool dialog, specify Helvetica Bold 72 point. Make sure that the Anti-aliased box is not checked. Enter the text **SHADOW**.

4. Click **OK**. The results are shown in Figure 3.7.

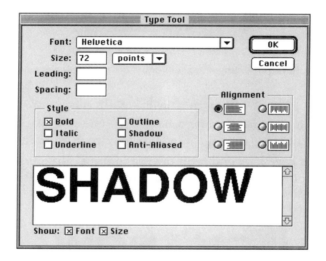

Figure 3.7 The Type Tool dialog showing the type entry with the Anti-aliased box unchecked.

5. Photoshop creates a new layer with the text at the point you clicked in the image. If you need to adjust the position of the text, select the Move tool (v) and drag the layer so that the text is approximately centered.

Look at the aliased type. The edges show distinct stair-stepping in every letter except the H, which is basically horizontal and vertical lines.

Now, do it again with anti-aliasing.

1. Change the foreground color to a medium gray. You can do this by clicking on a gray swatch in the Swatches palette (as we did in Figure 3.8), by

specifying gray in the Colors palette, or by clicking on the foreground color in the Toolbox and choosing gray from the color picker. (I know that all these options are confusing, but you'll find what's most convenient for you as you become more familiar with Photoshop.)

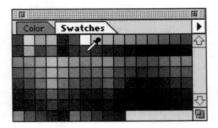

Figure 3.8 Selecting a medium gray from the Swatches palette.

2. With the Type tool still selected, click in the image again.

3. The Type tool dialog should have the same information you entered before. Click on the **Anti-aliased** box to select it and click **OK**.

4. Now you have a second layer of type in front of the first layer. Use the Move tool (v) to adjust the position of this layer just above and slightly to the right of the first text layer as shown in Figure 3.9.

Figure 3.9 This is how your image should look with one black layer of aliased type and a gray layer of anti-aliased type.

Examine the two layers of type. One is smooth-edged and the other jagged. The gray type has added intermediate values of gray to fill in the jagged edges.

Select the **Zoom** tool (z) and click on the image. Click again to zoom in further, as in Figure 3.10.

SHADOW
SHADOW

Figure 3.10 The two type layers compared: anti-aliased in gray, aliased in black.

The only way to draw diagonal or curved aliased lines is with jagged edges. At low resolution or high magnification this is painfully obvious.

You'll also notice that at high magnification, the anti-aliased type is distinctly blurry (or indistinctly sharp). Sometimes the blurriness of anti-aliasing can be a disadvantage, causing a loss of detail. That's why Photoshop gives you a choice.

DISTINGUISHING FOREGROUND AND BACKGROUND, (OR AMBIGUITY CAN BE FUN)

In our shadow text image, it's difficult to say by looking which is the foreground and which the background.

Select the **Move** tool (v) and slide the gray text down as indicated in Figure 3.11.

SHADOW

Figure 3.11 The ambiguous figure-ground relationship from before now looks like gray text with a black shadow.

You now have gray text casting a black shadow, because the gray layer is on top. But a fuzzy foreground would be unlikely to cast a focused shadow. We need to reverse the foreground and background.

1. Move the pointer over **Layer 2** in the Layers palette. If the palette isn't open, select **Show Layers** from the Window menu.

2. Click and drag Layer 2 until it is below Layer 1, but not below the background layer. A bold black line indicates when you're in the right place. See Figure 3.12.

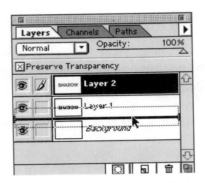

Figure 3.12 Moving Layer 2 so that it is under Layer 1. The darker black line indicates the moved position of the layer.

3. Release the mouse button and the layers are reversed. Now you have sharp black text casting a diffuse gray shadow.

It's evident from this little exercise that layers determine the foreground and background as far as Photoshop is concerned. But what about foreground and background colors?

USING FOREGROUND AND BACKGROUND COLORS

At this point in the lesson, the foreground color has been set to medium gray and the background is still white. There are three layers, two text and one background, and Layer 2 is active. You can also open the file **BLACK_SH.PSD** in the Lesson03 folder if you've interrupted the lesson or experimented with the preceding image.

Now, let's change the drop shadow to be embossed.

1. Click on the **Exchange Colors** arrow (x) in the color control section of the Toolbox. This puts gray in the background and white in the foreground.

2. Make Layer 1 the target layer by clicking on its name in the Layers palette.

3. From the Edit menu, choose the **Fill** command. This opens the Fill dialog. The default options should be right, so click **OK**. Refer to Figure 3.13 for the correct settings.

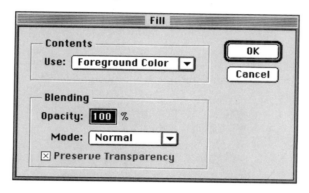

Figure 3.13 The Fill dialog indicating a 100% fill using the foreground color.

This fills the entire black text layer with the foreground color, white. You now have what looks like embossed text (Figure 3.14).

$$\text{SHADOW}$$

Figure 3.14 Filling the foreground image with the same color as the background layer yields an embossed look.

The reason the Fill command didn't obliterate everything underneath it is that the Preserve Transparency box is checked in the layers palette. This is the default when Photoshop creates a new text layer, and it renders everything that isn't text transparent.

It's interesting that this effect is produced by sandwiching a layer of background color between two layers of foreground color. You can achieve the same effect with any colors, as long as the topmost text layer and the background layer are filled with the same color.

DOODLING WITH BLENDING MODES

Here's your chance to experiment with the 18 variables called *blending modes*. I'm told that blending modes become known as painting modes when used with any of Photoshop's brush tools, which makes the terms essentially interchangeable. I've supplied a background suitable for blending experimentation, a rainbow of lines.

Open the file called **RAINBOWB.PSD** from the Lesson03 folder on the CD (shown in Figure 3.15) and start experimenting.

Figure 3.15 In case you have trouble finding it, a grayscale version of the Rainbow Background looks like this. Happy doodling.

You can select different painting tools from the Toolbox, various brushes from the Brushes palette, any foreground color from the Color or Swatches palettes or from the color picker. And don't forget the 18 blending modes selected from the dropdown menu of each tool's options palette.

Paint right onto this background and see how the colors interact. (You'll need to add a layer for the Behind mode to be usable.) When things get really messy, choose **Revert** from the File menu and your slate will be wiped clean.

Brushes

In this chapter...

- Selecting brushes
- Manipulating brushes
- Brush files

Photoshop's brushes—the Paintbrush, Pencil, Airbrush, and Eraser—are a diverse and highly adaptable set of tools. You can use them to paint freehand or straight lines and smooth, fuzzy, or rough-edged lines. Brush shapes can be round, oval, calligraphic—any shape you create. Paint can be applied continuously or intermittently as a dotted line, and its weight can range from opaque to completely transparent. You can even paint in different brush modes that allow you to lighten or darken only selected pixels in an image. There are a seemingly limitless number of brush effects to use to express your creativity.

All painting tools are used essentially the same way. Click in the image and drag to make a stroke. The effect of each stroke depends on the tool selected, the options chosen from the Brushes and Options palettes, and the colors selected.

NOTE A straight line can be created with any of the paint tools by clicking once to define the starting point and then shift-clicking to define the endpoint. If you move the pointer again and shift-click, Photoshop will continue to connect the lines. If, on the other hand, you hold down the mouse button and drag the pointer while pressing the **Shift** key, Photoshop will paint a vertical or horizontal line.

SELECTING BRUSHES

The Brushes palette contains all the currently defined brushes and works with all eight Photoshop painting tools. Each tool can be set to a differently-sized brush, but all are selected from the same palette (Figure 4.1).

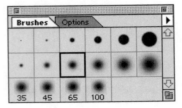

Figure 4.1 The Brushes palette lists all open brushes and expands to accommodate as many custom brushes as you'd like. The numbered brushes at the bottom indicate the diameter in pixels of brushes too large to preview in the palette.

To select a brush:

- Make sure the Brushes palette is open. If it isn't, select **Show Brushes** from the Window menu.
- Click on one of the painting tools in the Toolbox and then on any of the brush shapes in the Brushes palette. To change shapes, click on another.

NOTE   The painting icon will match the tool you chose. To use the precise cross-hairs icon without going to the Preferences dialog boxes, depress the **Caps Lock** key before you paint.

MANIPULATING BRUSHES

Photoshop comes with 16 ready-made brushes in the default Brushes palette. But, like the Swatches palette, the Brushes palette can be expanded by creating custom brushes of different sizes, shapes, angles, and degrees of hardness. The Brushes Palette Options menu is shown in Figure 4.2.

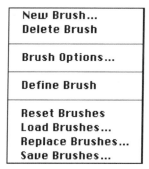

Figure 4.2 The Brushes Palette Options menu. Not every command in the menu is available at all times.

 All brush tools use the same brush shapes as shown in the Brushes palette, except that the Pencil tool only uses hard-edged brushes. Brush shapes that are too big to fit in a palette square are shown with a generic icon and a number indicating the brush diameter in pixels.

To create a new brush, choose **New Brush** from the Brushes Palette menu or double-click in an empty space in the Brushes palette. The New Brush dialog box (Figure 4.3) includes a preview box and lets you define custom brushes based on five variables.

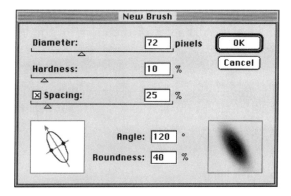

Figure 4.3 The New Brush dialog box showing the five options. The preview on the left can be manipulated directly to change the brush diameter and angle. The preview on the right shows the "true" brush shape and changes magnification automatically to show larger brushes.

- Diameter—The maximum width of the brush from 1 to 999 pixels. Note that the Diameter slider adjusts in one-pixel increments from 1 to 100, two-pixel increments from 102 to 200, 10-pixel increments from 210 to 500, and 25-pixel increments from 525 to 999.

- Hardness—The percentage of the brush from 0 to 100 that has a hard or solid center. Real-life paintbrushes are soft, 0% hardness, while pencils are 100% hard.

- Spacing—Defines the space between the brush marks in a stroke from 1% to 999% of the brush diameter. Small spacings create overlapping brush marks, while larger spacings create dotted or discontinuous strokes. Spacing can be turned on and off by clicking in the **Spacing** check box. When it is off, spacing is determined by the speed at which the stroke is painted.

The spacing specification cannot be previewed in the dialog box.

NOTE

- Angle—The tilt of an elliptical brush in degrees. Type in a number or drag anywhere in the left preview box to change the angle. This can be used to simulate the angle at which you might hold a brush. Photoshop measures angles from 180° to −179°.

- Roundness—The ratio of an elliptical brush's short and long dimensions. 0% creates a line brush, while 100% is a perfectly circular brush. Type in a number or drag the diameter of the circle in the left preview box to specify the roundness.

The right preview box shows the actual brush being defined and automatically reduces the size of a brush as it becomes too large to fit in the box.

NOTE

To define a custom brush shape:

1. Select part of an image. If you want your custom brush to be purely object-shaped, it's best if the object selected is on a white background.

2. Choose **Define Brush** from the Brushes Palette menu. A new brush of the shape you've selected is added to the palette.

3. Double-click on the new brush to open the Brush Options dialog box.

4. Set the Spacing parameter to achieve the desired effect. This is the only parameter available for custom brush shapes. A spiral brush shape is shown in Figure 4.4.

Figure 4.4 A spiral brush shape with spacing set to **25**, **50**, **75**, and **100**. (The size of the spiral brush is affected by the pressure applied to the pressure-sensitive pen used to make these strokes.)

You can select the **Anti-Aliased** option with custom brush shapes, but it doesn't work with very large shapes. The maximum size for custom brush shapes is 1000 x 1000 pixels.

N O T E

The variety of brush shapes is endless, though not all shapes make good brushes. Many can be used to create interesting effects by increasing the spacing.

To modify an existing brush shape, double-click on any brush in the Brushes palette or select a brush by clicking once, then select **Brush Options** from the Brushes Palette menu. Make modifications in the Brush Shape dialog box and click **OK** to save your changes.

To delete a brush:

• Hold down the **Command** key (Macintosh) or **Ctrl** key (Windows) and move the pointer over the Brushes palette. The cursor becomes a scissors icon. Click on a brush to delete it.

- With a brush selected, choose the **Delete Brush** command from the palette menu.

BRUSH FILES

You can create custom brush files for the different kinds of work that you do—for specific jobs, or to take with you and load on other machines that you may be using.

To save custom brushes:

- Select **Save Brushes** from the Brushes Palette menu.
- From the File dialog box (Figure 4.5), you can name your palette and choose any location to store it, but you might want to keep all your brushes in the **Brushes & Patterns** folder, in the **Goodies** folder within the **Adobe Photoshop 4.0** folder.

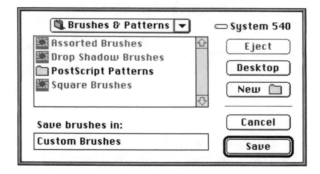

Figure 4.5 The standard File dialog box showing Photoshop's default brush files and location.

To Reset, Load, or Replace Brushes

The **Reset Brushes**, **Load Brushes**, and **Replace Brushes** commands are all executed from the Brushes Palette menu.

The **Reset Brushes** command sets the brushes in the palette back to Photoshop's default sizes and configurations or lets you append the defaults to the existing palette.

The **Load** and **Replace Brushes** commands let you open brush files saved on disk and use them in Photoshop. **Load** actually appends the new file to the existing brushes, while **Replace** replaces the previously opened brush file with the new one.

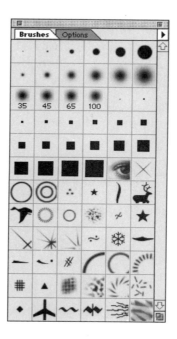

Figure 4.6 The Brushes palette expanded by the addition of two of Photoshop's custom brush palette files, including square brushes and some whimsical custom brush shapes.

NOTE You can add brushes to the palette without saving them as a file. Photoshop saves your changes and loads them each time the program is open. But if you revert to the default palette shapes, your changes will be lost.

Brushes are saved in shades of gray so that they can be used to paint with any color. If you create a custom brush stroke while using a color brush, it will appear as a gray brush shape in the palette and will seem semitransparent when you paint with it, even when you paint with solid black paint. The bottom line: If you want a custom brush to be totally opaque when used, create the brush in black.

Lesson 4: Using Brushes

Finally, you get to do something creative—actually make a painting in Photoshop. But Photoshop is not a big deal because of its painting tools. These tools are extremely capable, but image creation barely scratches the surface of Photoshop's power. Nonetheless, a knowledge of the brushes and the tools that use them is fundamental to working with Photoshop.

WILLOW TREE

We're going to paint a willow tree, so start with a clean canvas and clean brushes.

1. Choose **File:New**. Use the following specifications (see Figure 4.7):

Width: **480 pixels**
Height: **640 pixels**
Resolution: **72 pixels/inch**

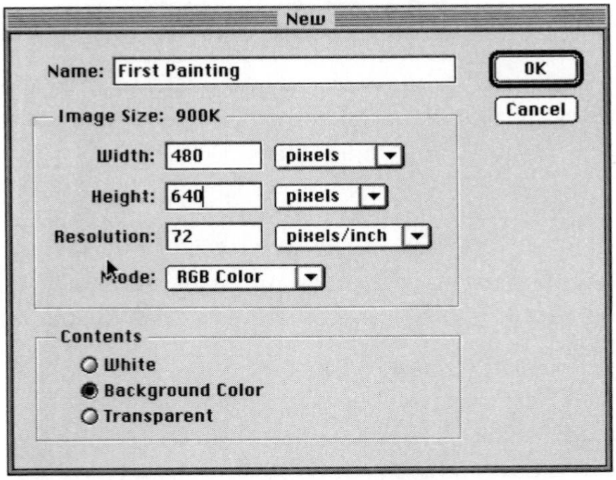

Figure 4.7 The New File dialog box showing the correct settings to begin this lesson.

2. Select the **Paintbrush** tool (b). If the Paintbrush Options palette isn't open, double-click on the tool or choose **Show Options** from the Window menu.

3. In the Brush Options palette, check the **Fade** box to turn it on, specify a **100** step fade, and choose **Fade to Background** in the Fade dropdown menu (see Figure 4.8).

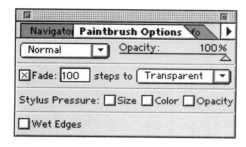

Figure 4.8 The Paintbrush Options palette showing the fade settings.

4. Click on the **Brushes** tab in the Options palette to select a brush (Figure 4.9).

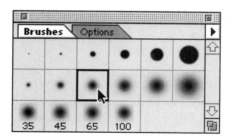

Figure 4.9 Choose a medium-sized soft brush to paint the trunk of the willow tree and a smaller brush for the drooping branches.

5. Click on the darkest brown on the bottom row of the Swatches palette (Figure 4.10). This sets the foreground color to brown. If the palette isn't open, choose **Show Swatches** from the Window menu or click on the **Swatches** tab if it's visible.

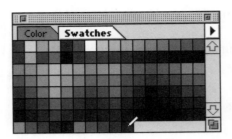

Figure 4.10 Sampling dark brown from the Swatches palette.

This is not the botanically correct color for the trunk of a willow, which is more gray, but we will use artistic license.

6. Start painting right in the middle of the image. Paint a center stroke going up until the paint fades out. Paint strokes on each side of the first. Make a few more pairs of strokes, letting them taper slightly as the strokes go up the trunk (Figure 4.11).

Figure 4.11 A tree trunk of fading brush strokes. It's not much, but we had to start somewhere.

7. Click on the next smaller brush in the Brushes palette.
8. Make the first layer of curving branches coming off the trunk (Figure 4.12).

Figure 4.12 The trunk with branches added. Yours should be a reasonable facsimile of this, or perhaps nicer.

9. Click on the smallest soft brush in the Brushes palette.

10. Click on the **Paintbrush Options** tab. Change the fade setting to **Fade to Transparent** in the Fade dropdown menu.

11. Make lots of branchlets, all curving down like a willow's (Figure 4.13).

Figure 4.13 A leafless willow tree made of fading brush strokes of three sizes.

ADDING LEAVES WITH A CUSTOM BRUSH SHAPE

Instead of adding lots of tiny brush strokes individually, we will create a brush that does this in single strokes.

1. Change the foreground color by clicking on the closest thing to willow-green you can find in the Swatches palette.

2. With the smallest brush still selected, deselect **Fade** in the Options palette, and paint a single leaf on the image. Paint it slightly away from the branches.

3. Choose the **Lasso** tool (l) and circle the leaf to select it (Figure 4.14).

Figure 4.14 The single leaf selected by drawing around it with the Lasso tool. It is ready to be turned into a custom brush shape.

4. In the Brushes palette, open the Palette Options menu, as indicated in Figure 4.15, and drag to select the **Define Brush** command. This turns the selected leaf into a custom brush shape and adds it to the Brushes palette.

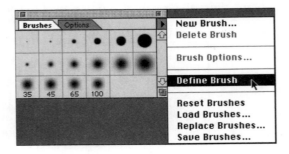

Figure 4.15 Selecting the **Define Brush** command from the Brushes Palette Options menu.

 All custom brushes are grayscale.

5. Choose **None** from the Select menu to drop the selection, **Command-d** (Macintosh) or **Ctrl-d** (Windows).

6. Double-click on the new custom brush shape in the Brushes palette, or select **Brush Options** from the Palette Options menu and set the spacing to **50%** in the Brush Options dialog box (Figure 4.16).

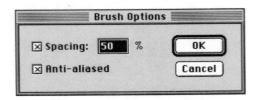

Figure 4.16 Setting a spacing of **50%** for the leaf-shaped custom brush shape in the Brush Options dialog box.

7. Start painting leaves by making curving strokes along the branchlets. Wow, the spacing option has made each stroke produce several leaves. (These are actually single compound leaves and leaflets, which is how willow trees grow.)

NOTE The custom brush shape is now a part of the Brushes palette until the palette is specifically reset. To save this useful willow-leaf brush, use the **Save** command in the Palette Options menu as described in this chapter.

Finish the leaves, and your willow tree is complete, a near masterpiece created solely with the Paintbrush (Figure 4.17). We've used the **Fade** option, several sizes of brushes, two colors, and a custom brush shape that we created.

Figure 4.17 The finished tree with compound leaves. Perhaps the trunk could be a little longer so that this didn't look like a vegetable, but it's clearly more willow than broccoli.

SAVE YOUR TREE

Choose **Save** from the File menu and put this resplendent willow someplace safe so that you can use it again for the next lesson.

Painting Tools' Options Palettes

In this chapter…

- Painting (blending) modes drop-down menu
- The opacity, pressure, and exposure sliders
- Setting fade
- Stylus pressure
- Check box options

In early versions of Photoshop, you could double-click on a tool icon in the Toolbox and bring up a dialog of tool-specific options. Starting with Version 3.0, all the options have been in the Options palette, and it changes when you select a tool. If the Options palette (see Figure 5.1) is closed, double-click on a tool to open to that tool's palette, or select **Show Options** from the Window menu to open the palette to the tool that is currently selected.

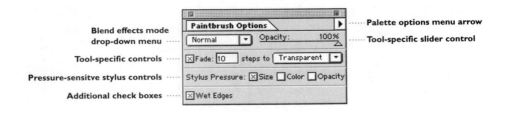

Figure 5.1 The paintbrush Options palette labeled to show the different sections. The painting tools share many options.

The Options tab in the Navigator/Info/Options palette group window changes names so you can tell which tool is selected without looking at the Toolbox— Paintbrush Options, Airbrush Options, and so on. As you set options, Photoshop retains your settings until you change them again.

To reset options to their default values, from the Palette Options menu, select one of the two commands shown in Figure 5.2. **Reset Tools** will return the values of the current palette's options to their default values. **Reset All Tools** resets all values in every palette, whether the palette is open or closed.

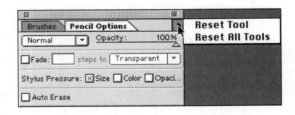

Figure 5.2 The Options menu for all the painting tools' Options palette has only two commands.

The Palette Options menu doesn't change as you select different tools. The only commands are **Reset Tools** and **Reset All Tools**.

N O T E

While each painting tool has a different set of options available in its palette, many of the options are the same across tools. Rather than discuss each palette individually, here is a guide to palette options and commands with information on how they apply to each tool.

PAINTING (BLENDING) MODES DROPDOWN MENU

This dropdown menu defaults to normal. Modes can be set separately for each tool by making a selection from the menu. The various modes and their actions (see in Figure 5.3) are discussed in Chapter 3.

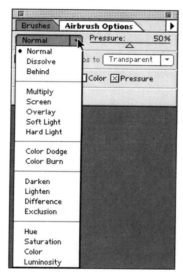

Figure 5.3 The Painting Modes dropdown menu and its 18 modes.

- The Paintbrush, Airbrush, Pencil, and Rubber Stamp tools can use all modes.
- The Smudge and Sharpen/Blur tools are limited to seven different modes (Figure 5.4).

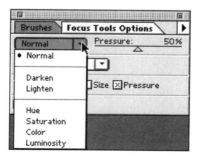

Figure 5.4 The Painting Modes dropdown menus with the seven modes used by the Smudge and Sharpen tools.

- The Eraser tool uses the effects modes—paintbrush, airbrush, pencil, and block—explained later in this chapter.
- The Toning tools—Dodge, Burn, and Sponge—use the tool operations, shadows, midtones, and highlights, explained later in this chapter.

THE OPACITY, PRESSURE, AND EXPOSURE SLIDERS

All eight painting tools include a slider control that can be moved back and forth with the mouse.

- The opacity slider ranges from 1% (transparent paint) to 100% (opaque paint) and is an option for the Paintbrush, Pencil, Eraser (when it's not in block mode), and Rubber Stamp tools. See Figure 5.5 for an example.

Figure 5.5 A grid of strokes made by the paintbrush at 20%, 40%, 60%, 80%, and 100% opacity.

- The pressure and exposure sliders range from 1% (weak effect) to 100% (strong effect). The Airbrush, Smudge, Sponge, and Focus tools have pressure sliders, while the Toning tools have an exposure slider. See Figure 5.6 for an example.

Figure 5.6 A grid of strokes made by the airbrush at 20%, 40%, 60%, 80%, and 100% pressure. Even though the same brush shape was used, you'll notice that the airbrush strokes are not as dense as the paintbrush strokes in Figure 5.5.

You can type in the percentage for any of the sliders.

N O T E

SETTING FADE

You can simulate the effect of exhausting the paint or ink by setting the **Fade** option for the Paintbrush, Airbrush, Pencil, and Eraser tools.

To create a fadeout:

1. Click in the **Fade** check box in the Options palette. The Paintbrush, Airbrush, and Pencil tools have Fade options, while the Eraser tool has a limited Fade option.

2. Type in the number of steps to a complete fadeout. This determines the rate of fade as indicated by one mark of the brush tip and can range from 1 to 9999.

3. In the Fade Options dropdown box, select either **transparent**, the default, or **background**. Note that this option is not available for the Eraser tool. See Figure 5.7.

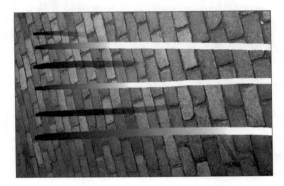

Figure 5.7 Alternating brush strokes of fade to transparent and fade to background with the number of steps set to **25**, **50**, and **75**. When fade to background is set, you can continue to draw using the background color, while fade to transparent gives the effect of running out of paint.

Your strokes will fade from the foreground color to nothing (transparent) or to the background color over the distance you've specified.

STYLUS PRESSURE

Digitizing tablets, such as those manufactured by Wacom, Kurta, and CalComp, feature pressure-sensitive styluses that vary the stroke width depending upon how hard you press. All eight painting tools include stylus pressure options.

There are three check box options. You can set them in any combination.

- **Size** allows the brush stroke to be thicker or thinner, depending on how much pressure is applied.
- **Color** changes the color of the brush stroke. Light pressure gives you the background color, medium pressure gives you a color between background and foreground, and the heaviest pressure yields the foreground color.
- **Opacity** makes the brush stroke more opaque with more pressure. See Figure 5.8.

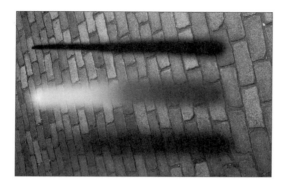

Figure 5.8 You may have noticed that the strokes in the previous illustrations varied in line width. As demonstrated in this figure, pressure-sensitive pens not only can vary line widths, but also color and opacity. In addition to these three settings applied individually, they can be used in combination.

Only the Paintbrush and Pencil tools include the **Opacity** option.

NOTE

CHECK BOX OPTIONS

The **Wet Edges** check box can be set for the Paintbrush and Eraser tool (when not in Block mode). This gives a watercolor effect, where paint builds up along the edges of the stroke, as shown in Figure 5.9.

Figure 5.9 Checking the **Wet Edges** option gives the paintbrush a more watercolor-like effect. Notice the darker stroke edges and overlapping effects.

The **Sample Merged** check box can be set for the Smudge, Rubber Stamp, and Focus tools. These tools sample pixels from the image as they paint and are capable of sampling from one layer as they paint into another. Checking the **Sample Merged** option forces sampling from all visible layers at once.

 Except for Clone options, the **Sample Merged** option works best when painting into a new layer.

N O T E

The **Auto-Erase** option works with the Pencil tool so that strokes beginning within the foreground color erase to the background color. With this option turned off, the Pencil tool always uses the foreground color.

Lesson 5: Painting Options

We've already examined the fade option in the previous lesson, so you've had some practice with painting options. This time we'll try out the modes and sliders. If you have a pressure-sensitive stylus, you can choose to use these options in this lesson.

TRICKS WITH MODES

I'm not happy with the colors we picked from the Swatches palette for our tree—too dark for a willow—and I'd like to put the tree on an island with a fish in the water.

Let's lighten the colors. There are numerous ways to do this, but the Soft Light blending mode should yield just the effect I'm looking for.

1. Open your willow tree from the previous lesson, or open the file called **WILLOW.PSD** from the Lesson05 folder on the CD. If this is your willow tree, use the **Save As** command in the File menu and give it a new name, so that you don't inadvertently overwrite it.

2. Select the **Airbrush** tool (a). If the Airbrush Options palette isn't open, double-click on the **Airbrush** tool or select **Show Options** from the Window menu. You'll also want to open the Brushes and Swatches palettes; use the **Show Brushes** and **Show Swatches** commands from the Window menu. Brushes and Swatches are in the same Palette group, so you can switch between them by clicking on their tabs in the Palette window. See Figure 5.10.

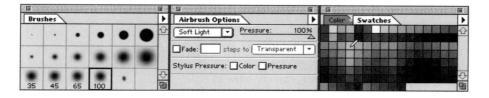

Figure 5.10 The three palettes you need to set to do this exercise: Brushes, Options, and Swatches. The Brushes palette has been dragged out of its palette group for this screen shot, as described in this chapter.

3. Move the pointer over the Painting Modes dropdown menu in the Airbrush Options palette. Hold down the mouse button and select the **Soft Light** mode.

4. Move the Pressure slider to 100% or type **0**.

N O T E Any number you type when a painting tool is active affects the slider. You can type a single digit to enter a percentage multiple of 10 or type two digits to enter an exact percentage. This doesn't work if you type 3 digits, so type **0** for 100%.

5. Choose the **100-pixel** brush from the Brushes palette.

6. Choose the **pale yellow**, fourth from the left and third from the top, from the Swatches menu. (See Figure 5.10.)

7. Move the pointer into the image over the tree. Hold down the mouse button and drag to spray with the Airbrush. You don't have to be very careful where you spray, because the Soft Light painting mode doesn't affect white pixels. Spray over the entire tree. The addition of yellow to the colors in the tree gives the effect of summer light, shown in Figure 5.11.

Figure 5.11 Your willow tree before and after painting with the Soft Light mode.

Now, let's put the tree on an island.

1. Change the painting mode to **Darken** by selecting it from the Modes drop-down menu in the Airbrush Options palette. Leave all other settings the same.

2. Move the pointer into the image, press down the mouse button, and paint the tree onto a sandy island, as in Figure 5.12. What's going on here? Now the yellow paints only in white areas, and the tree is unaffected. This is because the Darken mode only affects pixels that have a lightness value less than 50%—the white pixels in this image.

Figure 5.12 You can paint an island under an existing tree by using the Darken mode.

3. Even though we haven't discussed the Paintbucket tool (b) yet, select it and set the Tolerance in the Options palette to **70**. The **Anti-alias** box should be checked.

4. Select **dark blue** off the top row of the Swatches palette by clicking on it.

5. Click in any of the white space around the island to create the water. The results are shown in Figure 5.13.

Figure 5.13 Filling a sea with the Paintbucket tool.

Next, we'll draw a fish (or borrow one).

1. Choose **Open** from the File menu and select **FISH_OUT.PSD** from the **Lesson05** folder on the CD. Make sure the Layers palette is open, that the Fish outline image is active, and that the image we are creating (the willow) is visible, but not active.

2. Drag the Green Fish layer out of the Layers palette and into the inactive, but visible, willow image window. Release the mouse button when a highlight border appears around the willow window as you drag into it. This creates a new layer in the willow image with the green fish in it and activates the image window, as shown in Figure 5.14.

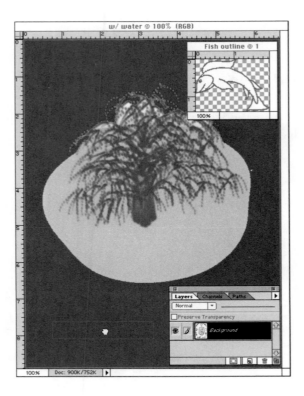

Figure 5.14 Copy the fish by dragging from the Layers palette of the Fish outline image into the willow image window.

3. Click on the **Preserve Transparency** box in the Layers palette. This makes it easy to paint the fish without spilling into the sea.

4. Select the **Airbrush** tool (a). Set the Transparency slider in the Options palette to **10%**. Set the Painting Mode back to **Normal** from the drop-down menu. The foreground color should still be set to **blue**.

5. Choose the **100 pixel** brush from the Brushes palette.

6. Paint over the fish in one or two passes, so that it blends in slightly with the sea (see Figure 5.15).

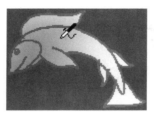

Figure 5.15 Apply a very light spray from the airbrush to blend the fish into the sea. Selecting **Preserve Transparency** in the Layers palette keeps the paint completely within the fish.

You can also just paint in your own fish if you're so inclined.

Finally, we'll stripe the fish.

1. Pick the **brightest yellow** from the fifth row of the Swatches palette by clicking on it, and then pick the **dark red** from the same row by **Option**-clicking (Macintosh) or **Alt**-clicking (Windows). You've now set the foreground and background colors.

2. Choose the **Paintbrush** tool (b). Open the Paintbrush Options palette, set the opacity to **80%**, and check the **Wet Edges** box.

3. Select the second smallest brush from the second row of the Brushes palette.

4. Paint slightly curving stripes in the shape of a fish, keeping a slight space between each stripe. See Figure 5.16.

Figure 5.16 Evenly spaced fish-shaped stripes. The effects of transparency on the darker brush strokes is more evident here.

5. Now select a harder brush, one size larger from the top row of the Brushes palette.

6. Turn off the **Wet Edges** option and set the Opacity slider to **50%** in the Paintbrush Options palette.

7. Click on the **Exchange** button (x) in the Color Selection area of the Toolbox to make red the foreground color.

8. Carefully paint red stripes in between the yellow stripes. Stripe the fins as well, and you have a fish in the water.

Using the Painting Tools

In this chapter...

- The big three in painting—Paintbrush, Airbrush, and Pencil
- The Eraser and its options
- Toning, Focus, and Smudge tools
- The multifaceted Rubber Stamp

In Photoshop, painting is the act of changing image information bit by bit. The painting division of the Toolbox includes eight tools that make this task easier and in many ways behave similarly to their more traditional namesakes. And while you may not consider a pencil a painting tool, in Photoshop, it paints in a pencil-like manner.

All the painting tools use the foreground color and are controlled by the options you set in the Options palette.

THE BIG THREE IN PAINTING

Photoshop has three basic tools that allow you to create strokes as if you were painting or sketching: the Paintbrush, Airbrush, and Pencil. They are designed to simulate the "real" tools of the same names, but each works similarly to the others and has similar options. However, the differences are notable, and you will use each tool for specific purposes in your images.

The Paintbrush allows you to create brush-like effects (see Figure 6.1). Choose a brush from the Brushes palette and a color from the Toolbox or color palettes group. Your strokes can vary from soft to hard, dark to light, wide to narrow, achieving various levels of perceived reality. The options you set affect how the strokes blend with the existing image. To avoid blending, apply your strokes to a new layer.

Figure 6.1 A paintbrush sketch of baby Wells. (Nothing fancy here, but notice how the paintbrush produces soft-edged strokes.)

The *Airbrush* simulates the dispersal of paint through an airbrush. It works very much the same way as the Paintbrush, except that paint appears to "build up" as you paint over the same area. Painting faster applies less paint, while moving more slowly applies a thicker coat of paint. Contrast this to the use of a pressure-sensitive pen that can be set to make a stroke thicker or thinner as you press harder or more softly. The Airbrush makes a stroke more or less opaque as you move the mouse slower or faster—it lays down more or less ink in whatever blend mode you have selected. See Figure 6.2.

Figure 6.2 While you can see the strokes the Airbrush made in this image, it is best at filling larger areas and creating textures. As with a real airbrush, you can work in much finer detail by using masks.

The *Pencil* (Figure 6.3) is like a hard-edged version of the Paintbrush. Even with a brush set to 100% hardness, the Paintbrush anti-aliases the edges to soften them while the Pencil does not. Only the size and shape of the brush can be adjusted when using the Pencil tool.

Figure 6.3 A pencil tracing of young Wells. Notice the hard-edged lines of the pencil stroke. You can adjust the opacity and fade of the strokes, but not the hardness.

THE ERASER AND ITS OPTIONS

The Eraser treats the image like a blackboard, so that in block mode (which used to be the default, but isn't anymore) it behaves like a hard-edged blackboard eraser, and anything you rub over reverts to the background color. Block mode uses a fixed size eraser.

By setting the Effect Mode in the eraser Options palette, you can make the eraser behave like the Paintbrush, Airbrush, or Pencil. This gives you access to painting-like options and lets you vary the Eraser size by selecting brushes from the Brushes palette. These modes turn the Eraser into a painting tool in reverse, painting with the background color. You get painting tool effects with eraser control. See Figure 6.4.

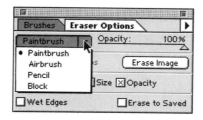

Figure 6.4 The Eraser tool's Options palette showing the eraser-specific options. Most of these options aren't available in Block mode.

You can cycle through the Eraser tool modes by **Option-clicking** (Macintosh) or **Alt-clicking** (Windows) on the Eraser tool icon.

The are two other unique options in the Eraser tools Options palette: Erase Image/Layer and Erase to Saved.

Click the **Erase Image/Layer** button to erase the entire image. This causes the image or the background layer to fill with the background color. If another layer is active, the layer is erased and set to transparent.

Erasing to a Saved Image

Many programs, including Photoshop, have a Revert command in the File menu that has the effect of removing all changes you made since you last saved the document. The Erase to Saved option allows you to revert selectively. (This used to be called the "magic eraser.")

1. Click on the **Erase to Saved** check box or hold down the **Option** key (Macintosh) or **Alt** key (Windows). The pointer changes into an eraser over a file icon.
2. Erase an area of the image. Instead of erasing to the background color, any changes you made since last saving the image are removed, and the saved image is restored.

TONING, FOCUS, AND SMUDGE TOOLS

The Toning tools include the Dodge, Burn, and Sponge tools. The Dodge and Burn tools (Figures 6.5 and 6.6) lighten and darken the image in the same way a photographer would when enlarging images in a darkroom. The Sponge tool (Figure 6.7) works the same way to change color saturation.

The toning tools—three figures showing the effects of dodging, burning, and sponging on Wells' Grandmother's cheekbone. The two circles in Figure 6.7 show the effects of the sponge's saturate and desaturate modes.

Figure 6.5 –6.7 Show the effects of dodging, burning, and sponging. The sponge in Figure 6.7 show the effectsof the sponge's saturate and desaturate modes.

To darken an area of an image:

1. Select the **Burn** tool, so called because more light from the enlarger was allowed to expose the paper in this area, thus burning the image.
2. Select **Shadows**, **Midtones**, or **Highlights** from the mode dropdown box in the Options palette. This determines the level of grays, dark, medium, or light, that are affected by the tool.
3. Pass the pointer over the area of the image you want to darken. The effect can be increased by passing the pointer over the image multiple times.

To lighten an area of an image:

1. Select the **Dodge** tool, so called because less light from the enlarger was allowed to expose the paper in this area, thus dodging the image.
2. Use it as you would the Burn tool.

To intensify/dilute color saturation:

1. Select the **Sponge** tool.
2. Select **Saturate** or **Desaturate** from the modes dropdown box in the Options palette.
3. Drag over the image to change the color saturation.

 The Toning tools have no effect on bitmap or indexed color images.

N O T E

The Focus tools include Sharpen, which increases the contrast between pixels, and Blur, which reduces detail by making it look fuzzy. You can also use filters to adjust image focus, but the tools allow you to work on areas of an image in an ad hoc manner. See Figure 6.8.

Figure 6.8 Before and after demonstration of the Sharpen and Blur tools.

The Focus tools have no effect on bitmap or indexed color images.

NOTE

The Smudge tool behaves like a finger being rubbed over wet paint. The color at the starting point of your stroke is smudged through any following colors, while following colors are picked up and smudged, as well.

The Smudge tool has no affect on bitmap or indexed color images.

NOTE

Finger Painting

With the Finger Paint option selected, the smudge starts with the foreground color instead of the image color under the pointer.

- Check the **Finger Paint** check box in the Smudge Tool Options palette.
- Hold down the **Option** key (Macintosh) or **Alt** key (Windows) to finger paint. See Figure 6.9.

Figure 6.9 Standard smudging and fingerpainting.

THE MULTIFACETED RUBBER STAMP

The Rubber Stamp tool is Photoshop's cloner. It paints by copying pixels from one area of an image to another area, or to a completely different image. This is referred to as *sampling*, and it provides a way to copy and paste without making a selection. This gives the tool special powers to clone with patterns, using an "impressionistic" style, or to revert to a saved image. Many of the standard painting modes and brush options apply to the Rubber Stamp tool.

To clone an image:

1. Select the **Rubber Stamp** tool.
2. Move the pointer to the source area for the clone and **Option-click** (Macintosh) or **Alt-click** (Windows) to set the source point.
3. Move the pointer to the destination area. Hold down the mouse button and start painting. The pixels painted are copied from the source area. In addition to the Rubber Stamp pointer, a crosshairs pointer indicates the clone source as you paint. See Figure 6.10.

To clone from one window to another:

1. Make sure that the destination window is active.
2. **Option-click** (Macintosh) or **Alt-click** (Windows) on the area of the inactive window you wish to clone.
3. Paint as usual.

Figure 6.10 Simple cloning with the Rubber Stamp tool.

The rubber stamp tool only clones from the active layer. If you wish to clone from all layers, check the **Sample Merged** box in the Rubber Stamp Options palette.

Rubber Stamp Options

There several ways to use the rubber stamp tool, and you can set these from the options dropdown box in the Options palette.

Aligned and Non-Aligned Cloning

Aligned cloning copies relative to the point at which you start painting. As you move the pointer, the source pointer moves with it, even if you stop and start cloning.

Non-aligned cloning copies relative to the original source point. This allows you to make copies of an area in several places on your image, because the source point returns to the original spot each time you start to paint again. See Figure 6.11.

Figure 6.11 The difference between aligned and non-aligned cloning.

To paint with a pattern:

1. Make a selection in any image.
2. Choose the **Define Pattern** command from the Edit menu.
3. Select the **Rubber Stamp** tool. (You can make sure the Options palette is open by double-clicking to select.)
4. Select **Pattern** from the Options dropdown menu in the Options palette. (Aligned and non-aligned patterns work as described above for standard cloning.)
5. Drag to paint with the pattern. Aligned patterns paint contiguous tiles, while non-aligned paint from the center of the pattern each time you start painting.

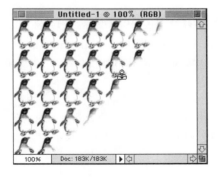

Figure 6.12 Painting with a pattern.

To Paint from a Snapshot

Each image has a snapshot buffer separate from your computer's Clipboard. You can use it to save a selection without overwriting the Clipboard.

1. Make a selection in an image.
2. Choose the **Edit, Take Snapshot** command.
3. Select the **Rubber Stamp** tool.
4. Select **From Snapshot** from the Options dropdown menu in the Options palette.
5. Drag to paint with the snapshot as the source image.

To Paint from a Saved Image

This option duplicates the function of the Erase to Saved option of the Eraser tool as described previously in this chapter.

To Use the Impressionist Option

Like the Saved Image option, the Impressionist option uses the last saved version of the active file. As you drag over the image, pixels from it and the saved version are "smeared" together to create an impressionistic effect.

NOTE You may experience a time delay using the Saved Image and Impressionist options while the saved image is read from disk. But if you click first, the image will be loaded into memory and you will experience no further delays.

Figure 6.13 Impressionist option.

Lesson 6: Using the Painting Tools

The lessons seem to be one step ahead of the chapters. In the previous lesson, you had a chance to use the Paintbrush and Airbrush tools, so we'll concentrate more on the Pencil, Eraser, and the manipulative painting tools in this lesson.

THE NAKED PENCIL

1. Open the file called **HARDY_SI.PSD** from the Lesson06 folder on the CD. Can you tell what Hardy is?

2. Click on the **Default Colors** button in the Toolbox to reset the foreground and background colors to black and white.

3. Select the Pencil tool (y). If anyone can tell me why the shortcut key for the Pencil tool is 'y,' I will be very grateful. Is it because most pencils are yellow or is it just that most of the other letters are assigned to more frequently used tools? If the Pencil Options palette isn't open, double-click on the **Pencil** tool.

4. Select the three-pixel brush, second from the left on the top row.

5. In the Pencil Options palette, click on the **Auto Erase** box to turn it on.

6. In the white background, draw the word **Hardy**. Add a flourish, if you're so inclined.

Figure 6.14 gives you a feel for what the pencil tool is like and what a completely hard-edged line looks like. Most Photoshop artwork one sees is smoothed, blended, or anti-aliased in various ways. You forget what an old-fashioned jagged line looks like.

But you're wondering why you turned the Auto Erase option on (and why the Pencil tool shortcut key is 'y').

Figure 6.14 The Pencil tool makes handwriting look as though it were done by a child. It is perhaps most useful when editing single pixels at high magnification, or when editing an image in bitmap mode.

Auto Erasing

1. With all the same settings, draw eyes, nose, head, leg, and tail onto the black body of the dog where they might go. Aha! When drawing on black, the same color as the selected foreground color, the pencil erases pixels to the background color, which happens to be white in this case (see Figure 6.15). This only works when you start the line on a black area.

Figure 6.15 This silhouette of Hardy looks a bit more dog-like after you draw in some features with the Pencil tool set to Auto Erase. The intelligent fix of the eyes was added by making single dots with a 9-pixel brush and then adding glints with a 3-pixel brush.

But what is the Auto Erase option actually useful for?

2. Select the **Zoom** tool (z) and click on the image until you can discern the actual square pixels, or drag over Hardy's head with the Zoom tool to enlarge the image.

3. Select the single-pixel brush (the smallest) from the Brushes palette.

4. Try touching up some of the jagged lines you've drawn with the Pencil. If you start to draw when the pointer is on a white pixel, the Pencil tool uses the foreground color and draws black. If you start on a black pixel, the opposite happens. This makes it easy to straighten out (or make more jagged) your lines without changing the foreground and background colors repeatedly (see Figure 6.16).

5. Save your image before starting the next section.

Figure 6.16 Editing at the pixel level with the Pencil tool. This image is magnified 300%,, larger magnifications make bit editing even easier. The drawback is that you can lose sight of the big picture.

THE ERASER STANDS ALONE

We'll continue to experiment on Hardy, so if you need to refresh your image, open the **HARDY_2.PSD** file from the Lesson06 folder.

1. Select the **Eraser** tool (e) from the Toolbox.

2. Select **Block Erasing** mode from the dropdown menu in the Eraser Options palette.

3. Drag through the hand-lettering. The black pixels are erased to the background color, which is white. This is archetypal eraser behavior, shown in Figure 6.17.

Figure 6.17 The Block mode for the Eraser tool hasn't changed since its original introduction with MacPaint in 1984.

4. Change the background color to red by **Option-clicking** (Macintosh) or **Alt-clicking** (Windows) in the Swatches palette.

5. Choose **Pencil** mode from the dropdown menu in the Eraser palette and set the Opacity slider to 50%.

6. Erase the flourish in the image window (see Figure 6.18). It's like painting with the background window and is, as far as I can tell, no different from using the Pencil tool.

Figure 6.18 The Eraser is a painting tool, too. On top, the Eraser in Block mode wiped a clean swathe through the text; below, changing the mode turned the Eraser into a Pencil that drew this wide gray line. The pointer icon is no longer indicative of the Eraser's size, which is set in the Brushes palette.

7. Now we've made a mess, so turn on the **Erase to Saved** option in the Eraser Options palette by clicking on it.

8. Erase over everything you've changed in this section, and it reverts to the last saved version. Be aware that there is a slight delay before reversion starts while Photoshop reads the saved version off the disk. Then notice how this selective reversion with Opacity set to 50% produces a curious result, like a ghost image. If you slide Opacity up to 100%, you end up entirely erasing the previous actions of the eraser.

THE ELECTRONIC DARKROOM

We've been working with Photoshop's metaphorical painting and drawing tools. It's time to tackle a new metaphor—photography and the darkroom.

Toning Tools

1. Open the file HARDY_BE.PSD from the Lesson06 folder on the CD. This is as close to living color as Scotties get. I want to reveal the shape of Hardy's head a bit more.

2. Select the **Dodge** tool (o) from the Toolbox.

3. Set the Exposure to 30% and leave the dropdown selection on Midtones in the Toning Tools Options palette (see Figure 6.19).

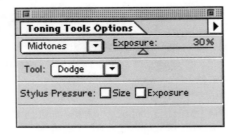

Figure 6.19 The Toning Tools Options palette set for the Dodge tool. You can change the tool by using the Tool dropdown menu.

4. Choose the 17-pixel soft brush from the Brushes palette, fourth from the left in the middle row.

5. Work over the left side of Hardy's face. (That's your left, not his.) Work in short strokes, because you'll have better control as the effects build up. You can lighten his beard a little more than his muzzle and cheek.

6. Now switch to the Burn tool (o), either by typing 'o' again, by using the dropdown menu in the Options palette, or by revealing the hidden tools under the Dodge icon in the Toolbar and selecting from there. Leave the options and brush selection the same.

7. Work over the neck, shoulder, and chest so that the contrast between body and head is more apparent.

The effects of the Dodge and Burn tools should be subtle. When they become obvious, generally you've gone too far.

Focus Tools

The Sharpen tool will allow us to give Hardy a clearer gaze and healthier look-ing nose.

1. Select the **Sharpen** tool (r) from the Toolbox and leave the default options and brush. You can choose **Reset Tool** from the Options Palette menu if the defaults have been changed.
2. Work over both eyes and the nose to make them look, well, sharper. Like the Toning tools, the Focus tools have a cumulative effect, but you can only sharpen so far.

Smudge Tool

I think Hardy's beard is a little too straggly. We'll smooth it out a little.

1. Select the **Smudge** tool (u) from the Toolbox and leave the default options and brush.
2. Work over the beard. While the Toning and Focus tools change pixels without regard to the motion of the mouse, the smudge tool actually moves pixels around to where you send them. So work in a consistently downward direction, using short strokes. You may even want to go back over your smudging with the Sharpen tool so that the strokes don't stand out from the rest of the image. Figure 6.20 shows the results.

Figure 6.20 Hardy, before and after. The changes are subtle, mere details, but these are techniques that can be applied to great effect.

Save your work, and that's it for Hardy. No dramatic, gee whiz effects—just some subtle improvements. Only obedience school can help now.

CLONING CLASS

Every good obedience class must supply treats, so we will clone plenty of them so as not to run out.

Aligned Cloning

1. Use the New File command to create a new image. In the New dialog, set the Height and Width to three inches and the Resolution to 144 pixels per inch, as shown in Figure 6.21.

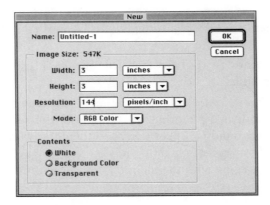

Figure 6.21 The New dialog showing the correct settings for this part of the lesson. The units are displayed in dropdown menus, so if you need to convert pixels to inches, hold down the dropdown menu and choose the units you want from the list.

2. Open the file **DOG_BONE.PSD** from the Lesson06 folder on the CD. Drag the window to the side so that you can work on both windows at the same time. Click on the **Untitled** window to make it active.

3. Select the **Rubber Stamp** tool (s) from the Toolbox. Double-click when selecting to make sure that the Rubber Stamp Options palette is open. We will use the default options for starters.

4. Select the 100-pixel brush from the Brushes palette.

   You need to set the cloning source first. Since the source and the destination are two different windows, we need to use a little trick.

5. Hold down the **Option** key (Macintosh) or **Alt** key (Windows) and click in the upper-left corner of the Dog Bone image (Figure 6.22). This allows you to set the source without activating the window.

Figure 6.22 Setting the image source in an inactive window by holding down the **Option** key (Macintosh) or **Alt** key (Windows).

6. Move the pointer back into the active Untitled window, hold down the mouse button, and drag the Rubber Stamp tool over the image.

Notice how a crosshairs pointer follows along in the Dog Bone window as you drag in the Untitled window, and that the area under the cross-hairs is cloned into the active window. Also notice that you can click and drag repeatedly to finish your clone, but that you can only clone in one place. This is because the source and target are aligned, the default setting for the Rubber Stamp tool.

Non-Aligned Cloning

1. From the Option dropdown menu in the Rubber Stamp Options palette, select the **Clone (non-aligned)** option (see Figure 6.23). Changing the option does not affect the cloning source.

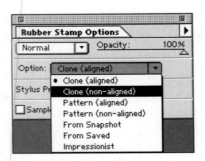

Figure 6.23 The Rubber Stamp Options palette showing the Option dropdown menu with aligned and non-aligned options.

2. Move the pointer into the Untitled window again and make another clone. This time you'll see that as you release the mouse button and start cloning again, the source returns to the starting point. You can clone bones all over the new image without resetting the source point, because the source and target are not aligned.

3. In the Rubber Stamp Options palette, set the Opacity slider to 50%. Set the blend mode to darken so that white edges won't show through if bones overlap. Make a few more bone clones. Lower the Opacity to 30% and clone some more. Make a few more clones with the Opacity set to 10% to finish up the background of this image. The results are shown in Figure 6.24.

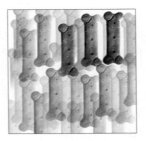

Figure 6.24 Many bone clones of varying opacities made with non-aligned cloning.

4. If you've still got the image window open from the previous section of this lesson, make it visible, or open the file **HARDY_AF.PSD** from the Lesson06 folder of the CD. Arrange the windows on your desktop so that both the Untitled window and Hardy After are visible. Click on the **Untitled** window to make it active.

5. Set the Option back to **Clone (aligned)** in the Rubber Stamp Options palette.

6. Set the Opacity slider to 70% in the Rubber Stamp Options palette. The mode should still be set to Darken.

7. **Option-click** (Macintosh) or **Alt-click** (Windows) on Hardy's face to set the cloning source point.

8. Move the pointer to the center of the Untitled window. Hold down the mouse button and copy Hardy's head over the bones. Follow the crosshairs in the Hardy After window as you clone. The Darken mode assures that none of the white background from the Hardy image will obliterate our carefully cloned dog bones. See Figure 6.25.

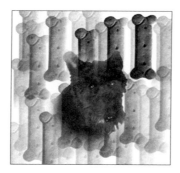

Figure 6.25 This hungry but well-behaved dog was created entirely with the Rubber Stamp tool.

Drawing, Filling, & Text Tools

In this Section:

- Drawing
- Filling
- Adding type to an image

Drawing

In this chapter...

- The Line tool
- The Pen tool

THE LINE TOOL

Like the constrained Pencil tool, the Line tool draws straight lines. The options for the Line tool are similar to other image creation tools, but the Line tool is not affected by brush shape and so is not a painting tool like the Pencil. You can set painting mode, opacity, line width, anti-aliasing, and add arrowheads to lines as you draw (see Figure 7.1).

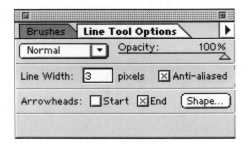

Figure 7.1 The Line tool's Options palette is similar to all other tool palettes, but the Line tool is not affected by brush shape.

To draw a straight line:

1. Select the **Line** tool from the Toolbox by clicking on it or typing l.
2. Click in the image window and drag. Photoshop follows your movements with a line as you drag.
3. Release the mouse button, and the line is drawn from the point where you clicked to the point where you released.

To constrain the angle of a line, hold down the **Shift** key as you drag to constrain the line to multiples of 45°.

   To specify line width:

1. Double-click the **Line** tool to show the options palette.
2. Click in the Line Width box and type in a width in pixels, from 1 to 1000.
3. Draw the line. Photoshop indicates the width of the line as you drag the cursor.

To create arrowheads:

1. Double-click the **Line** tool to show the options palette.
2. In the Arrowheads check boxes, select either **Start**, **End**, or both.
3. Click on the **Shape** button to edit the appearance of arrowheads (see Figure 7.2).

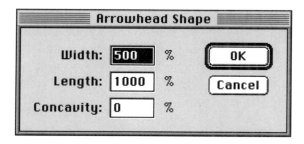

Figure 7.2 The Arrowhead Shape dialog for editing the appearance of arrowheads in relation to the line they're attached to.

4. The Arrowhead Shape dialog allows you to specify width, length, and concavity of the arrowhead(s) within the following parameters:

   • Width is specified as a percentage of line width from 10% to 1000%.
   • Length is specified as a percentage of line width from 10% to 5000%.
   • Concavity is specified from -50% to +50% and defines the curvature of the arrowhead from the widest part to the point where the arrow head meets the line.

5. Draw the line after specifying the arrowhead. Photoshop draws the image of the line and arrowhead as you drag. Figure 7.3 shows some examples.

Figure 7.3 A selection of arrowheads with varying specifications.

THE PEN TOOL

The Pen is special among Photoshop's image creation tools, because it doesn't paint with pixels. Instead, it draws paths and works just like the drawing tools in Adobe Illustrator.

Paths are composed of straight and curved line segments drawn between control points. Instead of painting directly on the image the way you would with the Paintbrush tool, you click to set anchor points and drag direction lines to create curves. If this seems to you like a counterintuitive way to draw lines, you are not alone. But the Pen tool and the paths it creates have some tremendous advantages.

NOTE Paths do not alter the pixels in the image in any way, and even though they are displayed with the image, they are not printed. Paths provide a means to make and save selections and it is these selections, not the paths that define them, that you can manipulate to affect your image. It's possible to turn a path into pixels, and this, as much as anything, explains why the Pen tool is included with the image-creation tools instead of the selection tools.

Paths retain their identity as objects and can be reshaped and moved without affecting the background or surrounding layers. The significance and details of working with paths are discussed in Chapter 18.

Drawing Straight Lines with the Pen Tool

1. Select the **Pen** tool from the Toolbox (p).
2. Click in the image window to set the starting anchor point.
3. Click again to set the next anchor point. Photoshop connects the two points with a straight line path.
4. You can continue clicking, and Photoshop will continue connecting the anchor points with straight line segments.
5. Click on the starting anchor point to close the path. Note the small circle that appears next to the pointer as it comes close to the starting point, indicating that the path will be closed if you click.

Drawing Curved Lines with the Pen Tool

1. Select the **Pen** tool from the Toolbox (p).

2. Click and drag in the image window to set an anchor point and create direction lines.

3. Click and drag again to set the next anchor point and its direction line. The direction lines determine the angle and direction of the curved segment.

Drawing curved segments is just like drawing straight segments, except that you simply click for the one, while you click and drag for the other. It's possible to mix straight segment anchor points with curved segments by clicking, or clicking and dragging, as you set down anchor points. You can try this out in Lesson 7, which also explains some of the finer points of direction lines.

Using the Rubber Band Option

The Pen tool has only a single option: the rubber band check box.

1. Double-click on the **Pen** tool (p) to open its Options palette.

2. Click in the Rubber Band check box to select it.

As you move the pointer, Photoshop indicates the curve that would be drawn if you were to click. This is simply a way to preview a curve before committing yourself by clicking.

Using the Hidden Pen Tools

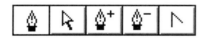

Figure 7.4 The Pen tool pop-up menu showing the default Pen tool and the four hidden tools.

The Pen tool hides four additional path creation tools: Direct selection, Add-anchor-point, Delete-anchor-point, and Convert-anchor-point.

Move the pointer over the Pen tool. Hold down the mouse button and the hidden tools menu pops up. Slide the pointer over one of the hidden tools to select it.

More information about the Pen tools is included in Chapter 18.

Lesson 7: Line & Path Exercise

LINE AND PATH EXERCISE

The Line and Pen tools are not like other image creation tools. They are purely electronic creations without precedent in the world of traditional drawing and painting media. While the Line tool is pretty straightforward, it can take a little practice to learn how to use the Pen tool effectively. Here's your chance.

Anchor Points and Direction Lines

We're going to trace over a template to practice using the Line and Pen tools.

1. Open the file **PEBNTEMP.PSD** from the Lesson07 folder on the CD.

   The squares represent anchor points, and they are aligned along a vertical guide for this exercise.

2. Select the **Pen** tool (p) from the Toolbox.

3. Move the pointer over the topmost anchor point. Click and drag to the right.

   This defines the first direction line for the curve to follow (Figure 7.5), but it takes two anchor points before Photoshop can actually draw a curved line.

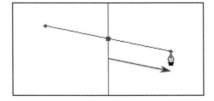

Figure 7.5 Click and drag in the direction of the curve. When the curve is drawn, it will follow the direction you've dragged.

4. Move the pointer over the next anchor point down. Click and drag to the left. As you drag, Photoshop draws a curve between the two anchor points, as shown in Figure 7.6.

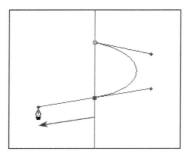

Figure 7.6 Two anchor points equal one curved line segment.

N O T E
Direction lines are vectors and therefore have properties of amplitude and directionality. Paths follow the direction of the direction line. When you drag to the right, the curve follows to the right at an angle determined by the angle of the direction line. The curve always follows behind the direction line.

5. Move to the next anchor point, click, and drag to the right again. Alternating sides this way creates a reverse 'S' curve, as shown in Figure 7.7.

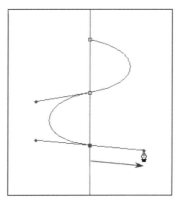

Figure 7.7 The number of curves equals the number of anchor points minus one. Here are three anchor points and two curved line segments creating a reversed 'S'.

6. Now **Option-click** (Macintosh) or **Ctrl-click** (Windows) on the third anchor point again. This allows you to change directions or make a sharp angle.

7. Let go of the mouse button, then click and drag to the left. Since the line will follow this direction line, you are about to create a second left-facing curve. See Figure 7.8.

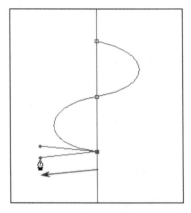

Figure 7.8 If you Option/Alt-click on an anchor point, you can change directions by dragging a direction line in the opposite direction. This does not add an anchor point, but lets you adjust the direction lines on both sides of it independently.

8. Click and drag on the next anchor point down to complete the double-bump (see Figure 7.9).

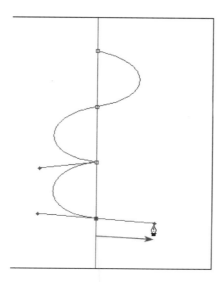

Figure 7.9 The result of changing directions leaves two curves on the same side of the line, like a '3' instead of an 'S'.

9. To add a straight line segment, **Option-click** (Macintosh) or **Ctrl-click** (Windows) on the fourth anchor point.

10. Move the pointer over the fifth anchor point and click to make a line segment, as shown in Figure 7.10.

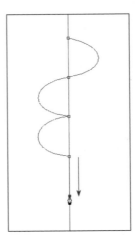

Figure 7.10 Changing directions can also mean changing from curved segments to straight and back again. By adjusting anchor points, you can continue a path without interruption.

It takes only two anchor points to create a curved line that subtends 180°, and one more anchor point takes you the rest of the way around 360°. So, for a smoother curve, use the fewest number of control points possible.

Now try moving some of the control points around to see what happens. **Option/Alt-click** on an anchor point to select it and its associated direction line(s). Selected anchor points are solid, while others are hollow. Drag the handles of a direction line around to see what effect this has. Use some of the hidden pen tools to add, delete, and convert anchor points. Use the Direct-selection tool to move anchor points around. Note the remarkable ease with which paths can be edited. It makes it possible to define a path quickly and then fine-tune it to meet your needs exactly.

Lines with Arrowheads

Since the template has some diagrammatic pointers, we'll practice by tracing over them as well.

1. Double-click on **Line tool** (n) to select and open the options for that tool.

2. Set the Opacity slider in the Line Options palette to 60%. Make sure the line width is set to 1 pixel and the Anti-aliased box is checked.

3. Click on the **End** check box as shown in Figure 7.11 to add arrowheads to the finishing end of every line you draw.

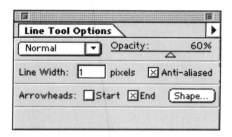

Figure 7.11 The Line Options palette as set for this exercise.

4. Click on the **Shape** button in the Line Options palette. In the Arrowhead Shape dialog (Figure 7.12), set the Width to 800%, Length to 1200%, and the Concavity to 30%. This will make an elegant arrowhead.

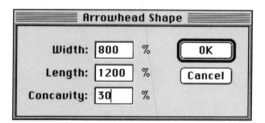

Figure 7.12 The Arrowhead Shape dialog as set for this exercise.

5. Start at the centerline in the Template file we've been working with and drag to trace the arrowhead. Photoshop previews the line and arrowhead as you drag.

Finish dragging arrowhead lines as indicated in the template. If we had wanted horizontal lines instead of angled lines, we would have held down the **Shift** key while dragging. You can also add step numbers using the Text tool if you wish.

Filling

In this chapter...

- The Paint Bucket tool
- The Eyedropper tool
- The Gradient tool

THE PAINT BUCKET TOOL

The Paint Bucket lets you fill large areas of an image with a single click—it's like spilling a bucket of paint onto the floor. When you click, contiguous pixels of the same color value are changed to the foreground color. When the fill reaches differently-colored pixels, the "spill" stops.

The Paint Bucket cannot be used in bitmap mode.

The Paint Bucket is a simple tool and most of its options are similar to the painting options, with the addition of a tolerance setting and pattern fill option (see Figure 8.1).

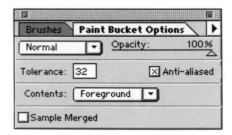

Figure 8.1 The Paint Bucket Options palette.

To set the tolerance, enter a number into the Tolerance field in the Options palette. Tolerance is measured from 0 to 255 corresponding to the similarity of color values necessary to determine the fill area. Smaller values require a closer match, while larger values will spread the paint farther before finding a border.

You can smooth the edges of a Paint Bucket fill by selecting the Anti-aliased box in the Options palette.

To fill with a pattern, select **Pattern** from the Contents dropdown box in the Options menu. The Paint Bucket will now fill with the chosen pattern rather than the foreground color. (Defining patterns is described Chapter 21.)

THE EYEDROPPER TOOL

The Eyedropper tool is used to set the foreground or background color by sampling colors from any open window (see Figure 8.2).

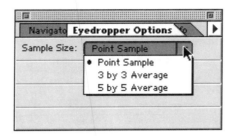

Figure 8.2 The Eyedropper Tool Options palette showing the sample size options.

To sample colors:

1. Select the **Eyedropper** tool (i) in the Toolbox.

 By holding down the **Option** key (Macintosh) or **Alt** key (Windows), the pointer becomes an eyedropper, ready to take a quick color sample no matter which tool is currently selected.

N O T E

2. Move the pointer to a color in your image and click to change the foreground color.
3. To change the background color, **Option-click** (Macintosh) or **Alt-click** (Windows).

If you want to change the sampling size, the Options palette for the Eyedropper tool has one dropdown menu for setting the sample size.

- **Point Sample** samples the color of a single pixel in the image.
- **3-by-3 Average** samples an area of 9 square pixels and averages the values.
- **5-by-5 Average** samples an area of 25 square pixels and averages the values.

THE GRADIENT TOOL

The gradient tool makes fills of graded color (see Figure 8.3) and has been substantially improved in Photoshop 4. Unlike the Paint Bucket, the Gradient tool requires a selection to define the limits of the gradient. Otherwise, the fill completely fills the active layer.

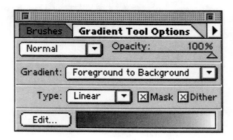

Figure 8.3 The Gradient Tool Options palette.

To make a gradient fill:

1. Select the Gradient tool and double-click to open the Gradient tool's (g) Options palette.

2. Choose a gradient from the Gradient dropdown menu. The options allow you to set painting mode and opacity like other painting tools.

3. To make a linear fill, select **Linear** from the Type dropdown box. Drag across the image, and the gradient will fill the active layer or selection with the gradient start and ending points matching the drag start and ending points.

4. To make a radial fill, select **Radial** from the Type dropdown box and drag a radius from the center point of the intended fill to the end. The active layer or selection will be filled with a circular gradient.

A gradient fill can either fill past the starting and end points with the starting or ending color, or will start or end the fill outside the image, depending on where you drag.

N O T E

To edit gradients:

1. Click on the **Edit** button in the Gradient Tool Options palette to bring up the Gradient Editor, as shown in Figure 8.4.

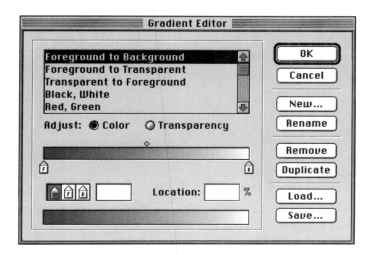

Figure 8.4 The Gradient Editor.

2. Choose the gradient to edit from the scrolling list at the top of the editor or click the **New** button to start from scratch. You can also duplicate a gradient, edit it, rename it, or remove gradients from the list by clicking on the appropriate buttons.

3. Choose the **Adjust Color** radio button. After adjusting the color, click the **Transparency** button to create a transparency mask for the gradient. The same controls are used to set transparency, but there are no color choices.

4. Click the leftmost square under the gradient bar to define the starting color.

   • Click on the **F-box** or **B-box** to start with the foreground or background color.
   • Click on the color box to bring up the color palette and select a color.
   • Click on any color in the Color or Swatches palette, or in any open image window.

5. Click the rightmost square under the gradient bar and use the same methods to set the ending color.

6. Click anywhere along the bottom of the gradient bar to add a color point. Define the color of this point and the blend becomes a three-color gradient. You can add as many color points as you need in this way. You can also drag color points to adjust them or type a number in the location box.

7. Drag the midpoint sliders at the top of the gradient bar to change gradient ramp, or type a number in the location box. These diamonds set the point at which the colors of two adjacent color points are mixed in equal parts.

8. Click **OK** to save the gradient.

    You can add your custom gradients to the default gradient list or, like custom brush palettes, custom gradients can be saved as files for use with other images or on other machines.

    - Click on the **Save** button to bring up the standard file dialog. Pick a location, name the file, and click **OK**.

    - Click on the **Load** button to bring up the standard file dialog. Pick the gradients file you wish to open and click **OK**.

Lesson 8: Fill, Color, and Gradient

In this lesson, you will use a pair of stock photos from the PhotoDisc collection. We'll take the color from one and use it to juice up a vintage black-and-white photograph entitled *The Setting Sun*, also called *Descending Night*. *The Setting Sun* is a 1914 photograph of a statue by New York Sculptor Adolph Alexander Weinmann. It stood atop a column in the Court of the Universe, the central court of the Panama-Pacific International Exposition in San Francisco in 1915. We'll shine a little sunlight on it.

Open both files.

1. Using the **File Open** command, open the files **CITRUS.PSD** and **SETTINGS.PSD** in the Lesson08 folder on the CD. Arrange the two image windows on your desktop so that you can work on both at the same time. Make sure that the Setting Sun is the active window by clicking on it.

For this lesson, the Setting Sun window will be active, and we will simply pick colors off the Citrus image window in the background.

Since we are colorizing a black-and-white photograph, we first have to change the mode.

2. Select **RGB Color** from the Mode submenu in the Image menu, as shown in Figure 8.5.

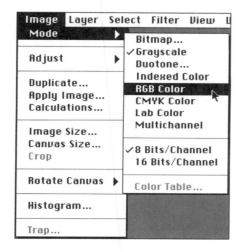

Figure 8.5 Converting to RGB mode from the Image Mode dropdown menu. This does not change the way the image looks, but allows us to add color to a previously colorless image.

3. Open the Color palette by clicking on the **Color** tab in the Color/Swatches/Brushes palette group window or by choosing **Show Color** from the Window menu.

Next, we'll pick a color.

1. Select the **Eyedropper** tool (i) from the Toolbox.
2. Change the Sample Size to **3-by-3 Average** in the Eyedropper Options palette. We don't need precise color picking control for this exercise.

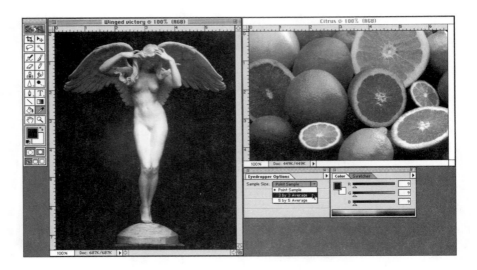

Figure 8.6 Here are the windows you will be using for this lesson, showing the Eyedropper Options palette and the Sample Size dropdown menu. You don't need to arrange the windows this way—you may not be able to if you have a smaller monitor.

3. Move the pointer over the Citrus image window. (Click and drag the Eyedropper around the image and watch the color palette as it's dynamically adjusted, as shown in Figure 8.7.) Pick a vibrant green from the rind of one of the limes.

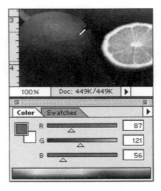

Figure 8.7 Sampling with the Eyedropper tool dynamically updates the Colors palette. You can really see the color you are picking before you select it.

Now, dump a color.

1. Select the **Paint Bucket** tool (k) from the Toolbox.

2. In the Paint Bucket Options palette, use the Painting Modes dropdown menu and select **Color**. Leave the other options at their defaults, as shown in Figure 8.8.

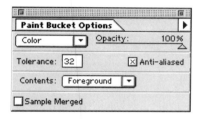

Figure 8.8 The Paint Bucket Options palette with the Color Painting Mode selected.

3. Move the pointer into the lower-left corner of the Setting Sun image. Click to dump paint from the Paint Bucket. Photoshop uses the tolerance setting from the Options palette to determine contiguous color. With the default setting of 32, most of the background is colorized, with a little bleed onto the wingtips, which we won't worry about.

4. Using the Paint Bucket again, click in the two background areas left uncolored: next to her left thigh and a small section in the upper-right corner of the image.

Finally, we'll make a semi-transparent gradient.

The new gradient features of Photoshop 4 allow you to create a transparency mask for gradients. How can we resist? But first we need to set the foreground and background colors.

1. Select the **Eyedropper** tool (i).

2. Move the pointer over the Citrus image and click on the brightest pink in the cut grapefruit. This sets the foreground color for the Setting Sun window without activating the Citrus window.

3. **Option-click** (Macintosh) or **Alt-click** (Windows) on the rind of an orange to set the background color. Choose an area that's not too light.

4. Select the **Gradient** tool (g). Since the Options palette is already open, it automatically switches to Gradient Options. Change the Type to Radial from the dropdown menu and select **Darken** from the Painting Mode dropdown menu, as shown in Figure 8.9.

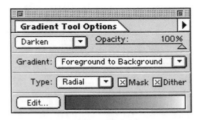

Figure 8.9 The Gradient Tool Options palette, showing the Darken mode selected and the Radial option set.

5. Click on the **Edit** button. We'll use the default gradient pattern of Foreground to Background but will create a transparency mask.

6. Click on the **Transparency** button in the Gradient Editor.

7. Click on the **left pointer box** under the gradient preview bar. Set the Opacity to 50% by typing it into the Opacity box.

8. Click on the **right pointer box** under the gradient preview bar. Set the Opacity to 80% by typing it into the Opacity box.

9. Click **OK** (see Figure 8.10).

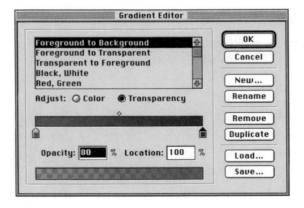

Figure 8.10 Creating a transparency mask in the Gradient Editor.

10. Move the pointer into the center of the Setting Sun image window. (You can see where the middle is by checking the rulers on the top and side of the image.) Click and drag from her left thigh straight down to her feet and release the mouse button. The Darken mode leaves the dark green background alone and fills the statue with our gradient.

CHAPTER

Adding Type to an Image

In this chapter...

- Type issues
- The Text tool
- The Text Mask tool

TYPE ISSUES

Photoshop is not known for its robust text entry capabilities; they're fairly rudimentary. But the effects you can achieve with text after it becomes part of an image are essentially endless. This chapter addresses some simpler aspects of adding text to an image.

Bitmap Type

It is the nature of painting applications like Photoshop to convert any type you add to bitmaps. This means that you won't get the nice scalable outline type you may be used to from using word processing or page layout programs (see Figure 9.1). PostScript or TrueType typefaces are actually type outlines that scale smoothly to any size or resolution.

Figure 9.1 Bitmap type in Photoshop versus outline type in Illustrator.

Using Adobe Type Manager (ATM) on either Macintosh or Windows can help alleviate scaling problems with PostScript Type1 typefaces, but cannot overcome the effects of resolution.

N O T E

However, since Photoshop is a pixel-oriented painting program (see the discussion of pixels versus vectors in Chapter 2), anything you add is converted to the resolution of the image. If your image has a resolution of 72 dpi, which is appropriate for Web-bound images, any type you enter will look jagged when you print the image on a 300 dpi printer. If you want to avoid jagged type edges, you can select the **Anti-aliased** option in the Type dialog.

Adding Type with Other Programs

The biggest limitation of bitmap type is that it becomes part of the image and cannot be edited as text, only as a layer of bits. One solution is to create the image in Photoshop and export the image to a page-layout program, then add type over it. You'll need to save your image in a format that your page-layout program can read; usually EPS or TIFF is fine. Then you can open or place the image and type right over it using the text tools of your program.

For type that you want to blend into your Photoshop image, it's sometimes helpful to create the text in Adobe Illustrator and then import it already formatted.

To place text:

1. Select the **Place** command from the File menu.
2. From the standard File dialog, select the Adobe Illustrator file you created with the text to be imported.

3. A preview of the imported file is placed on your image and is selected for manipulation. Move or rotate the image into place.

4. Click anywhere on the Toolbox to place the image. A new layer is created as a container for the placed text.

THE TEXT TOOL

Entering text in Photoshop has remained a fairly straightforward process. Photoshop 4 automatically adds text as a new layer, which simplifies editing. The Text tool adds text in the foreground color wherever you click.

To add text:

1. Select the **Text tool** (t) from the Toolbox.

2. Click in the image approximately where you want the text to go. The Type Tool dialog appears (see Figure 9.2).

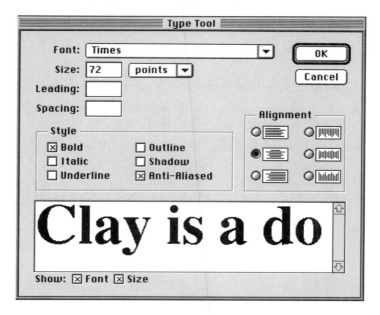

Figure 9.2 The Type Tool dialog.

3. Type in the text, including any line breaks. You can set the font, size, leading, spacing, style, and alignment for the entire text selection, but you cannot adjust individual letters. You can also preview the text by clicking the font and/or size boxes at the bottom of the window.

4. Click **OK**, and the text is entered as a new layer. You can adjust the placement of text on the image by selecting the **Move tool** (v) and sliding the layer or by nudging the layer with the arrow keys.

N O T E

While there are no options for the Type tool, you can set type opacity from the Layers palette.

THE MASK TYPE TOOL

The Mask Type tool, while new to Photoshop 4, is an adaptation of features already available in previous versions. It automatically creates a type mask that has the effect of a border selection. You can use this to create special type effects.

To create a type selection border:

1. Select the **Mask Type** tool (t), which is a hidden tool under the Type tool.
2. The Mask Type tool is used exactly as the Type tool, except that when you press OK, a selection is created in the shape of the text.
3. Use the **Edit Fill** or **Edit Stroke** commands to fill or stroke the text.

Lesson 9: Three Text Additions

This lesson adds text to an image in three different ways to suit three distinct purposes.

Basic Text for a Basic Cow

1. Open the file **BROWN_CO.PSD** from the Lesson09 folder on the CD.

2. Make sure the foreground and background colors are set to their defaults by clicking on the **Default Colors** button (d) in the toolbox. Then swap the foreground and background by clicking on the **Exchange** button (x). The foreground should be white and the background black. See Figure 9.3.

Figure 9.3 Exchanging colors in the Color Control area of the Toolbox.

3. Select the **Text** tool (t) from the Toolbox.

4. Move the pointer into the cow image and click to open the Text Tool dialog. Click near the cow's shoulder to put the text in approximately the right place.

5. Use the following settings in the Text Tool dialog:

   Font: Times

   Size: 72 point

   Alignment: Left

   Style: Anti-aliased

   Type the word **Cow** into the text field and leave all other fields blank or unchecked (see Figure 9.4). Click **OK**.

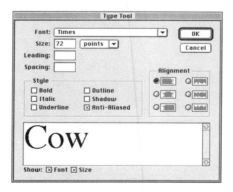

Figure 9.4 The Text Tool dialog handles only simple text formatting. Here are the correct settings for this exercise.

6. Hold down the **Command** key (Macintosh) or **Ctrl** key (Windows) to turn the pointer into the Move tool, then drag the text into the middle of the cow itself. This is possible, because Photoshop 4 puts text on a new layer that you can move around without affecting the background. See Figure 9.5.

Figure 9.5 A properly labeled cow. The text and the cow are on different layers, which allows you to position the text without getting kicked by the cow.

Masked Text for a Refined Cow

1. Select the **Mask Text** tool (t). Since this is a hidden tool, either type **t** to toggle between Text and Mask Text tools or hold down the mouse over the text tool to pop up the hidden tools menu, and drag to select the **Mask Text** tool.

2. Click on the **Background layer** in the Layers palette (see Figure 9.6). We want to put the masked text right on the cow, not up in the air.

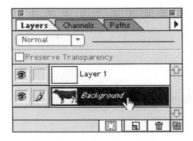

Figure 9.6 Notice how the icon for Layer 1 appears blank. This is because the only thing in the layer is white text on a transparent background.

3. Click again in the same place on the cow.

4. The Text Tool dialog will contain the information you entered before, which is fine. Click **OK**.

    Instead of text on a new layer, the Mask Text tool enters text right on the active layer as a selection. So you must manipulate this text as a selection rather than a layer.

5. Move the pointer inside the text selection border. It changes shape to a move cursor. Drag the text so it can be used as a drop shadow of the first text, as shown in Figure 9.7.

Figure 9.7 Moving the text selection into position to become a drop shadow.

6. Press the **Delete** key. This erases everything within the selection to the background color, black.

7. Choose **None** from the Selection menu, **Command-d** (Macintosh) or **Ctrl-d** (Windows), to deselect the text and complete the drop shadow (Figure 9.8).

Figure 9.8 Our cow with a black drop shadow of text in the background layer and white text in its own layer floating above.

Once the text is deselected, it can't be moved or adjusted. Its pixels are part of the background, while the text layer above can still be moved or adjusted independently from the background.

NOTE

Adding Text

I would like to add a poem to this composition, but typesetting it with Photoshop's type tools would be a nuisance. So I have typeset it in Adobe Illustrator, and now we will place it into our image.

1. Select the **Place** command from the File menu. This opens a standard file dialog. Choose the file called **BOVINE_I.AI** from the Lesson09 folder on the CD.

   Photoshop puts a selection rectangle on a new layer centered in the image. The diagonal lines indicate that this is a placed image. The Illustrator image is previewed as it as placed, so you can see what you're doing.

2. Put the cursor inside the rectangle, hold down the mouse button, and move the placed text to the bottom left corner of the image, as shown in Figure 9.9.

Figure 9.9 Moving the selection from the center of the image, where Photoshop placed it, to the lower-left corner.

3. Press **Enter** to place the image. Since the placed text is on its own layer, you can still adjust the placement by using the Move tool (v) or by nudging with the arrow keys. See Figure 9.10.

Figure 9.10 The finished image with text, text mask, and imported text.

If you'd like to see this image on your screen, open the file **COW_SENT.PSD** in the Lesson09 folder on the CD.

Selecting

In this section...

- Area selection tools
- Adjusting selection borders
- Editing selections

SELECTION ISSUES

Photoshop allows you to work on an entire image or to edit and manipulate parts of an image by making selections or by using layers (layers are discussed in Chapter 15). Selections can be made in a number of ways, with any of Photoshop's selection tools. A selection is indicated by a border marquee of "marching ants" and may be edited or manipulated using any of Photoshop's tools or commands for these purposes.

The selection tools are grouped in the topmost division of the Toolbox and are subdivided into marquee (straight-edged) selectors and lasso (freeform) selectors. There is also the Magic Wand tool (w), which selects by color, and the Move tool (v), which is used to adjust the position of selections. The way in which selections are made differs, but the results are the same. All commands that operate on selections are available, regardless of the tools you used to make the selection.

While there is only one kind of selection, there are two types of selection commands: *image-oriented commands* that can be used with or without a selection, and *selection-specific commands* that change the selection marquee rather than the image itself.

We will start this section by discussing the selection process and finish with some of the selection-specific commands. Image-oriented commands are discussed in the chapters of Section V.

CHAPTER

Area Selection— Straight-Edged and Freeform

In this chapter...

- The Marquee and Single-pixel Marquee tools
- The Lasso and Polygon Lasso Freeform selectors
- The Crop tool

THE MARQUEE AND SINGLE-PIXEL MARQUEE TOOLS

The most obvious way to make a selection is to erect a sort of enclosure, the bits within the enclosure constituting the selection. And the most basic border erector is the Marquee tool (m). You click and drag out a rectangle and everything within the rectangle is selected. The Marquee tool includes a number of options that make this simplest of tools more flexible.

To select with the Marquee tool:

1. Choose the Marquee tool (m) from the Toolbox.
2. Click in the image at the upper-left corner of your selection and drag to the bottom-right corner. Release the mouse button. The results are shown in Figure 10.1.

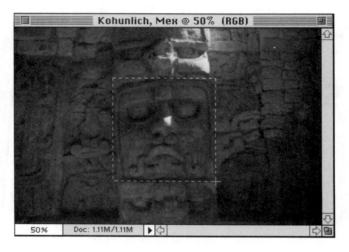

Figure 10.1 A selection made with the Marquee tool.

The Marquee tool includes three selection styles: Normal, Constrained Aspect Ratio, and Fixed Size. To change Marquee selection styles, choose a style from the Style dropdown menu in the Marquee Options palette (Figure 10.2). Normal style is the typical marquee method; click and drag a rectangle of any size.

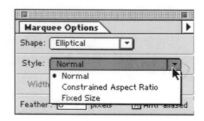

Figure 10.2 The Marquee Options palette with the Style dropdown menu.

N O T E

The Rectangular and Elliptical marquees can be constrained to a square or circle by holding down the Shift key as you drag. This only works if there are no other active selections.

By holding down the **Option** key (Macintosh) or **Alt** key (Windows) you can make a selection by dragging from the center outward.

With the Marquee tools you can toggle between the Rectangular and Elliptical marquees by pressing the **m** key, but the Single-pixel Marquees have no keyboard shortcut. They must be selected from the hidden pop-up tools.

To select using the Constrained Aspect Ratio style:

1. Select **Constrained Aspect Ratio** from the Style dropdown menu in the Marquee Options palette.
2. Enter numbers in the boxes for Height and Width. These numbers represent the two sides of a ratio and not actual sizes. If you enter 2 for Height and 1 for Width, your selection is constrained to a height twice the width. Numbers can range from .001 to 999.99.

To select using the Fixed Size style:

1. Select **Fixed Size** from the Style dropdown menu in the Marquee Options palette.
2. Enter numbers in the boxes for Height and Width. This is the actual size of the selection in pixels from 1 to 30,000. Bear in mind that the resolution of the image will affect the dimensions of a fixed size selection.
3. Instead of clicking and dragging, you simply click, and the exact selection rectangle appears. Continue to hold the mouse button down and you can drag the selection rectangle around the image.

Other Marquee Options

- **Feather**—in its effect, feathering is like anti-aliasing, but you can control the amount of feathering. According to Adobe's technical notes, feathering produces a Gaussian blur of the Quick Mask channel (channels are discussed in Chapter 17). This extends the blurring effect of the feather on both sides of the selection to create a more gradual transition along the selection border. You can enter a size in pixels for the extent of feathering from 1 to 250.

 If there is a value in the Feather option before you make a selection, the selection is automatically feathered.

- **Anti-aliased**—gives the appearance of a smooth selection border by partially selecting pixels. This hides the stair-stepping that's often visible when using the selection tools by filling in the gaps with partially selected (shades of gray) pixels. There is no loss of detail with anti-aliasing unless you anti-alias a feathered selection. Anti-aliasing is not a factor with rectangular selections as it is for diagonal or curved selections. Because there is no stair-step effect to hide with vertical or horizontal lines, this option is not available for the rectangular marquees.

Figure 10.3 shows the Marquees options.

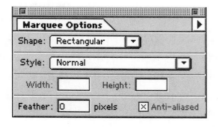

Figure 10.3 The Marquee Options palette with two option boxes at the bottom.

Changing the Marquee Selection Shapes

The hidden Marquee tools include the Ellipse and Single-pixel marquees, as well as the Crop tool, which is discussed later in this chapter. These tools (except Crop) can also be selected from the Marquee Options Shape dropdown menu. You can also select hidden tools by **Option-clicking** (Macintosh) or **Alt-clicking** (Windows) on the Marquee tool in the Toolbox, or by holding down the mouse button on the Marquee tool and picking from the Marquee pop-up menu. Figure 10.4 shows the options.

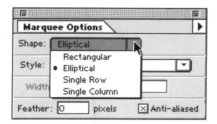

Figure 10.4 The Shapes dropdown menu in the Marquee Options palette.

The Rectangular and Elliptical Marquees work the same way, except for the shape of the resulting selection. The single-pixel row and column tools select only a single row or column of pixels. This is obviously useful for detailed work. If you can't see a single-pixel selection, try magnifying the image view with the Zoom tool.

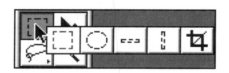

Figure 10.5 The Marquee tool and its pop-up menu in the Toolbox.

THE LASSO AND POLYGON LASSO: FREEFORM SELECTORS

Not every selection you'll make fits neatly into a rectangle or ellipse. The Lasso and Polygon Lasso are the freeform equivalents of the Marquee tools. Both behave somewhat like the Pencil or Pen tools.

The only options for these two tools are the same two check boxes available for the Marquee selection tools: Feather and Anti-aliased, as shown in Figure 10.6.

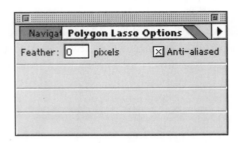

Figure 10.6 The Lasso and Polygon Lasso Options palettes are essentially the same, with only two options.

To make a freehand selection:

1. Select the **Lasso** tool (l) from the Toolbox.
2. Click and drag around the area you wish to select. The exact path of the Lasso tool becomes your selection border. If the starting and ending points of your selection don't meet (Figure 10.7), Photoshop automatically closes the selection with a straight line between the two open endpoints.

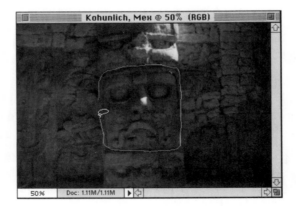

Figure 10.7 Using the Lasso tool to make a freeform selection is like drawing with the Pencil tool, except that any path you draw is automatically closed when you release the mouse button.

To make a straight-edged selection:

1. Select the **Polygon Lasso** tool (l) by option-clicking on the **Lasso** tool in the Toolbox or by holding down the mouse on the Lasso tool and choosing it from the Lasso pop-up menu. You can toggle between the Lasso and Polygon Lasso tools by pressing on the l key.

2. Click in the image to define the starting point.

3. Click again to set the endpoint for the first line segment of the selection. Continue clicking to mark additional endpoints and lines. The selection continues until you close the selection path.

4. To complete the selection, move the pointer over the starting point. A small circle appears next to the pointer when you get close. Click to close the selection path.

5. Double-click to close the selection border. Figure 10.8 shows a closed section.

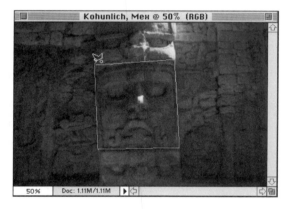

Figure 10.8 The Polygon Lasso tool makes straight-edge selection boundaries. Notice the small circle next to the pointer which indicates that it is near the start and that clicking will close the path.

Mixing Freehand and Straight-Edge Paths in a Selection

Holding down the **Option** key (Macintosh) or **Alt** key (Windows) with either the Lasso or Polygon Lasso tool selected gives you the best of both worlds. Dragging makes freehand selections, while clicking makes polygon selections. As long as you hold down the **Option/Alt** key, you can mix techniques in a single selection without changing tools. Figure 10.9 shows an example.

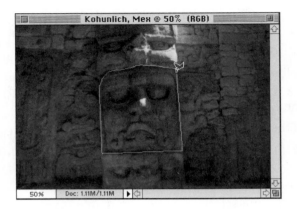

Figure 10.9 A mixed Lasso selection of freehand and straight-edged lines.

THE CROP TOOL

Although the Crop tool makes selections, you can't edit the bits enclosed within the border of "marching ants." All you can do once a cropping "selection" has been made is to crop the image. Here's how it works.

The Crop tool works slightly differently than in previous versions of Photoshop.

To make a cropping selection:

1. Select the **Crop** tool (c) from the hidden Marquee tools in the Toolbox.
2. The Crop tool selects exactly as the rectangular Marquee tool does; click and drag from the upper-left corner to the lower-right (see Figure 10.10).

Figure 10.10 A crop selection showing eight adjustment handles and the double-headed pointer ready to adjust the corner.

You can constrain the crop selection to a square by holding down the **Shift** key as you drag. The resulting selection remains a square, even as you make adjustments to it.

N O T E

You'll notice that the "marching ants" around a crop selection have eight handles (little boxes), one at each corner and on each side. These allow you to adjust the selection boundary.

If you have set a Fixed Target Size in the Marquee options, there are only four selection handles.

N O T E

1. Move the pointer over one of the handles. The pointer turns into a two-headed arrow indicating the direction the handle can be moved.

2. Hold down the mouse button and move the handle: up and down or in and out for sides, or any direction for corners. You can continue adjusting as long as the selection is active.

3. Move the pointer outside the selection rectangle, and it becomes a curved double-headed arrow. Click and drag in a clockwise or counterclockwise direction, and the entire selection rectangle rotates as much as 45° (see Figure 10.11).

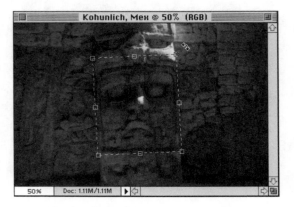

Figure 10.11 Rotate a crop selection by placing the pointer anywhere outside the selection rectangle and then moving it in a clockwise or counterclockwise direction.

 You can't rotate a bitmap image using the Crop tool.

NOTE

4. Move the pointer inside the selection rectangle, click, and drag. The entire selection rectangle can be moved around the image without changing its size.

To crop an image:

• Once a selection is made, either press the **Return** or **Enter** key (only **Enter** works in Windows).

If you try to select another tool while a crop selection is active, Photoshop asks you if you want to crop the image, continue adjusting the crop, or forget it. This is the only way to cancel a crop once a selection has been made. The Select None command is not available.

- Select the **Crop** command from the Image menu (Figure 10.12). This is the only manipulative command available when a crop selection is active.

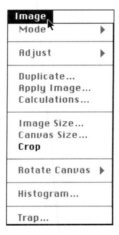

Figure 10.12 The Image Crop command. All other commands are grayed out and unavailable.

You can use the Crop command with any rectangular selection, including those made with the rectangular Marquee tool, to crop an image.

The Cropping Tool Options palette allows you to set a target size for the cropped image (see Figure 10.13). This is not the size of the crop selection, but the size of the image *after* you execute a crop.

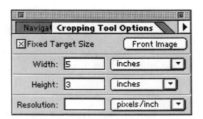

Figure 10.13 The Cropping Tool Options palette with a Fixed Target Size specified. With the resolution blank, Photoshop will calculate the maximum resolution from the size of the selection and the size of the target image.

The Target Size options must be set before a crop selection is started.

NOTE

To crop and resample simultaneously:

1. Click on the **Fixed Target Size** check box in the Cropping Tool Options palette.

   - If you wish, click on the **Front Image** button and Photoshop fills the options with the vital statistics of the current image.
   - You can type in numbers for Width, Height, and Resolution.
   - You can change units from the dropdown boxes next to eachfield. (The columns unit in the Width field is calculated from the width and gutter sizes specified in the Rulers and Units Preferences, described inChapter 26.)

2. Make your selection and execute the crop. The resulting image will be resampled to fit the exact size you specified in the Options palette rather than the size you selected. If you leave the Resolution field empty, Photoshop will calculate the resolution. If you only specify the resolution, Photoshop will calculate the width and height.

Lesson 10: Area-Selection Exercises

You will find as you work with Photoshop that you spend as much time making careful selections as doing anything else. This is why there is such a range of selection tools and options. This lesson gives you some practice with basic selection methods. Later lessons will give you the opportunity to refine selections and then actually do some more interesting things with them.

First, lets do some Marquee exercises.

1. Open the file **3_EGGS.PSD** from the Lesson10 folder on the CD. This is taken from the PhotoDisc Object series.

2. Select the **Rectangular Marquee** tool (m) from the Toolbox.

   We will surround the three eggs with a selection marquee.

3. Move the pointer above and to the left of the three eggs. Click and drag to just below and to the right of the eggs (see Figure 10.14). If you misjudge the starting point, click outside the selection rectangle to deselect it and try again.

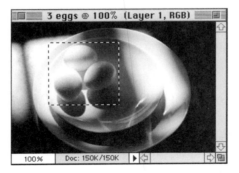

Figure 10.14 A plain vanilla rectangular selection.

You can copy, cut, transform, apply filters or various other alterations to this selected rectangle of three eggs, but that's not the point of this lesson.

4. Deselect by clicking outside the selection rectangle or by choosing **None** from the Selection menu.

Now, make a similar selection with the Polygon Lasso.

1. Select the **Polygon Lasso** (l) tool from the Toolbox. The l key will toggle between the Lasso and Polygon Lasso tools, or you can click, drag, and select the tool from the pop-up menu on the Lasso square of the Toolbox.

2. Click at the four points around the egg outlined by the rectangle of light from what one assumes is a window.

3. Close the selection by clicking again at the starting point (see Figure 10.15). The pointer icon has an additional small circle to indicate that you will close the selection by clicking.

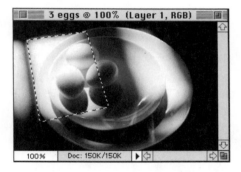

Figure 10.15 Why use a rectangle when you really want a quadrilateral? The Polygon Lasso can inscribe any polygonal shape.

If we select this very bright area, we can use a filter or one of the Image commands to bring out more of its detail.

Next, make an egg-shaped selection.

1. Select the **Lasso Marquee** (l) tool from the Toolbox.

2. Trace around the topmost egg to make a selection border. Since the Lasso is a freehand tool, it doesn't work well for making clean-edged selections. It's very useful for making complex selections or for adding or subtracting selection areas, as you'll see later in this section.

3. Deselect, as you did in step 4 above.

4. Select the **Elliptical Marquee** tool (m) from the toolbox as described above in step 5 for the Lasso tool group. You can also use the Shape dropdown menu in the Marquee Options palette to select.

5. Click above and to the left of the top egg and drag to surround the egg in an elliptical marquee. Estimating the starting point for an elliptical selection can be tricky, because the area you drag over actually constitutes a rectangle that contains the selection ellipse. So you have to imagine the rectangle around the egg and start where the upper-left corner would be (see Figure 10.16).

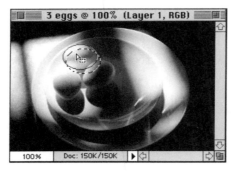

Figure 10.16 You can make a selection like this one with the Elliptical Marquee tool and adjust its placement by moving with the pointer or nudging with the arrow keys.

If your selection misses the egg, you can start again the way we did with the rectangular selection in step 3, or you can drag the correct shape, release the mouse button, move the pointer into the selection, and drag to put it over the egg. Either way, you have to estimate, and the best you can hope for is a close approximation of the exact shape.

6. Deselect as described above.

EXERCISING OPTIONS

1. Choose **Constrained Aspect Ratio** from the Style dropdown menu in the Marquee Options palette.

2. Enter a Width of 4 and a Height of 3.

3. Enter a Feather size of 5 pixels. Figure 10.17 shows the dialog box.

4. Now select the same egg. Notice that you can make the selection any size, but it maintains the 4:3 aspect ratio set in the option, which is about right for this egg. But what does the feather option do? I'm glad you asked.

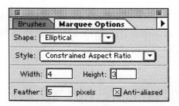

Figure 10.17 The Marquee Options dialog with options set to constrain the aspect ratio and feather the selection.

5. Put the pointer inside the selection, and hold down the mouse button and the **Command** key (Macintosh) or **Ctrl** key (Windows). The cursor turns into a scissors icon. Drag the selection and drop it on the black background. (We'll talk more about this shortcut for cutting and pasting a selection in Chapter 12.)

    Notice how the image is softened around the edges. You couldn't see it in context, but on the black background it should be obvious, as shown in Figure 10.18.

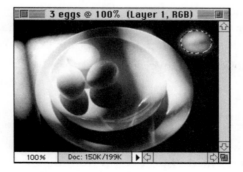

Figure 10.18 A feathered selection cut from its original location and dragged into the corner to show what five pixels of feathering look like.

To crop:

1. Open the file **WINDOW_D.PSD** another PhotoDisc image, from the Lesson10 folder on the CD.

2. Select the **Crop** tool (c) from the hidden menu under the Marquee tool in the Toolbox.

3. Crop this door by putting the pointer at the upper-left corner of the door, pressing the mouse button, and dragging to the lower-right corner. Initial selection is exactly the same as with the Rectangular Marquee.

4. Fine tune your selection by adjusting the handles in and out to select the exact door outline. Don't worry about the little bit of the door latch that's being cropped off. In fact, since this old door isn't perfectly square, you'll need to shave off some wood to ensure a clean crop. See Figure 10.19.

Figure 10.19 A door framed by a cropping selection border.

5. Press **Return** or **Enter** (Macintosh) or **Enter** (Windows) to execute the crop.

This door just begs to have something in the window panes. You can see that selecting each pane might be made easier if you set the Fixed Size option in the Marquee Options palette. Try 29 by 29 pixels and see what happens. Hold down the **Shift** key to select the second pane without deselecting the first.

Wouldn't it be easier to make this selection using the Magic Wand tool? Save this cropped image and go to Chapter 11 to find out.

CHAPTER

Selecting by Color

In this chapter...

- The Magic Wand tool

THE MAGIC WAND

Do you think Adobe would have had sufficient whimsy to name a tool the Magic Wand? The Knoll brothers did, but then again John Knoll was working at a place called Industrial Light and Magic when he designed Photoshop. (Thomas Knoll's name still appears first on the Photoshop credits list, but John Knoll's seems to have disappeared.) We take the Magic Wand tool for granted now, but I found it pretty magical when I first saw it.

NOTE If you hold down the **Command-Option** keys (Macintosh) or **Ctrl-Alt** keys (Windows) and click on the top button of the Toolbox, you can view the complete credits for Big Electric Cat, Photoshop's code name.

The Magic Wand tool makes selections based on color. You don't have to drag or trace, you just click and a selection is made. This is immediately useful if your image has well-defined areas of color. For instance, a still life of melons photographed on a simple black background is difficult to trace, but a single click on the background with the Magic Wand can make this selection instantly (see Figure 11.1).

Figure 11.1 You can quickly select the black background with the Magic Wand tool and save yourself the trouble of tracing around all these melons.

The Magic Wand tool uses two variables to calculate a selection—tolerance and adjacency.

- *Tolerance* is a setting in the Magic Wand Options palette. It can be set from 0 to 255 and is a measure of color similarity. A setting of 0 selects pixels of exactly the same color, while 255 selects everything. The default setting is 32, which limits the selection to very similar colors, without being too limiting.

- *Adjacency* is not measured; it refers to neighboring pixels. The Magic Wand selects the pixel you click on and then looks at all the neighboring pixels, testing each for tolerance. For each pixel that meets the tolerance setting, this process continues recursively until no more neighbors satisfy the tolerance test. This makes it possible to select a cantaloupe on one side of a still life without selecting a casaba at the same time. (The Similar command described later ignores adjacency.) See Figure 11.2.

Figure 11.2 The Magic Wand allows you to select this cantaloupe without getting the casaba at the same time. (You'll have to take my word for it. They're just about the same color.)

To make a Magic Wand selection:

1. Select the **Magic Wand** tool (t) from the Toolbox. Double-click on the tool if the Options palette isn't open.
2. Click in the image in an area of color you wish to select.

    It's often useful to extend a Magic Wand selection by adding more color.

3. Hold down the **Shift** key and click outside the selection to expand it.
4. Hold down the **Option** key (Macintosh) or **Alt** key (Windows) and click inside the selection to reduce it. It's often useful to reduce the tolerance setting before doing this.

Magic Wand Options

The Tolerance setting is the main Magic Wand option. There are also two option check boxes (see Figure 11.3).

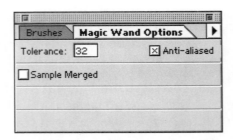

Figure 11.3 The Magic Wand Options palette with default settings.

- **Tolerance**—can be set with values ranging from 0 and 255 as previously-described. You can change the tolerance at any time. This does not affect the previous selection.

- **Anti-aliased**—with the Anti-aliased box checked, the selection includes an anti-aliased border.

- **Sample Merged**—the default setting makes selections from the active layer of an image only. Check the **Sample Merged** option to select from all visible layers.

The Color Range command in the Selection menu, described later in this section, also makes selections based on color. While its pointer icon is the same as the Magic Wand tool, it is not affected by the Toolbox or any of its tools.

Lesson 11: A Quick Magic Wand Selection

At the end of Lesson 10, I wondered for you if the selection couldn't have been made more easily with the Magic Wand tool. Once again, I'm glad you asked this question.

To make a quick Magic Wand selection:

1. Use the image you saved from Lesson 11, or open the image **CROPPED.PSD** from the Lesson11 folder on the CD.

2. Choose the **Magic Wand** tool (w) from the Toolbox. Set the Tolerance to 0—we only want to select the white areas. Leave the Anti-aliased box checked and the Sample Merged box unchecked.

3. Click in the white area in the middle of the door. A selection this obvious is pretty much automatic with the Magic Wand tool.

4. Choose the **Similar** command from the Selection menu. We'll talk about the selection commands later in this section. The Similar command ignores adjacency and selects all pixels in the image that match the original selection color. This is an extremely quick way to select the windowpanes in this door, as shown in Figure 11.4.

Figure 11.4 The complete selection after executing the Similar command. Note how each windowpane is selected by a separate marquee, but that multiple marquees are treated like a single selection.

5. Press the **Delete** key or choose **Cut** from the Edit menu (**Command/Ctrl-x**). This cuts the background and makes it transparent, as indicated by the checkerboard fill pattern. This is a special situation. When the bottom layer of an image has any name other than Background, cutting the background out results in a transparent fill.

6. Deselect by clicking outside the selection or by choosing **None** from the Selection menu, or press **Command-d** (Macintosh) or **Ctrl-d** (Windows).

The rest of this lesson has nothing to do with selections and concerns tools and commands that haven't been discussed yet. But you're welcome to follow along, because these are basic Photoshop methods that you will use over and over again.

7. Open the file **SKY.PSD** from the Lesson11 folder on the CD.

8. Make sure the Layers palette is open by choosing **Open Layers** from the Window menu. (If the Layers palette is already open, the command will say Hide Layers.) Make sure that, even though the Sky image is active, the Door image is at least partially visible.

9. In the Layers palette, click on the words **Layer 0** to select the layer. Drag the layer to the Window Door image, and release the mouse button. This copies the Sky image to the Door image and places it over the door as a new layer, called Layer 1. The Door image is now active (see Figure 11.5).

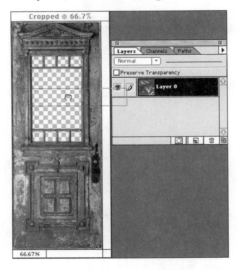

Figure 11.5 Dragging a layer from the active image (the sky) into another (the door). This activates the door window and copies the sky to it as a new layer.

10. Click on **Layer 1** in the Layers palette and drag it underneath the layer called **door**. Now this sky layer, still active, is on the bottom and should be showing through the selection (see Figure 11.6).

Figure 11.6 This is what the Layers palette should look like, with the sky layer on the bottom, but still active.

11. Select the **Move** tool (v) and move the sky layer so that it fills the window selection. Figure 11.7 shows the results.

Figure 11.7 This is the finished composition. The ability to make complex selections gives Photoshop remarkable flexibility when it comes to creating an atmosphere that suits your purpose.

If you'd like more practice with the Magic Wand tool, open the file **MELONS.PSD** from the Lesson11 folder on the CD. This is the image used for the screen shots in Chapter 11. Try making selections by changing the Tolerance setting in the Magic Wand Options palette. You'll see that adjacency is not always a friend, that the color of one melon is sometimes not as distinct from another as it seems. Getting the right tolerance can be a matter of trial and error. We'll learn later in this section how to make more refined selections without a lot of guesswork.

CHAPTER

Adjusting Selection Borders

In this chapter...

- Moving a selection border
- Expanding a selection
- Contracting a selection
- Selecting a portion of a selection

It is the nature of Photoshop's selection tools that a single pass rarely achieves the exact selection you're looking for. This makes the process of refining selections as important as making them to begin with. Fortunately, there are numerous short-cuts and commands for adjusting selections. We've already seen some of these in the lessons where selection borders needed to be moved or expanded.

Note that once a selection marquee is active in an image, it doesn't matter what tool was used to create it. All selection adjustments apply equally, and you can switch among tools to refine selections. You can also switch options, but this can lead to odd results if you change feathering or anti-aliasing.

Before we go on, we need to make the distinction again between the selection border and the active selection—they exist independently. The border is the line of "marching ants" known as the selection marquee. The bits surrounded by this border constitute the active selection (Figure 12.1). You can make numerous adjustments to the selection border without affecting any bits in the image. Nothing happens to the active selection until you execute a command to adjust it.

Figure 12.1 The marquee is just a border; it can be moved, expanded, or contracted. It surrounds the active selection, which contains the actual bits of the image. Any commands or tools you use while a selection is active affect only the active pixels of this image—the almond—and nothing else.

Moving a Selection Border

A selection border can be moved around on an image without affecting the shape of the border or any bits of the image.

To move a border:

1. With any selection tool active, move the pointer within the selection border. The pointer becomes the move cursor.
2. Click the mouse button and drag the selection border to any location within the image, as shown in Figure 12.2.

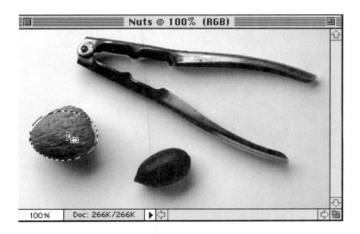

Figure 12.2 Moving a selection border does not affect the shape of the border or any pixels within the image itself.

N O T E You can constrain movement to increments of 45° by holding down the **Shift** key while you drag. (You must hold down the mouse button before the Shift key or you will end up adding to the selection instead of moving it.) You can move a selection border in 1-pixel increments by using the arrow keys, and if you hold down the **Shift** key while using the arrow keys, the selection border moves in 10-pixel increments.

EXPANDING A SELECTION

The ability to expand selections makes it easier to select complex outlines and to combine tools when making single selections.

To expand any selection:

1. Make a selection using any selection tool. Continue using the same tool, or select a different tool from the Toolbox.

2. Hold down the **Shift** key. A small plus sign is added to the selection cursor to indicate that you are adding to a selection.

3. Make an additional selection. The selection may overlap the original or be completely separate.

The second selection is added to the first (see Figure 12.3). You can continue making additions until you have selected all the bits you wish to modify.

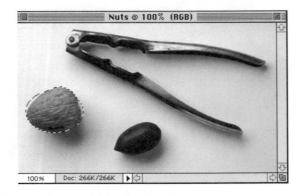

Figure 12.3 It's not only possible to expand a selection, but also to make discontinuous selections. All pixels within all selection borders are active.

CONTRACTING A SELECTION

As easily as selections can be added, they can be subtracted.

To contract a selection:

1. You can start with any selection and any selection tool.
2. Hold down the **Option** key (Macintosh), or **Alt** key (Windows). A small minus sign is added to the selection cursor to indicate that you are subtracting from a selection.
3. Make your selection. The area is removed from the previous selection border; it is deactivated. It's possible to remove an area within an area using this method which creates a doughnut-like selection (see Figure 12.4).

SELECTING A PORTION OF A SELECTION

A second way to contract a selection is to select part of that selection. This is subtraction by selective inclusion, the inverse of the exclusion method discussed earlier.

To subtract from a selection:

1. Use any selection tool.
2. Hold down the **Shift-Option** keys (Macintosh), or **Shift-Alt** keys (Windows). A small *x* appears next to the selection icon.
3. Select the part of the previous selection you wish to remain selected. Release the mouse button, and the excluded area is deselected. See Figure 12.5.

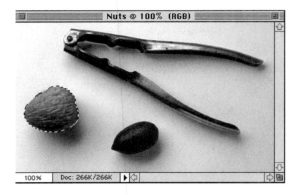

Figure 12.4 Subtracting from a previous selection can create doughnut-like selections or can simply be used to adjust a selection border.

Figure 12.5 Selecting part of a selection can be useful when the Magic Wand tool has found more areas of adjacent color than you were trying to select, as in this before image on the top. On the bottom, part of the selection has been selected using the Elliptical Marquee tool.

Lesson 12: Several Tools for a Single Selection

In this lesson, we will work with a very silly snapshot containing the lion's head mask and Timo's spectacles. We will cut out this image using several selection tools to make a single, complex—but not too complex—selection.

There is no single most efficient selection method. Whatever works best for you in a given situation is most efficient. This exercise will not even attempt to use the fewest possible steps to make a complex selection. Our goal is to try out a number of different tools to achieve our end.

For this lesson, open the file **LION_HEA.PSD** from the Lesson12 folder on the CD.

I'm sure there are many experienced users who would think nothing of tracing around this mask with the Lasso tool alone or drawing a path with the Pen tool to make this selection. In some cases this would be your only choice, but not this time.

START BIG

We'll make the largest, most general selection first. It makes sense to start with cruder selections and make finer adjustments later. For all selections in this lesson, we'll use the default options, which will result in an anti-aliased selection.

1. Select the **Elliptical Marquee** tool (m) from the Toolbox. This is a hidden tool that can be selected using the **m** key to toggle between Elliptical and Rectangular marquees. Or hold down the mouse button over the Marquee tool and select the ellipse from the pop-up menu, or choose **Elliptical Marquee** from the Shape dropdown menu in the Marquee Options palette, which also changes the tool in the Toolbox.

2. Move the pointer to the middle of the image. You can turn on the rulers and do this exactly, or just put the pointer in the middle of the Lion's nose, and you've got it.

3. Start dragging, and then hold down the **Option** key (Macintosh) or **Alt** key (Windows). This turns the starting point of the selection into a center point and your drag line into a radius of the selection ellipse.

   As you drag out the elliptical selection, you'll notice that the nose is not quite centered, so select a little too much on the right and leave a little unselected on the left, as in Figure 12.6.

Figure 12.6 Making a selection using the Elliptical Marquee tool. It's nearly impossible to judge the exact starting point for a selection like this, so we've compensated by estimating the correct selection border, which can be moved into position as a second step.

4. Move the pointer inside the selection. The pointer turns into the Move icon. Press the mouse button and drag the marquee slightly to the left so that the selection is properly centered over the lion's beard (Figure 12.7). You can also nudge the selection marquee into place using the arrow keys.

Figure 12.7 Moving the selection marquee into the correct position.

5. Move the pointer to the top of the first selection circle. Press down the **Shift** key to add another ellipse to the selection, press the mouse button and start dragging, and then hold down the **Option/Alt** key to select from the center point. Notice how the cursor changes so that it now includes a plus sign.

   Drag to enclose the lion's ears. You now have a keyhole-shaped selection enclosing the entire mask, as shown in Figure 12.8.

Figure 12.8 Adding a second elliptical selection that will enclose the entire mask within the marquee.

GET SMALLER

It's time to whittle away at the selection so that it matches the outline of the mask more closely.

1. Select the **Rectangular Marquee** tool (m) from the Toolbox. We're going to trim the parts of the keyhole selection that stick out most.
2. Move the pointer to the upper-left corner outside the selection marquee.

3. Hold down the **Shift-Option** keys (Macintosh) or **Shift-Alt** keys (Windows). This allows us to select the selection. The *x* next to the selection icon (seen in Figure 12.9) indicates that you are making an intersecting selection.

Figure 12.9 Making an x selection. Everything within both selections remains selected. Everything else is deselected or left unselected. The result of intersecting selections is subtractive.

4. Click the mouse button and drag to enclose the entire selection, while trimming the selection on both sides. The resulting selection marquee includes everything within both selections. You may need to Undo and try again if your first attempt doesn't yield the correct results, shown in Figure 12.10.

Figure 12.10 This shows the result of the intersecting selection. Note that it is a subtractive process .

FINE TUNING

Now, we'll just sand away the rough edges to make a final selection.

1. Select the **Polygon Lasso** tool (l). We'll work on both sides of the selection, but one side at a time.
2. Hold down the **Option** key (Macintosh) or **Alt** key (Windows) to make a subtractive selection.

3. Click below an ear and drag along the side of the face.

4. Click a second time when you've dragged down to the intersection with the active selection marquee (Figure 12.11).

Figure 12.11 The first segment of a subtractive selection being made with the Polygon Lasso tool. The small circle beside the icon indicates that it is near the starting point, and clicking will close the selection.

5. Now drag out to the side away from the face and above the starting point. Double-click to complete the subtraction selection or drag one more segment to the starting point and click. The marquee is redrawn, as shown in Figure 12.12.

Figure 12.12 The selection marquee with one side reduced by a subtractive selection and the other yet to be altered.

6.   Repeat the process for the other side of the face.

The selection marquee is now a pretty fair approximation of the lion's head. For you sticklers who wish to continue fine-tuning, select the **Lasso** tool (l) and using the **Option/Alt** key to subtract and the **Shift** key to add, make small selections around the ears and the top of the head to refine the selection further.

At this point, you could copy the selection, open a new file, and paste the lion into it for safekeeping, or do a million other things with the current selection. Try the **Save Selection** command from the Select menu to see what it does. We'll discuss this and all the other Select commands in Chapter 13.

Open the file **HEAD_SEL.PSD** in the Lesson12 folder on the CD. The Quick Mask has been turned on to show the selection more clearly (Figure 12.13). If you want to see the "marching ants," click the **Mask Off** button at the bottom of the Toolbox.

Figure 12.13 A complex selection made using several tools in an additive, subtractive, and multiplicative way. This screen shot was made in Quick Mask mode (click on the **Quick Mask** button in the Toolbox) to emphasize the selection. Once a selection is made, the real work of transforming the image begins.

Selection Commands

In this chapter...

- Whole image commands
- Color Range dialog
- Border adjustment commands
- Saving selections

Selections can be modified by using the commands in the Select menu (see Figure 13.1). These commands allow you to adjust an active selection in various ways that would be difficult using the selection tools alone.

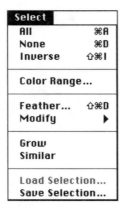

Figure 13.1 The Select command menu. Only the Color Range command is available when no image selection is active.

WHOLE IMAGE COMMANDS

At the top of the Select menu are three basic commands that make selections over the entire image:

- **Select All**—The **All** command, **Command-a** (Macintosh) or **Alt-a** (Windows), in the Select menu puts all pixels in the active layer within a selection marquee.

- **Select None**—The **None** command, **Command-d** (Macintosh) or **Alt-d** (Windows), drops any active selections leaving no marquee and no pixels selected.

- **Select Inverse**—The **Inverse** command, **Shift-Command-I** (Macintosh) or **Shift-Alt-I** (Windows), inverts any selections so that selected pixels are dropped and inactive pixels are selected. This is useful when it's more convenient to select a background and then invert to select the object on the background.

COLOR RANGE DIALOG

In addition to the Magic Wand tool, Photoshop includes the Color Range command for making more refined selections by color. This command lets you select colors from the entire image or a selection. You can sample colors or select from a preset range.

Even though the Color Range command is similar in many ways to the Magic Wand tool, all selecting is controlled from the Color Range dialog box. While the dialog is open, you can sample colors and preview your selection within the box or from the actual image. The big difference is that the Color Range command makes its selections as semi-transparent masks.

Briefly, areas within a semi-transparent mask selection are partially selected. It's as though you had used a transparency setting as a gradient across the selection and applied it according to color value. This is a somewhat abstract concept that we won't discuss in great detail here, but it is taken up again in Chapter 17. For now, it's only important that you understand that it's possible to partially select pixels and that this creates the effect of semi-transparency. See Figure 13.2.

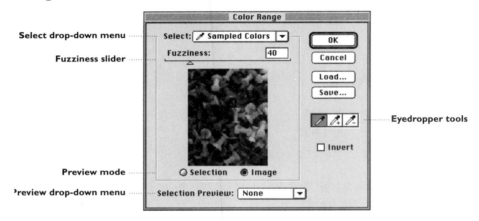

Figure 13.2 A diagram of the Color Range dialog showing settings and the preview area.

Clear Thinking about Fuzzy Selections

The Fuzziness slider in the Color Range dialog controls the selection tolerance. Why is Color Range fuzzy while the Magic Wand and Paint Bucket tools are tolerant? This has to do with the difference between a standard selection bordered by marching ants and the semi-transparent mask selection that the Color Range command makes.

The Fuzziness slider in the Color Range dialog can be adjusted from 1 to 200. This roughly corresponds to tolerance settings of 0 to 256. When you adjust the slider or type in a number, the selection is adjusted dynamically to reflect the changed setting (see Figure 13.3).

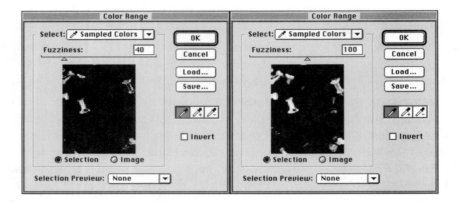

Figure 13.3 The same Color Range selection with the fuzziness set to 40, the default, on the left, and 100 on the right.

The Preview Area

The preview area provides an alternative to the "marching ants" used for most selections. There are two preview modes selected from the radio buttons below the preview area:

- **Selection mode** previews the actual selection in grayscale. White areas are selected, while black areas are not. Gray areas are partially selected. This means that they are part of the semi-transparent mask selection.

- **Image mode** previews the actual image, but does not show selection information. This is useful when the image window is magnified and you want to sample color from an area that is not visible.

You can toggle between Selection and Image modes in the preview area by holding down the **Command** or **Control** key (Macintosh) or **Ctrl** key (Windows). Click the **Invert** checkbox to change the preview from the grayscale view to negative grayscale.

Preview Modes

There are several preview modes for the image window as selected from the Selection Preview dropdown menu. These allow you to preview the selection one way in the preview area and another in the image window:

- **None** provides no selection preview in the image window. This is the default.
- **Grayscale** turns the image window into a grayscale preview as described above under selection mode.
- **Black Matte** (Figure 13.4), shows the image through a black matte, where the selection is not matted and therefore shows in color, while the rest of the image is either viewed through a grayscale matte when partially selected or obscured by the black matte when unselected.

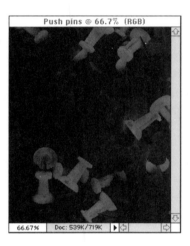

Figure 13.4 The Black Matte preview shows unselected areas in grayscale and selected areas in color. Since this screen shot is not in color, it looks exactly like the Grayscale and Quick Mask previews.

- **White Matte** (Figure 13.5), like Black Matte, shows the selection in color but the rest of the image in reverse grayscale fading to white.

Figure 13.5 The White Matte preview is the inverse of the Black Matte.

- **Quick Mask** previews the selection in Quick Mask mode using the current Quick Mask settings as described in Chapter 16.

 You can change the Selection Preview as you make color selections using the Color Range dialog.

N O T E

To sample a color range:

1. Choose the **Color Range** command from the Select menu.
2. Choose settings in the Color Range dialog box.

- The Select dropdown menu should be set to the default, which is Sampled Colors. Other settings use color selection presets and do not allow sampling.

- To view the selection in the preview area, check the **Selection Mode** radio button. This is the default.

- To preview the selection in the image window, choose one of the Selection Preview options from the dropdown menu as described above, or leave this set to None.

3. You can sample color from either the preview area of the dialog or from the actual image:

- Move the pointer to the actual image. The pointer turns into an eye-dropper icon. Click on the color you wish to select.
- From the two buttons below the preview area, click on the **Image** button. Move the pointer inside the preview area and click on the color you wish to select.

4. Adjust the Fuzziness slider to include a larger or smaller range of colors in the selection.

5. Click **OK** to apply the selection to the image. Areas that are more than 50% selected are bordered by "marching ants," but this is not necessarily the entire selection. Remember, the Color Range command makes selections as semi-transparent masks. The only way to view the entire selection once you dismiss the dialog is to turn on the Quick Mask mode or channel. This will all be clearer when you've read Chapters 16 and 17 on channels and masks.

Adding or Subtracting from a Selection

You can also add to or subtract from a selection. This is similar to the selection methods described in the previous chapter, except that you can only use the Eyedropper tools provided within the Color Range dialog box (see Figure 13.6).

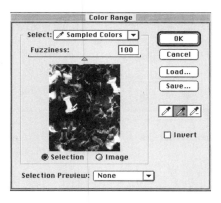

Figure 13.6 Expanding the color range of a selection using the Plus Eyedropper.

1. Choose either the **Plus Eyedropper** tool or the **Minus Eyedropper** tool.
2. Click in either the preview area or the image.

   - To add, click on a color area that is outside the current selection area.
   - To subtract, click on a color area that is inside the current selection area.

 Holding down the **Shift** key temporarily activates the Plus Eyedropper, and holding down the **Option** key (Macintosh) or **Alt** key (Windows) temporarily activates the Minus Eyedropper.

Making Preset Color Selections

The Color Range dialog includes preset color selections, which are available from the Select dropdown menu. These can be used to make quick selections based on standard color or tonal ranges (see Figure 13.7).

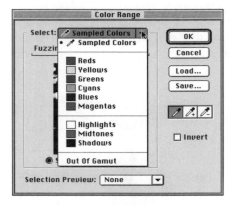

Figure 13.7 The Select dropdown menu showing the preset color selections.

 You cannot make adjustments for fuzziness or add/subtract from selections made using these presets. The default Select setting is Sample Color, which does not use any presets.

To select using preset colors, move the pointer over the Select dropdown menu, hold down the mouse button, and drag to select one of the ten presets, six color ranges, three tonal ranges, and Out of Gamut. This last preset can be used in RGB or Lab mode to find unprintable colors.

NOTE You can use the Color Range command on a selection. This means that you can use the Color Range command recursively to refine the colors selected within a selection. The preset color selections are especially useful in this situation.

Saving and Loading Range Settings

Photoshop includes the ability to save and load different settings and selections. This allows you to define a selection range and use it for multiple images.

To save and load range settings:

- Click on the **Save** button to save your color range as a file.
- Click on the **Load** button to make a selection using a color range previously defined and saved as a file.

Saving color ranges creates a file that can be saved anywhere on disk.

BORDER ADJUSTMENT COMMANDS

The Select menu includes two groups of two commands each that are used to adjust selection borders in various ways: Feather, Modify, and Grow and Similar. All of these commands affect the active border selection of an image. When no marquee is active, these commands are grayed out and not available.

Feather

The Feather command is the same as the Feather option for the Marquee and Lasso tools described in Chapter 10, except that it affects a selection *after* it is made, whereas the option must be chosen *before* making a selection.

To feather a selection border:

1. With a selection marquee active, choose **Feather** from the Select menu.
2. In the dialog box, type in a feather amount from 0.2 to 250.0 pixels.
3. Click **OK** to apply the feather.

The Feather command can be used to fill in small "holes" in a selection that was made using one of the color selection methods. See Figure 13.8.

Figure 13.8 A selection before and after applying the Feather command.

Modify

Modify is actually a submenu (shown in Figure 13.9) that includes four commands: Border, Smooth, Expand, and Contract. Each uses a dialog box to control the amount of modification applied to the active selection marquee.

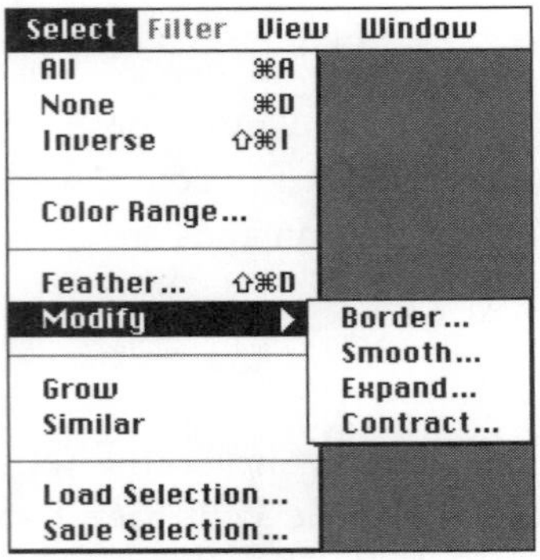

Figure 13.9 The Select menu with the Modify submenu commands expanded.

To modify a selection border:

1. Choose one of the commands from the Select Modify submenu.

   • **Border** turns the selection marquee into a selection of itself. This creates a selection frame in the width specified in the dialog (Figure 13.10), from 1 to 64 pixels.

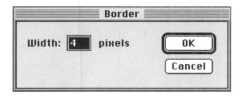

Figure 13.10 Turning a selection marquee into a border selection; just specify the width.

   • **Smooth** removes selection anomalies like rough selection borders made with the Lasso tool or stray pixels left after a color selection. This command is useful when blending, cloning, or in making tran sitions appear seamless. Enter a sample radius from 1 to 16 pixels. Photoshop examines the radius of pixels you specify around each pixel in the selection border. If most of the pixels are within the selection, all are added. If most are not, all are deselected. See Figure 13.11.

Figure 13.11 A selection before and after smoothing.

• **Expand** enlarges the selection border by the amount you specify, from 1 to 16 pixels. See Figure 13.12.

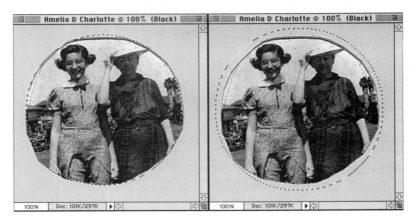

Figure 13.12 The effects of the Expand command are evident in these before and after screen shots.

• **Contract** shrinks the selection border by the amount you specify, from 1 to 16 pixels, as shown in Figure 13.13.

Figure 13.13 Contract is the opposite of Expand, shrinking the selection.

2. Type in an amount in pixels. This is the only variable.

3. Click **OK** to apply the modification.

NOTE The "real" area a Modify command affects is dependent on the image resolution. Adjusting a selection by 8 pixels for a 300 dpi image is much less noticeable than for a 72 dpi image.

Grow and Similar

The Grow and Similar commands expand a selection based on color similarity. The tolerance setting in the Magic Wand Options palette is used to determine color matches. These commands have no dialog box and are affected by no other variables.

To grow a selection by color:

1. Make a selection.
2. Choose the **Grow** command from the Select menu.

Photoshop calculates the amount of growth by looking at pixels adjacent to the selection and adding those that fall within the tolerance setting of the Magic Wand Options Palette. The selection border expands to include all selected pixels. Figure 13.14 provides an example.

Figure 13.14 The Grow command grabs more pixels that match the current selection, enlarging the border marquee.

To select all similarly colored pixels:

1. Make a selection.
2. Choose the **Similar** command from the Select menu.

Photoshop looks at all pixels in the image regardless of adjacency to the active selection. All pixels of similar color, as determined by the tolerance setting of the Magic Wand Options palette, are surrounded by one or more selection borders (see Figure 13.15). The Color Range dialog makes its selections exactly the same way.

Figure 13.15 The Similar command ignores adjacency and finds pixels throughout the image that match the selection.

You can continue to expand a selection by executing the Grow or Similar commands multiple times.

N O T E

SAVING AND REUSING SELECTIONS

The Load Selection and Save Selection commands are another example of the Load/Save capabilities of Photoshop. These do not create selection files, but instead save selection borders with the image itself for reuse whenever you open the file.

To save a selection:

1. Make a selection.
2. Choose the **Save Selection** command from the Select menu.
3. In the Save dialog, name the selection and click **OK**.

NOTE You are saving the selection as an additional channel to the image, not as a separate file. Photoshop names selection channels numerically; if there are already three channels, the selection is named #4. You can change the name in the Channels palette as discussed in Chapter 17.

To load a selection:

1. Choose the **Load Selection** command from the Select menu.
2. The Load dialog allows you to specify a source and a method, which Photoshop refers to as an *Operation*.

   - For the source, you can choose any saved selection from any open document. Both are specified from dropdown arrows. You can also choose the inverse of the selection by clicking in the **Invert** check box.
   - The default operation is New Selection, which deselects anything you had previously selected and activates the saved selection border. You can also choose to Add, Subtract, or Intersect the selection by click ing the appropriate radio button.

Saving and loading selections can be useful when you're working with channels to create masks. This is discussed in Chapter 17.

Fill and Stroke Commands

The Fill and Stroke commands are both found in Photoshop's Edit menu. Fill works similarly to the Paint Bucket tool, but acts on a selection or layer rather than contiguous pixels. Stroke is just like the Fill command except that it creates a border of pixels around a selection or layer rather than a uniform fill.

Both commands are applied either to the active selection or, if there is no selection, the target layer. Both can be adjusted for transparency and can be applied using the blending modes discussed in Chapter 3.

You can fill a selection or layer using keyboard shortcuts.

With an area or layer selected, do one of the following:

- To use the foreground color to fill, press the **Option-Delete** keys (Macintosh) or **Alt-Backspace** keys (Windows).

- To use the foreground color and preserve transparency, press the **Shift-Option-Delete** keys (Macintosh) or **Shift-Alt-Backspace** keys (Windows).

- To use the background color to fill, press the **Command-Delete** keys (Macintosh) or the **Ctrl-Backspace** keys (Windows).

- To use the background color and preserve transparency, press the **Shift-Command-Delete** keys (Macintosh) or the **Shift-Ctrl-Backspace** keys (Windows).

To fill a selection or layer using the dialog:

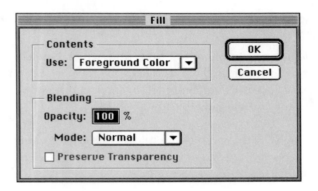

Figure 13.16: The Edit Fill dialog.

1. With an area or layer selected, choose Fill from the Edit menu or press the **Shift-Delete** keys (Macintosh) or **Shift-Backspace** keys (Windows).
2. Specify the fill from the **Contents Use** dropdown menu.

Figure 13.17: The Use menu from the Fill dialog. Pattern and Snapshot are only available when those buffers are in use.

Choose **Foreground Color** or **Background Color** to use one of the current color choices in the Toolbox.

The next three choices, Pattern (Edit Define Pattern), Saved, and Snapshot (Edit Take Snapshot), use Photoshop's buffers, explained in Chapter 21. You must first define a pattern or save a snapshot for these options to be available.

The last three choices are simply Black, 50% Gray, and White.

3. Make blending choices by typing in an Opacity percentage and choosing a blending mode from the dropdown menu. Select the **Preserve Transparency** check box to leave empty pixels unfilled.

4. Click OK.

To stroke a selection or layer:

1. With an area or layer selected, choose **Stroke** from the Edit menu.

2. Specify a Width in whole pixels from 1 to 16.

3. Choose a Location. Inside creates a stroke inside the selection, Center centers the stroke on the selection, and Outside creates a stroke outside the selection.

4. Specify an Opacity, select a blending mode, and click on the Preserve Transparency check box as desired.

5. Click OK.

Figure 13.18 shows the Edit Stroke dialog box.

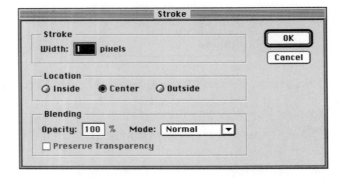

Figure 13.18: The Edit Stroke dialog.

Lesson 13: Manipulating Selections

We're not going to attempt to use all of the commands in the Select menu, but I'll indicate where you can try out more of them if you wish. All the commands in this lesson are in the Select menu, except the File Open command.

To ignore precision:

1. Open the image **WATER_LI.TIF** from the Lesson13 folder on the CD. This image is from KPT's Power Photos collection.

2. Choose the **Magic Wand** tool (w) from the Toolbox.

3. Use the default options to make your selection. The tolerance should be 32, with the Anti-aliased option selected.

4. Click on a lily pad (see Figure 13.19).

Figure 13.19 A selection made with the Magic Wand tool's default options.

5. Choose the **Grow** command. Remember, this command uses the tolerance setting from the Magic Wand Options. Notice how the selection expands to include adjacent pixels within the tolerance setting, as shown in Figure 13.20.

Figure 13.20 The selection expanded after using the Grow command to enclose all the adjacent pixels within the color tolerance.

6. Choose the **Similar** command. This time adjacency is ignored and all the lily pads are pretty well selected, as shown in Figure 13.18. We didn't really need to use the Grow command first, but it points out the difference in these two commands.

Figure 13.21 The Similar command ignores adjacency and selects all the lily pads, because they contain the only matching green pixels in this image.

7. Choose the **Feather** command. Type in **2** pixels for the feather amount in the dialog box (Figure 13.22). This will fill in the holes left from the Similar command (Figure 13.23).

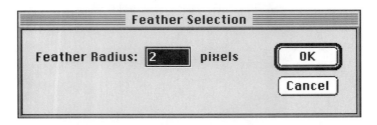

Figure 13.22 The Feather dialog has a single option for setting the extent of feathering.

Figure 13.23 The result of feathering this selection eliminates most of the holes left from the Similar command.

8. Select the **Inverse** command. Now everything but the lily pads is selected (Figure 13.24).

Figure 13.24 The selection marquee looks almost the same before and after inversing the selection. The only noticeable difference is that the marquee around the frame changes.

NOTE You can tell what's selected and what isn't by moving the pointer around. When it's over selected areas, the pointer turns into the move icon; when it's over non-selected areas, the pointer reverts to the active tool's icon.

9. Choose the **Save Selection** command. Accept the default settings in the dialog by clicking **OK**. This does not save a file, but adds a channel to the existing image. All RGB images have four default channels (0-3), so the selection channel is added as #4. See Figure 13.25.

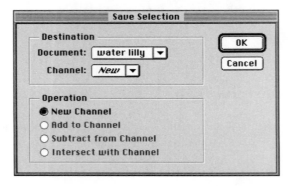

Figure 13.25 The Save Selection dialog allows you to add channels to the image and then reload the selection at any time.

Here's your chance to play with the Modify subcommands. Try each one: Border, Smooth, Expand, and Contract. Since each of these alters only the selection border, choose the **Load Selection** command (Figure 13.26) to revert to the original selection.

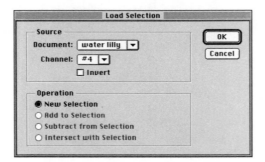

Figure 13.26 The Load Selection command defaults to channel #4. If there were more channels, you could make your selection from the dropdown arrow, but in this case just click **OK**.

Subtle Selections

You can make subtle selections with the Color Range command. We'll exercise this command only minimally, since the significance of this tool will become clearer when you know more about channels and masks.

1. Open the file **ELEPHANT.TIF**. We won't make any selections, except with the Color Range command.
2. Choose the **Color Range** command.
3. From the Select dropdown menu, choose **Yellows**. You can see the effect of this selection in the Preview Area.

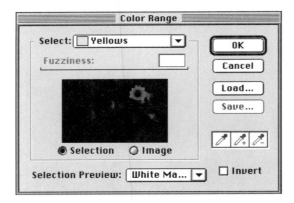

Figure 13.27 The Color Range dialog with a preset selection chosen and the Selection Preview set to White Matte. The Preview Area shows the selection mask in grayscale.

The preset selections do not allow you to adjust for fuzziness. If you'd like to play with this setting, choose **Sampled Colors** from the Select dropdown menu. Click on the sunflower petals to select a yellow color. Slide the Fuzziness slider to see how it affects the selection. See if you can find a setting that closely matches the Yellow preset. It won't be the same, because the hues are different.

4. From the Selection Preview dropdown menu, choose **White Matte**. This shows the transparent mask selection very clearly in the image window (see Figure 13.28).
5. Click **OK**. Only some of the sunflower's petals (shown in Figure 13.29) are selected by the selection marquee. Don't worry, the transparent mask is still there.

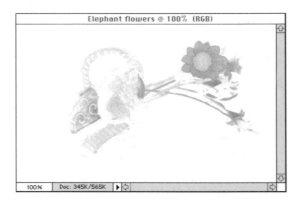

Figure 13.28 The Image window set to preview the selection as a White Matte. Everything that's not white is part of the selection mask.

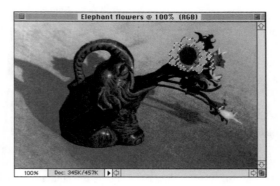

Figure 13.29 The actual selection marquee shows only pixels that are at least 50% selected. Pixels less than 50% selected are still part of the transparent mask.

6. If the Swatches Palette isn't open, choose **Show Swatches** from the Window menu, hold down the **Option** key (Macintosh) or **Alt** key (Windows), and click on the bright yellow swatch in the top row to select a background color.

7. Hit the **Delete/Backspace** key. This replaces the selection with the background color. But since the selection is really a transparent mask, the substitution is partially transparent. This makes all the yellow in the image perceptibly brighter, but maintains the image's integrity.

8. Choose **Select None** to deselect. The yellow flowers and tusk are distinctly more yellow, but they do not stand out from the rest of the image. Since it is difficult to discern the difference in a grayscale image, you may want to check your work by opening the image **ELEPHANT.PSD** from the Lesson13 folder on the CD.

Palettes

In this section...

- Colors & Swatches
- Layers
- Channels & Masks
- Paths
- Info
- Navigator
- Actions

PALETTES GENERALIZED

Photoshop has five default palette groups: Brushes/Options, Colors/Swatches, Layers/Channels/Paths, Info/Navigator, and Actions. We have already discussed palettes generally in Chapter 1, and since the details of the Brushes and Options palettes were covered in Sections II and III, I won't discuss them in this section. I'll briefly recap the general behavior of palettes and then discuss the specifics of each palette in the chapters of this section.

The operation of the palettes has been refined over several versions of Photoshop, and Adobe has generalized their behavior for use across most of its product line. So while the Navigator and Actions palettes are new with version 4, they share the properties of all palettes in Photoshop.

 The Toolbox shares all these same properties, except that it has no tab and therefore cannot be grouped.

N O T E

Palette groups or windows float freely around the desktop in a layer above all open image windows. They can be dragged around by the title bar, collapsed or expanded by clicking on the resize box (upper-righthand corner), or closed using the close box (upper-lefthand corner). They can also be shown or hidden by using commands in the Window menu.

Palettes can also be rearranged using their tabs—the palette title within the palette group window. Click on a gray tab to activate a palette and deactivate any other palette in the group window. Drag a tab to remove it from the group window and open it as new palette window. You can also drag a tab from one palette window into another, creating a new grouping. All of this allows you to customize your Photoshop desktop to suit the way you work and the amount of screen real estate you have.

Every palette has a palette menu with palette-specific commands. This dropdown menu is accessed by moving the pointer over the menu arrow (near the upper-righthand corner) and pressing the mouse button. You can also access context-sensitive menus by holding down the **Control** key (Macintosh) with the mouse button, or by holding down the right mouse button (Windows).

Colors & Swatches

In this chapter…

- Color Pickers
- Colors
- Swatches

I lied. I said I would discuss each palette in a separate chapter, but the Colors and Swatches palettes are so closely related that I thought it best to keep them grouped. I'll also use this opportunity to discuss Photoshop's use of different color picking systems.

COLOR PICKERS

The color picker allows you to select foreground and background colors by sampling or by entering numerical specifications in any of Photoshop's supported color models. (The color models are discussed in Chapter 2.) There are a number of different ways to specify or choose colors, including support for various commercially available custom color systems.

To open Photoshop's Color Picker:

- Click on the foreground or background color in the color selection box of the Toolbox.
- Click on the front color selection box in the Color palette.

Figure 14.1 shows the Color Picker.

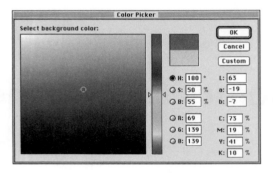

Figure 14.1 Photoshop's Color Picker. The Color Picker tells you whether you are picking the foreground or background color.

Selecting Colors by Sampling

Since all color models exist in more than two dimensions, it's impossible to represent them all in a two-dimensional display. Photoshop shows two dimensions of color in the square color field and lets you adjust for the third dimension using the color slider. This system works for both RGB and HSB color models.

To select a color by sampling:

1. Drag the white triangles alongside the slider to set the first dimension of color, or click on a color within the slider.
2. Click inside the color field to pick the color. This becomes either the foreground or background color, depending on which you clicked on to open the Color Picker.

To the left of the OK and Cancel buttons in the color dialogs, Photoshop displays the previous color (bottom) and current color (top) selections in swatches.

Changing Color Dimensions

The three color dimensions used by Photoshop's Color Picker can be changed by clicking on one of the six radio buttons next to the HSB and RGB fields. The selected button is the dimension represented by the slider, and the other two dimensions of the color model selected become the two axes of the color field.

To change color dimensions, click on one of the radio buttons to change the slider and color field displays.

Specifying Colors by Number

Photoshop's color picker includes numerical fields for all four color models supported, HSB, RGB, Lab, and CMYK.

To specify colors by number, type numbers into any of the specifications fields in the Color Picker. Specify a value for each of the components for the model you're using. The chosen color is updated each time you enter a new value.

Choosing Custom Colors

Photoshop includes color palettes for the PANTONE Matching System, the TRUMATCH Swatching System, the FOCOLTONE Colour System, the Toyo 88 ColorFinder 21050 System, the ANPA-Color system, and the DIC Color Guide. These systems are used by printers to specify ink colors or spot colors.

Custom colors are chosen from the Custom Color dialog. You can toggle between this and the Color Picker. Custom Colors are stored as files in the Palettes folder within Photoshop's Goodies folder. This allows you to update palettes or add new custom color files, like a palette of the 217 non-dithered World Wide Web colors.

1. Click on the **Custom** button in the Color Picker to toggle to the Custom Color dialog.
2. Select a custom color model from the Book dropdown menu (see Figure 14.2).

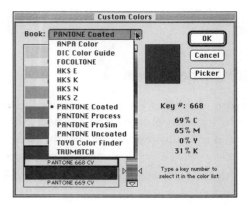

Figure 14.2 The Book dropdown menu showing the custom color systems included with Photoshop 4..

3. Drag the white triangles alongside the slider (Figure 14.3), or click on the **Up** or **Down arrow** to adjust the slider.

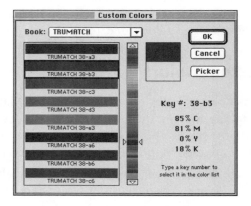

Figure 14.3 The Custom Colors dialog. You can toggle between this and the Color Picker. Whichever was the last open will remain chosen the next time you click on the foreground or background color selector.

4. Click on a color patch in the display area to select it. You can also type a Key # to specify an ink color.

5. Click on the **Picker** button to toggle back to the Color Picker.

When you select a color, the CMYK values used by Photoshop to represent the ink color are listed in the dialog. These are the values Photoshop will use to display and print the color with non-ink systems.

Gamut Warnings

As discussed in Chapter 2, each color system has a gamut of printable colors that is smaller than the 16 million colors you can view on your monitor. Photoshop has the gamut information built in and warns you if the color you select is outside the printable range.

If the selected color is out of gamut, a warning triangle with an exclamation point appears next to the current color swatch (Figure 14.4). Beneath the warning triangle is a small square showing the closest color within the printable gamut. Click on the triangle or square and Photoshop adjusts the current color selection automatically.

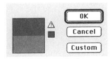

Figure 14.4 The bottom color swatch shows the previous color selection; the top color swatch shows the current selection. The warning triangle shows that the current selection is out of gamut.

Changing Pickers

If you'd rather use the Macintosh or Windows color pickers, open the **General Preferences** dialog from the File menu. Use the Color Picker dropdown menu to change pickers. Click **OK**. Instead of the Photoshop Color Picker, the system color picker will be used. To learn about using your system picker, read the documentation that came with your system.

THE COLOR PALETTE IN DETAIL

We've used the Color palette already in several of the lessons and discussed it briefly. It offers most of the flexibility of Photoshop's color picker in an abbreviated format.

To open the Color palette, choose **Show Color** from the Window menu or click on the **Color** tab in the Color/Swatches palette group.

As with the Color Picker, there are a number of different ways to choose colors from the Color palette. The palette primarily uses sliders to define colors. There are different sets of sliders for each of Photoshop's supported color models (see Figure 14.5).

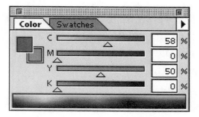

Figure 14.5 The Color palette in CMYK mode. Note the highlighted square around the foreground color swatch indicating that it is the color you are editing.

To choose a color from the Color palette:

1. Choose the color model from the Color palette menu—Grayscale, RGB, HSB, CMYK, or Lab (Figure 14.6). This sets the sliders in the Color palette. The default is RGB.

Figure 14.6 The Color palette menu.

2. Set the value for each color component by sliding the triangles under each color scale or by typing in a number in the fields at the end of each slider. Values for RGB sliders are from 0 to 255. Values for Grayscale, HSB, and CMYK are in percents. Lab values are from 0 to 100 for the 'L' axis, while the other two axes are from -128 to +127.

You can also pick colors directly from the color bar at the bottom of the Color palette. To use the color bar:

Using the Color Bar

1. Choose the Color Bar command from the Color palette menu (Figure 14.7) and drag to select a color bar representation.

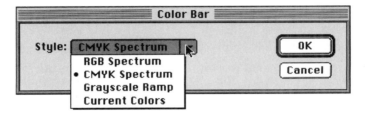

Figure 14.7 The Color Bar dialog is used to change the representation of the color bar in the Color palette.

2. Move the pointer into the color bar at the bottom of the Color palette and click to select a color. The Grayscale ramp limits your selection to shades of gray, while the Current Color bar shows a color ramp between the foreground and background colors and limits your selection to these colors.

The two overlapping color swatches in the Color palette show the current foreground (on top) and background (underneath) colors.

Specifying Foreground and Background Colors

Click on a swatch to make the foreground or background the active selection. The active selection is indicated by a highlighted line around the swatch. Any color selection affects only the active swatch.

As with the Color Picker, out-of-gamut colors are flagged with a warning triangle. Click on the triangle or the color square beneath it to bring the color back within the printable gamut.

CUSTOMIZING THE SWATCHES PALETTE

As described earlier, the Swatches palette can be used to select foreground or background colors simply by clicking on a swatch. The swatches in the palette can be customized to suit your work in general or a specific image.

To open the Swatches palette, choose **Show Swatches** from the Window menu or click on the **Swatches** tab in the Color/Swatches palette group.

As you move over the colors in the Swatches palette, the pointer turns into an eyedropper icon to indicate that clicking will select a color.

- To select a foreground color, click on any swatch.
- To select a background color, **Option-click** (Macintosh) or **Alt-click** (Windows) on any swatch. See Figure 14.8.

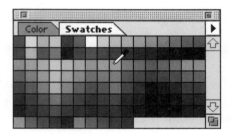

Figure 14.8 Selecting a color from the Swatches palette. The Eyedropper icon indicates that clicking will make a selection.

Every time you modify a swatch to add or change a color, the foreground color is used.

To modify a swatch, select the color you want to add, using any method to change the foreground color—Color Picker, Color palette, or by sampling with the Eyedropper tool in an image.

Deleting colors does not leave a blank space in the palette. Instead, all colors are shifted up and over to fill the void.

To add a new color swatch:

1. Move the pointer over one of the empty swatch squares at the bottom of the Swatches palette. The icon turns into a Paint Bucket.

2. Click to fill the empty square with the current foreground color (see Figure 14.9).

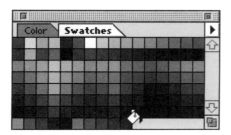

Figure 14.9 Adding a color to the end of the Swatches palette. The Paint Bucket icon indicates that you are adding a color.

To modify an existing color swatch:

1. Move the pointer over the swatch you wish to modify.

2. Hold down the **Shift** key. The icon changes to a Paint Bucket.

3. Click to replace the color, as shown in Figure 14.10.

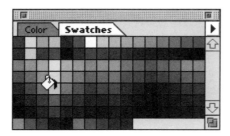

Figure 14.10 Modifying an existing color swatch. The Paint Bucket icon indicates that you are adding a color, but in this case it will replace the current swatch color.

To insert a new color swatch:

1.   Move the pointer over the swatch where you wish to insert a new color.
2.   Hold down the **Shift-Option** keys (Macintosh) or **Shift-Alt** keys (Windows). The icon changes to a paint bucket.
3.   Click to insert a new swatch. All swatches after the insertion are shifted to make room for the inserted swatch.

NOTE   The pointer icon does not change when you are inserting a new color swatch.

To delete a color swatch:

1.   Move the pointer over the swatch you wish to delete.
2.   Hold down the **Command** key (Macintosh) or **Ctrl** key (Windows). The icon turns into scissors, as shown in Figure 14.11.

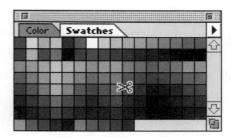

Figure 14.11 The scissors icon indicates that clicking will delete the color swatch.

3.   Click to delete the swatch. All following swatches shift up a place to fill the void.

Saving and Loading Palettes

The Swatches palette menu (Figure 14.12) includes several commands that allow you to save, load, and append custom palettes. There are four commands.

```
Reset Swatches
Load Swatches...
Replace Swatches...
Save Swatches...
```

Figure 14.12 The Swatches palette menu with commands for saving and loading palettes.

- **Reset Swatches** loads Photoshop's default swatches. A dialog box asks if you wish to replace the current swatches completely. Click **OK** to replace the palette of swatches. All changes to the current palette are lost. Click **Append** to add the new swatches after the existing swatches.
- **Load Swatches** allows you to locate any palette file you have on disk and append it to the current palette's swatches.
- **Replace Swatches** allows you to locate any palette file you have on disk and use it to replace all the current swatches.

You can expand the Swatches palette to display more colors by clicking on the Resize box, or you can scroll through the swatches using the scroll bars in the palette.

- **Save Swatches** saves the current swatches as a file. You can save the file anywhere you like, but you might want to keep it with Photoshop's other color palettes in the Goodies folder.

Any changes you make to the Swatches palette are saved when you quit Photoshop and are opened in the same state when you launch it next.

Lesson 14: Picking Colors

Pick a color, any color. This lesson won't deal with any specific images, but will guide you through some of the items you learned about in this chapter. You won't even need to open a document to follow this lesson.

TOURING THE COLOR PICKER

Reset the foreground and background colors to their defaults by clicking on the **Reset** button in the Toolbox.

1.　Click on the Foreground color in the Toolbox to open the Color Picker. The Color picker will say "Select foreground color:" over the Color Field, as shown in Figure 14.13.

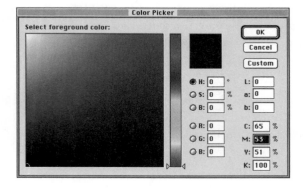

Figure 14.13 Photoshop's default black,as specified in the Color Picker.

There is a small round circle in the Color Field that indicates the current pick. It's all the way down in the bottom lefthand corner, and all color values are zero, except in the CMYK fields. You would expect the K value to be at 100% for black, but what about the CMY values? Many artists like to specify CMY values when they pick a black to avoid trapping problems or create an especially rich black.Photoshop uses 65% cyan. 53% magenta, and 51% yellow for the default black because of the seperation set up in Chapter 27.

2. Type **0** in the K field. Many things change when you make this single change. Suddenly all of the numeric fields have values, the current color changes to a medium gray, and the selection circle in the Color Field moves to a new location. Notice that Hue and Saturation remain 0 (1% saturation is close enough), and only the Brightness value has changed. The selected color is 66% gray. Figure 14.14 shows the changes in the Color Picker.

3. Click in the upper righthand corner of the Color Field. Since the H radio button is selected, this corner represents 100% saturation (S) and 100% Brightness (B). (If you've previously changed the Color Picker, H might not be the current selection. Click on the H radio button now and continue with this lesson.) Notice that Hue is still 0 and the white triangles on the color slider are still at the bottom (Figure 14.15).

4. The warning triangle indicates that this is an unprintable color using CMYK inks. Look at the CMYK values, then click on the triangle to bring the color back into the printable gamut.

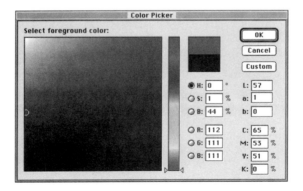

Figure 14.14 Changing the K value to 0 yields gray.

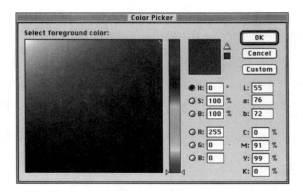

Figure 14.15 From gray to red in the same Color Field, while the Hue remains 0.

Curiously, none of the CMYK values change, but all the other values do (Figure 14.16). This is because the conversions from one system to another are approximate. There are no values of CMYK to equal a perfect bright red, and that is why it is out-of-gamut.

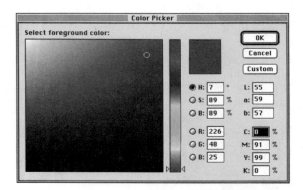

Figure 14.16 Bringing unprintable red into the printable gamut does not change the CMYK values.

5. Click on each of the radio buttons to see how it affects the Color Field and Color Slider. The selected color doesn't change, but the selection circle jumps around as the axes change.

LOTS OF CUSTOM COLORS

1. Click on the **Custom** button in the Color Picker. This toggles to the Custom Colors dialog and picks the custom color closest to the cur-

rently selected color. The default custom color palette in the Book drop-down menu is PANTONE uncoated. The closest it offers to our printable red is number 1665. You can see from the color swatches and from the CMYK values that this is not an exact match (Figure 14.17).

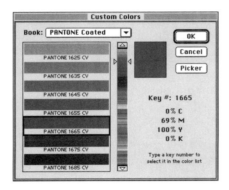

Figure 14.17 The printable red from the Color Picker translates into this very orangey PANTONE color.

2. From the Book dropdown menu, choose the FOCOLTONE color palette. You can see from the CMYK values that FOCOLTONE 3495 is a closer match to our original color. If you really wanted red instead of orange, click a little higher on the slider where the red bars are. You'll find that FOCOLTONE 3470 is an equally good match in terms of percentages, and is a much better red. See Figure 14.18.

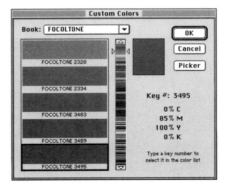

Figure 14.18 FOCOLTONE provides a closer approximation for this color, but more important is the variety of choices the Custom Colors dialog provides.

N O T E

This is probably not the way you'll pick colors from the Custom Colors dialog. You're more likely to use the color system that your printer is using or the one that experience has told you yields the best results.

3. Try scrolling through the swatches. You can click or drag in the slider, click on the arrow keys or press on the **Up** or **Down Arrow** keys on your keyboard.

4. Click on the **Custom** button to toggle back to the Color Picker. The CMYK values will match exactly what you picked from the Custom Colors dialog.

5. Eventually, you'll have found the color you want. Click **OK**, and the foreground or background color is updated.

PICKING FROM PALETTES

Open the Color palette by choosing **Show Color** from the Window menu or by clicking on the **Color** tab in the Swatches/Color palette group.

It's possible to do the same things we did with the Color Picker using the Color palette, although no custom colors are available.

Click on the **Reset** button in the Toolbox to set the foreground and background colors to their defaults, and let's get started again. The palette's default will have RGB sliders set to match the foreground color, black. Notice that all three sliders are at zero.

1. Move the pointer over the right-pointing triangle near the upper right corner of the palette. Hold down the mouse button to open the palette menu, and drag to select CMYK Sliders (Figure 14.19).

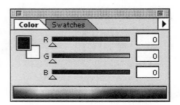

Figure 14.19 Changing the Color palette display by selecting CMYK sliders from the palette menu.

The CMYK sliders represent black with the same color values as in the Color Picker.

2. Change the K quantity to 0, either by moving the slider or typing in the amount. See Figure 14.20.

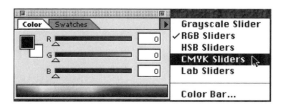

Figure 14.20 This medium gray is the same as that produced using the Color Picker as shown in Figure 14.14.

This achieves the same result that we got in the Color Picker, but we now have different feedback. Each slider contains dynamic color information so that you can see what the result of changing a single slider will be.

We can see that the bright red from the exercise above cannot be achieved by adjusting a single slider. However, there are several ways to get there.

3. The most direct route to red is simply to click at the left end of the Color Bar across the bottom of the palette where red is. A more exact route is to switch back to **RGB Sliders** by selecting it from the palette menu, and adjusting the sliders to 255 for red and 0 for green and blue.

Once again, we've achieved unprintable bright red. If you switch back to CMYK sliders, you can see that the percentages shown in Figure 14.21 are the same as they were in the exercise above.

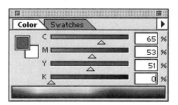

Figure 14.21 Bright red cannot be printed using the CMYK process. The closest approximation to red that CMYK can achieve is orange.

4. Click on the warning triangle to select the closest printable color. Notice that even though the color changes, the CMYK sliders don't.

Ordinarily you won't find it useful to switch back and forth between RGB and CMYK colors. Since the gamuts don't match exactly, it's usually best to work in one mode and only switch when you have to. Switching back can cause color confusion.

CUSTOM SWATCHES

While there's no way to use custom colors in the Color palette, the Swatches palette is a different story. We've already picked foreground and background colors from the Swatches palette in previous lessons, but we haven't customized the palette.

1. Click on the **Swatches** tab in the Color/Swatches palette group. There are no colors highlighted and no indication of the current foreground and/or background colors. You have to look at the Toolbox to see what they are, because the Swatches palette is purely for picking.

2. Open the Swatches palette menu and drag to select **Replace Swatches**. From the dialog, open the **FOCOLTONE** colors file in the Color palettes folder of Photoshop's Goodies folder. This replaces the current default swatches with the FOCOLTONE palette of swatches.

3. There are a lot of FOCOLTONE colors, so click on the **Resize** box in the upper right corner of the palette to enlarge the palette window.

   How do we find FOCOLTONE 3470 in this large palette? First, you can see where the reddest colors are, but the exact shade may be difficult to discern.

4. Move the pointer over the swatches. It turns into the Eyedropper icon to indicate that clicking will select the swatch. But more importantly for our search, notice how the palette tab changes to indicate the name of the custom color the Eyedropper is passing over. As you pass over the second row of magenta swatches, you'll find that the fourth swatch (Figure 14.22) is FOCOLTONE 3470, the exact swatch we're looking for. Click to select it.

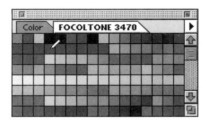

Figure 14.22 Here is FOCOLTONE 3470 positively identified in the Swatches tab.

Suppose we wanted to save this color with the default system swatches so that we could use it frequently.

5. Open the Palette menu and drag to select **Reset Swatches**. In the dialog, click **OK** to replace the FOCOLTONE swatches. Click the **Resize** box to reduce the size of the palette again.

6. Move the pointer over the white, unfilled swatches on the bottom row of the palette. The icon turns into a Paint Bucket, as shown in Figure 14.23.

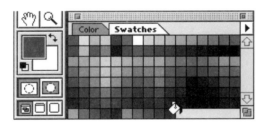

Figure 14.23 Moving the pointer over an unfilled swatch allows you to add any color to the palette simply by clicking.

7. Click to fill a new swatch with the foreground color.

This addition will stay loaded in the Swatches palette until you replace or reload. Choose **Save Swatches** from the Palette menu if you want to save your changes as a file.

CHAPTER

Layers

In this chapter...

- Understanding layers
- A tour of the Layers palette
- Working with layers

UNDERSTANDING LAYERS

Layers are fundamental to Photoshop and have become a standard feature of many graphics programs and most of Adobe's software. Photoshop's layers act as independent images within a single file. You can move, transform, edit, or apply any of Photoshop's filters to individual layers without affecting the rest of the image.

The comparison is often made to layers of acetate that are transparent until drawn on and can be rearranged, added to, or deleted as needed. Essentially, layers provide a convenient means for keeping elements of an image discrete so that you can continue to work on them. Before Photoshop implemented its layers scheme, all the bits of an image merged together and all sense of individual objects was lost.

When you open a new image, it has a single layer named Background (see Figure 15.1). A background layer cannot be transparent or use blending modes and cannot be moved. There can only be a single background layer for any image, and it must be the bottom layer. However, not every image needs to have a background layer, and you can change the name of the background if you wish to use the layer in a way that would otherwise be impossible.

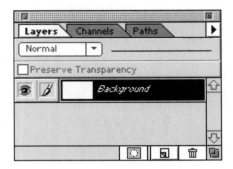

Figure 15.1 A new document opens with only a background layer, which has certain unique characteristics.

As you work with an image, you will add layers for different purposes. You can add new layers in different ways. There are also situations where Photoshop automatically creates new layers, as when you use the text tool or copy a layer or selection from another image.

Layers are viewed, controlled, and manipulated from the Layers palette, which is part of the Layers/Channels/Paths palette group. Many of the properties of layers are similar to properties discussed in earlier chapters about tools and selections. Layers are affected by transparency, blending modes, and masking, which we have mentioned only briefly, but are discussed in detail in Chapters 16 and 17.

It's important to know that there is one, and only one, active or target layer. This is the layer you are working on at any given moment, and you can identify it in the Layers palette, because it is highlighted, as shown in Figure 15.2. While you can link and move multiple layers simultaneously, you can only change the actual pixels on the single active layer.

It's easy to add type to an image by typing it right in or by importing type from another source.

Lesson 15

or better or worse, Photoshop is responsible for sparking the current photo montage rage. Here three images on three layers are combined with a text layer.

The selection process in Photoshop is as important as any of the image creation tools. Here, a color selection was made of the window panes and

Sky Writer

ling type with a background is only
he most obvious use of Photoshop's
clipping paths, while hiding a frog
under a fern frond is easily accom-
lished by painting on a layer mask.

Lesson 17

Lesson 21

This image takes advantage of both color and
alpha channels. Color channels were used to

Photoshop's built-in text tools
are supplemented by the

Lesson 22

Every photograph brought into Photoshop will require a certain amount of image correction. At the top, a badly scanned photo is corrected using the Image Adjust Levels, Curves, and Color Balance commands. Above, a 70-year-old photograph has been turned into a sepia-like print using the Colorize option of the Hue/Saturation command.

Lesson 23

The effects available using Photoshop's built in filters are endless. This image is the result of applying a series of filters to a simple stock photo.

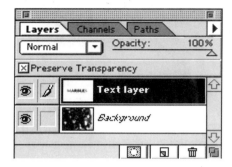

Figure 15.2 Two layers: a background with one layer above it that is selected and therefore active. Active layers have a brush icon in the second column.

Since layers are additive, order is significant. You can't see through an opaque layer to a lower layer in the palette. This means that transparency is especially important when working with layers. Photoshop 4.0 takes further advantage of transparency with Adjustment Layers. This new feature allows you to preview image adjustments to all layers simultaneously.

NOTE Photoshop layers can only be saved using Photoshop's native file format. All other file formats flatten multiple layers into a single layer. This is one way in which layers and channels (discussed in Chapter 17) differ.

Each layer that you add to an image represents additional pixels and therefore requires additional memory. The dimensions of the image don't change, but its use of system resources does. The info bar at the bottom of each image (see Figure 15.3) changes as you add layers to show how much memory the image requires with and without layers. Bear this in mind as you add layers, because the convenience of using layers will eventually be outweighed by the inconvenience of an overtaxed system.

Figure 15.3 The information panel in the active window shows that this two-layer image uses 732k, but would only use about half that (315k) if the image were flattened to a single layer.

A TOUR OF THE LAYERS PALETTE

Open the Layers palette by choosing **Show Layers** from the Window menu or by clicking on the **Layers** tab in the Layers/Channels/Paths palette group. Figure 15.4 shows the palette.

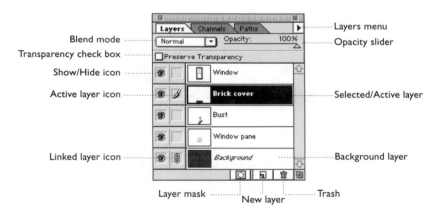

Figure 15.4 A diagram of the Layers palette.

Each layer is listed in the Layers palette, and the list can expand to include as many layers as your machine has memory to create. Adjustment layers and floating selections are also listed as layers, and you can manipulate them like any other layer until they are applied or deselected.

The options at the top of the Layers palette can be set for each layer individually.

- The Blend Mode dropdown menu uses the same blending/painting modes discussed in Chapter 3, and they work the same way but on adjacent layers. The active layer provides the blend color, all layers beneath it become the base color, and the resulting color is what you see in the image window.

- The Opacity slider is identical to the Opacity slider in the various Option palettes (see Chapter 5). It's used to make entire layers semitransparent in relation to the layers below them.

- The Preserve Transparency check box prevents you from changing any transparent pixels in a layer. So if you have a layer with an object surrounded by transparent pixels and you check **Preserve Transparency**, you can change the pixels in the object, but not in the rest of the layer.

Beneath the three layer options is the layers list, with layers listed in order. There are three columns.

The first column controls layer visibility.

While you can have only a single target layer, any number or combination of layers can be made visible.

N O T E

To show/hide layers:

- Click in the square in the first column to hide a layer. Hidden layers are not visible, do not print, and will not be sampled when you use a tool with the Sample Merged option checked. Hiding layers can speed up Photoshop, because there is less information to redraw as you make changes.

- Click in the square again to show a layer. An eye icon appears in the square to indicate that the layer is visible.

- Drag through several squares to make a group of layers visible or hidden.

- **Option-click** (Macintosh) or **Alt-click** (Windows) the visibility column to show just that layer and hide all others. **Option/Alt-click** again to make all layers visible. See Figure 15.5.

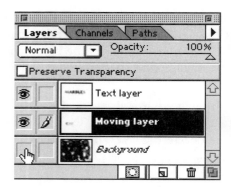

Figure 15.5 Clicking in the visibility column to hide a layer. Hidden layers have no eye icon in this first column.

The second column controls linking, but it is also used to display the active layer and mask icons.

The active layer is indicated with a brush icon in the second column. Since there can only be a single target layer, only one layer can display the brush icon. This is controlled from the third column in the layers list.

When you create a mask layer using the Mask button or command, a mask icon appears in the second column. Masks are discussed in Chapter 16.

To link layers:

- Click in the second column of a non-active layer. This links it to the active layer, and the chain link icon appears, as shown in Figure 15.6. Linked layers can be moved together when either is active. You can link as many layers together as you wish. When no linked layer is active, the icon is not displayed.

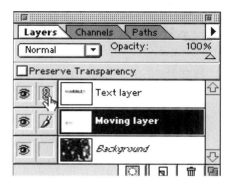

Figure 15.6 Clicking in the second column puts the chain link icon in the box and links the layer to the active layer. Linked layers can be moved together.

- Click on the chain-link icon to delete a link.

The third column identifies the layer and displays a thumbnail image of the layer with its name. By clicking and dragging in this column, a layer can be moved around in the Layers palette, as discussed later in this chapter.

To activate a layer, click on a layer's thumbnail image or name. The third column is highlighted, and a brush icon appears in the second column. Activating any other layer deactivates the previously active layer.

Across the bottom of the Layers palette are three buttons: Layer Mask, New Layer, and Trash. As you might expect, these allow you to turn a layer into a mask, create new layers, and delete layers. They all have command equivalents.

To delete a layer:

- Click on the **Trash** button and then confirm by clicking **OK** in the alert box. This deletes the active layer.
- **Option-click** (Macintosh) or **Alt-click** (Windows) on the Trash button to delete the active layer without an alert box.

- Drag any layer to the Trash button. When the Trash button is highlighted, release the mouse button. Click **OK** in the alert box and the layer is deleted.

- Choose **Delete Layer** from the Layers palette menu or from the Layer menu. There is no alert to confirm. If the layer contains a floating selection, this command changes to Delete Selection.

Whenever you create a new layer it becomes the active layer and is added to the layers palette above the previously active layer.

To create a new layer:

- Click on the **New Layer** button. This automatically adds a layer without opening a dialog box.

- **Option-click** (Macintosh) or **Alt-click** (Windows) on the **New Layer** button to open the New Layer dialog.

- Choose **New Layer** from the Layers palette menu or from the Layer New submenu. This also opens the New Layer dialog before creating a new layer.

   New layers are transparent unless otherwise specified.

N O T E

Using the New Layer Dialog

The New Layer dialog (Figure 15.7) lets you name the layer, set the opacity and blending mode, and group the new layer with the previous one. All of these features can be changed at any time or added to a layer later, as discussed earlier in this chapter.

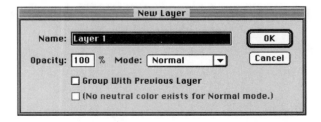

Figure 15.7 All of the options in the New Layer dialog can be specified when you create a layer or modified later.

If the image has no designated background layer, the Mode dropdown menu has an additional Background option (Figure 15.8). Choose this mode to create a new layer with all the properties of the default background layer.

Figure 15.8 The Mode dropdown menu has the same choices as the Painting Mode menu in the various Options palettes, except when an image has no background layer. Then you can designate background mode from this menu.

There is also a Fill With Neutral Color check box, shown in Figure 15.9. Some effects, like the blending modes, are not available if a layer is transparent and therefore has no pixels. Since new layers are usually transparent, this option allows you to fill the layer with neutral-colored pixels—white, black, or gray, depending on the mode selected.

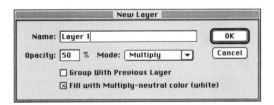

Figure 15.9 Some modes have the option of filling a new layer with a neutral color so that you can apply effects without actually painting on the layer.

NOTE The Fill With Neutral Color check box is not available for Normal, Dissolve, Hue, Saturation, Color, or Luminosity blending modes.

The Mask button allows you to create clipping groups where the upper layers are masked by the lowest grouped layer. This feature is discussed in Chapter 16.

The Palette Menu Commands

The last stop on our tour of the Layers palette brings up the Palette menu (Figure 15.10). There are four groups of commands within this menu. These commands are all available from the Layer menu as well and are discussed in various places in this chapter, except for the Palette Options command, which we'll cover right here.

```
New Layer...
New Adjustment Layer...
Duplicate Layer...
Delete Layer

Layer Options...

Merge Linked
Merge Visible
Flatten Image

Palette Options...
```

Figure 15.10 The Layers palette menu contains four groups of commands. The first three groups are all also available from the Layer menu.

There is only a single option in the Options command, and it allows you to change the thumbnail display. Thumbnails are a useful means for keeping track of layers. Smaller icons take up less space in the layers palette, but are less distinct. Figure 15.11 shows the options.

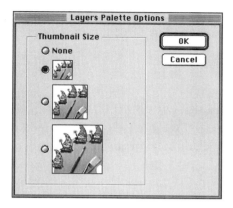

Figure 15.11 The only Palette Option available is for Thumbnail size. Choose one and it applies to all layers.

To change the thumbnail display:

1. Choose **Palette Options** from the Layers palette menu.
2. Click a size—small, medium, or large—or none, then click **OK**. The none option hides the thumbnail images, displaying only the layer name in the Layers palette.

The thumbnail size option affects the display of all layers.

N O T E

WORKING WITH LAYERS

While the layers palette does not manipulate the pixels in an image, the order and display options you specify for layers are essential elements of Photoshop image creation.

NOTE

All of these manipulations will apply to multiple layers if you link them first, using the link box for each layer.

Moving layers around within the Layers palette is a straightforward process; you simply drag and drop. Except for the background layer, you can move any layer to any position, including floating selections.

To change the order of the layers:

1. Move the pointer over the name or thumbnail image of the layer you want to move.

2. Drag to the new location in the Layers palette. As you drag, a highlighted bar appears between layers to indicate the new location of the layer, as shown in Figure 15.12.

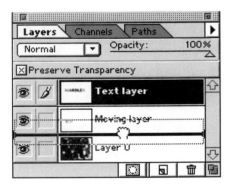

Figure 15.12 Moving the active layer by dragging. The highlighted bar indicates the new location.

3. Release the mouse button when the layer is where you want it to be.

You can also rearrange layers by using the commands in the Arrange submenu of the Layer menu.

1. Select the layer or layers you want to move in the Layers palette.

2. Choose one of the four commands from the Layer Arrange submenu.

- **Bring to Front**, **Command-]** (Macintosh) or **Alt-]** (Windows), moves the layer to the top of the layers stack.

- **Bring Forward**, **Shift-Command-]** (Macintosh) or **Shift-Alt-]** (Windows), moves the layer up one level in the stack.

- **Send Backward**, **Shift-Command-[** (Macintosh) or **Shift-Alt-[** (Windows), moves the layer down one level in the stack.

- **Send to Back**, **Command-[** (Macintosh) or **Alt-[** (Windows), moves the layer to the bottom of the stack, just above the background layer.

By default, the Background layer cannot be moved and must remain at the bottom of the stack. However, it is often useful to move the information on this layer or to create a different Background layer.

To move the Background layer:

1. Select the Background layer.
2. Double-click or choose **Layer Options** from the Palette menu.
3. Rename the layer or accept the default name, layer 0. Once a layer is no longer called Background, it loses all of the default background properties and may be moved about with abandon.

You can also copy the Background layer as described below.

Once you have renamed the Background layer, you can create a new Background layer by using the **New Layer** command and specifying Background mode.

N O T E

To copy layers:

- Drag the layer by the name to the New Layers button at the bottom of the Layers palette (see Figure 15.13). A new layer is created above the copied layer, and copy is appended to the name.

- Choose **Duplicate Layer** from the Palette menu. This brings up a Duplicate dialog that lets you rename the copy before it's created and choose a destination other than the current image, as described below.

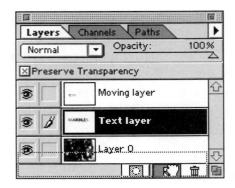

Figure 15.13 Duplicating a layer by dragging it to the New Layer button. Note the moving hand icon over the grayed button that indicates that releasing the mouse button will create a duplicate layer.

You'll probably find copying layers to other images one of the most useful features of the Layers palette, because it allows you to copy between images with a single drag and drop.

To copy layers to another image:

- Drag the layer by its name, but instead of dragging to a new location within the Layers palette, drag directly to the image window. You must be able to see the image you are dragging to for this method to work.

- Choose **Duplicate Layer** from the Palette menu. In the dialog, choose the new image location from the Destination Document dropdown box. You may also name the copied layer.

- You can also copy an entire layer or part of it by making a selection and using Copy and Paste from the Edit menu.

While floating selections automatically become temporary layers, you can turn any other selection into a permanent layer. To turn sections into layers:

1. Make a selection.
2. Choose **Layer Via Copy** or **Layer Via Cut** from the Layer New submenu (see Figure 15.14). Copy creates a copy of the selected pixels in a new layer, while Cut cuts the pixels from the previous layer and pastes them into a new one.

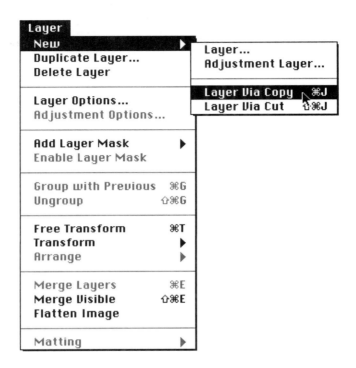

Figure 15.14 The Layer menu shows the New submenu and the commands that turn selections into new layers by copying or cutting. These are some of the few commands in the Layer menu that do not have alternatives.

Setting Layer Options

Not only are there palette options, but there are layer options, as well. These are set in a dialog box that can be opened in the usual ways:

- Double-click on a layer in the Layers palette to open the Layer Options.
- Select a layer and choose **Layer Options** from the Palette menu.
- Select a layer and choose **Layer Options** from the Layer menu.

Figure 15.15 shows the Layer Options dialog.

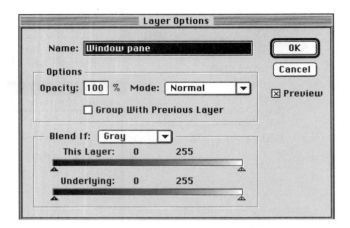

Figure 15.15 The Layer Options dialog is very similar to the New Layer Dialog, with the addition of some powerful blending options and a preview button so that you can see what you're doing.

The Layer Options dialog allows you to change all the options that were available in the New Options dialog, plus it includes a Blend If option that allows you to control the blending of one layer into another. There are two sliders—one for the selected layer and one for the underlying layers—that allow you to set the range of pixels that are visible and invisible or blended.

The scales are measured from 0, black, to 255, white. This is another example of an 8-bit grayscale channel. There are triangle sliders at each end of the scales. Drag the sliders away from the ends to exclude pixels.

There is a further refinement in that the triangles are split into two halves. Dragging moves both halves, but if you **Option-drag** (Macintosh) or **Alt-drag** (Windows) you can drag half the triangle in either direction. The space between the two halves of the triangles is partially blended as a gradient.

Click the **Preview** check box to see the effects of the Blend If sliders while you adjust them.

You can also limit blending by color channel. The default setting in the Blend If dropdown menu is gray, which affects all channels. You can also select red, green, or blue channels if you're working in RGB mode, or cyan, magenta, yellow, or black if you're working in CMYK mode. Each channel can be adjusted individually.

Merging Layers

There are times when it's convenient or even necessary to combine multiple layers into a single layer. For instance, it's a good way to save system resources. Combining the pixels from two or more layers is called *merging* in Photoshop. There is no visible effect on the image, but all pixels that were hidden under another layer are lost.

There are three merge commands, and they are available from the Palette menu and the Layer menu.

- **Merge Down** combines the active layer with the layer immediately beneath it in the stack. The result is that there is one fewer layer.

- **Merge Visible** combines all visible layers into a single layer. Hidden layers are unaffected, so any layer you don't wish to merge should be hidden by clicking in the Show/Hide column first.

- **Flatten Image** merges all layers, regardless of visibility. You must flatten an image before saving it in any format other than Photoshop's native file format. This means that if you have hidden layers, the information they contain will be discarded without affecting the image. Changing from a color display mode to grayscale or bitmap mode will automatically flatten the image.

Lesson 15: A Roman Bath in Layers

Would collage now be as popular as a graphic design technique if it weren't for Photoshop? It's so easy to put images together into a single composition, or to borrow pieces from work you've done before, that it's sometimes difficult to justify spending time to create everything from scratch.

The image we'll create in this lesson is cobbled together out of recycled art. Yet the final image might have been taken as a single photograph.

1. Open the file **BRICK_BA.PSD** from the Lesson15 folder on the CD. This will be the background for the image. It is taken from Letraset's Phototone series.

2. Open the file **L15_OBJE.PSD**, which contains the images we'll copy. This is a three-layered image, introducing the background, window, and noblest Roman (Figure 15.16). Both image windows should be visible. The Window is from PhotoDisc's Object Series.

Figure 15.16 The file L15_OBJE.PSD.

3. Make sure the Layers palette is open, either by choosing **Show Layers** in the Window menu or by clicking on the **Layers** tab in the Layers/Channels/Paths palette group.

4. Copy the Window layer by selecting it in the Layers palette and dragging it into the brick background image window, as shown in Figure 15.17. This creates a new active layer in the brick background image and activates the window.

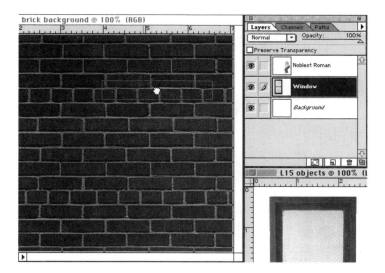

Figure 15.17 Drag the Window layer from the Layers palette to the BRICK_BA.PSD image window. The source window, L15_OBJE.PSD, is active, while the target window, BRICK_BA.PSD, is not.

5. Either hold down the **Command** key (Macintosh) or **Ctrl** key (Windows), or select the **Move** tool (v) from the Toolbox and drag the window into the middle of the image so that it fits nicely between the brick courses. You can use the **Arrow** keys to nudge the layer into position.

6. Select the **Magic Wand** tool (w) from the Toolbox. Make sure that the Options are set to the defaults (Tolerance 32 and Anti-aliased checked). If the Magic Wand Options palette isn't visible, double-click on the Magic Wand tool to show it.

7. Click in the lower pane of the window. This should select nearly all of the pane. This is fine, because the edges will not be moved and therefore will blend without showing.

8. Choose **Layer By Cut** from the New submenu of the Layer menu (Figure 15.18). This cuts the selected pane from the Window layer and creates a new layer out of it. The cut area is filled with the current background color, which should be white.

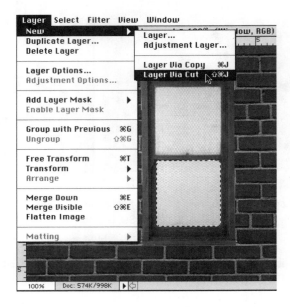

Figure 15.18 Choosing the **Layer Via Cut** command after selecting the lower windowpane with the Magic Wand tool.

Now put the noble Roman in front of the window.

9. Make the L15_OBJE.PSD window active, either by clicking on it or by choosing it from the Window menu.

10. Drag the Roman layer from the Layers palette to the brick background image, just as you did for the Window layer.

11. With the **Command** key (Macintosh) or **Ctrl** key (Windows) held down or the **Move** tool (v) chosen, position the bust so that his head is fully over the lower windowpane, his shoulders below it (see Figure 15.19).

Figure 15.19 Moving the bust into position in front of the window.

The problem is, we really want the noble Roman behind the window and not in front of it. See what happens when you drag the Window layer to the top of the stack. The bust is hidden behind the white fill. We could select the white area and delete it to reveal the bust and windowpane beneath, but then we would still have to deal with the parts of the bust that are sticking out below the window.

There's an easier way to solve this problem. It wasn't discussed in Chapter 15, so this will give you a preview of what's coming up in Chapter 16. We're going to create a clipping group out of the bust and windowpane. First put the layers back to their original order: Background, Window, Layer1 (the windowpane), and Noblest Roman.

12.   Hold down the **Option** key (Macintosh) or **Alt** key (Windows) and move the pointer so that it is on the line between the top two layers in the Layers palette (see Figure 15.20). The icon turns into two intersecting circles to indicate that you are about to make a clipping group.

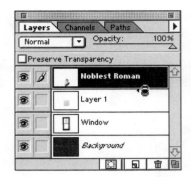

Figure 15.20 Making a clipping group in the Layers palette.

13. Click the mouse button to create the clipping group. The windowpane layer, Layer 1, will be underlined, the Noblest Roman layer is indented, and the line between the two is dotted to indicate that they are part of a clipping group (see Figure 15.21).

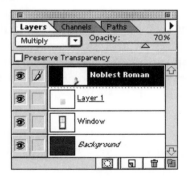

Figure 15.21 This is what the Layers palette looks like after making the clipping group and modifying the Noblest Roman layer.

The effect is that the outline of the windowpane layer clips the bust above it so that none of it spills out over the window frame or the brick wall. This is exactly what we wanted, except that the bust still looks as if it is in front of the windowpane.

14. Select the **Noblest Roman** layer. In the Layers palette, move the pointer over the blend dropdown menu, click, and drag to select Multiply mode. This allows the wires in the glass to blend through.

15. Change the Opacity for the Noblest Roman layer, either by typing a **7** or by dragging the Opacity slider to 70%. The image now looks like Figure 15.22.

Figure 15.22 The image after defining a clipping group. Notice how the image of the bust is completely confined within the area of the windowpane, the layer beneath it in the Layers palette.

This is an interesting situation. The bust really looks as if it's behind the window, but it is in fact the top layer of the image. The viewer doesn't need to know what tricks you used to create the image. It's like the smoke and mirrors of a magic act. You've made it look as if there's a person behind the window, and, therefore, there is.

Now we'll add a text layer and blend it into the background using the Layer Options. But first, we'd better move the window over to leave room for the text.

16. Link all three layers above the background layer by clicking in the Link box in column two of the Layers palette (Figure 15.23). Click only on the two layers that aren't active, and this links them to the active layer. Activating any of the three layers maintains the links.

17. Choose the **Move** tool (v), or hold down the **Command** key Macintosh or **Ctrl** key (Windows) and move the linked layers to the right. They should still be lined up with the mortar joints in the brick wall.

Figure 15.23 Linking layers to the active layer. Layer 1 is already linked, and the Window layer is about to be by clicking in the Link box.

18. Choose the **Eyedropper** tool (i), and click on the Window frame to set the foreground color to a worn blue-gray, not too dark.

19. Choose the **Text** tool (t) and click on the image. This opens the Text dialog and will create a new text layer in the image.

20. In the Text dialog, I've specified Adobe's Trajan Bold, but you can use any Roman font, like Times. The size for Trajan that fits nicely is 58 points with 72 points of leading. You may need to make slight adjustments if you're not using Trajan. Click the **Anti-aliased** box in the Style options and the vertically centered option in the Alignment options (see Figure 15.24).

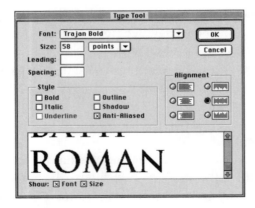

Figure 15.24 The Type Tool dialog with font, size, alignment, and style choices made. By clicking the preview buttons at the bottom, the text is shown in the correct font and size.

221. Type the word **BATH**, then a carriage return, then the word **ROMAN**. Photoshop enters vertically aligned text from right to left. (This feature was first added to the Japanese version of Photoshop, and right to left vertical text is the norm in Japan.) Click **OK**.

22. Choose the **Move** tool (v) and center the text to the left of the window.

    Now we'll make the text look like old paint on the brick wall by using the Layer Options to let some of the brick pixels show through.

23. The text layer was automatically named Layer 2 when it was added to the image. Double-click on this layer in the Layers palette to open the Layer Options dialog.

24. Make the following settings in the Layer Options dialog. Check the **Preview** box so you can watch what happens in the image.

    • Change the name by typing **Text Layer** into the field.

    • Change the Opacity to 90% so the lettering looks like cheap paint.

    • Choose **Screen** from the Mode dropdown menu to mix the color of the paint with the color of the bricks beneath.

    To give the appearance of paint wearing off, we'll set the Underlying slider in the Blend If option so that some of the brick and mortar pixels show through.

    • Move the white slider to the left until it's at 65. This lets the lightest colored brick and mortar pixels show through.

    • Move the black slider to the right until it's at 30. This lets some of the darker shadow pixels show through.

    • Click **OK**.

You now have a finished image composed of three recycled photographs and some blended text. A careful look reveals that the shadows are falling at different angles, and we haven't taken the time to blend the window into the wall fully. But at a quick glance, it's pretty convincing.

Save your composite if you wish. You can also have a look at the image **ROMAN_BA.PSD** in the Lesson15 folder on the CD.

CHAPTER

Masking for Clipping, Adjusting, and Selecting

In this chapter…

- About masks
- Clipping groups
- Layer masks
- Adjustment layers
- Quick masks

This chapter is not specifically aimed at a single palette; it lies in between the Layers and Channels palette chapterss. It discusses the masking features of the Layers palette and serves as an introduction to masking in the Channels palette. The vocabulary of masking is the same across all the various Photoshop masking techniques.

ABOUT MASKS

Masking in Photoshop is generally associated with channels, but several mask types—clipping groups, Layer, Adjustment, and Quick Masks—don't use the channels palette. Yet all masks work similarly. They are 8-bit grayscale channels containing pixels that range from nearly transparent to opaque, or areas with no pixels that are completely transparent. This allows you to work through cutouts and screens to prevent effects and paint from affecting areas you don't want them to bleed into. It's very similar to silk screening or the use of friskets for traditional air brushing.

Quick masks provide a more flexible way to display selections. As we've seen before, the "marching ants" style of selection is either on or off and provides no mechanism for displaying partially selected pixels. Quick masks are the alternative.

The purpose of the Mask and Adjustment Layers is to allow you to overlay information with a test layer—the mask—and experiment with various options before making any permanent changes. They are scratch layers. Layer masks work with single layers, while an Adjustment layer uses information from all layers beneath it.

A clipping group also creates a mask, but between grouped layers. The effect is the same, though, because it allows you to mask pixels without changing them until you have achieved the effect you want.

CLIPPING GROUPS

The clipping group is the classic mask. A selection or shape in the base layer acts like a window through which the grouped layers above it are revealed. Pixels outside this view are masked (see Figure 16.1).

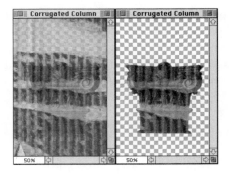

Figure 16.1 The effect of a clipping group is to fill the background figure with whatever is in the foreground layers. These two figures show the image before and after clipping.

Clipping groups are commonly used for effects such as putting text under a texture. With a clipping group, the texture is clipped so that it's only visible through the text. The result is readable text, filled with the texture above it rather than a color or blend.

Definig a Clipping Group

To define a clipping group, create the layers that will be turned into the group. This takes some forethought, but such is the nature of group activity. There are three ways to group layers:

- Hold down the **Option** key (Macintosh) or **Alt** key (Windows). In the Layers palette, move the pointer to the line above what will become the base layer. The pointer turns into the clipping group icon—two overlapping circles, shown in Figure 16.2. Click to group the two layers.

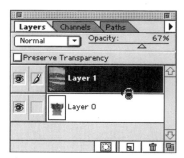

Figure 16.2 When the pointer icon turns into the overlapping circles icon, it indicates that clicking will group two adjacent layers in a clipping relationship.

- Select the layer above the base layer and choose **Group With Previous**, **Command-g** (Macintosh) or **Ctrl-g** (Windows), from the Layer menu.
- Double-click on the layer above the base layer, or select the layer and choose **Layer Options** from the Palette menu. Click on the **Group with Previous Layer** check box.

You can add layers to the group by repeating any of the steps above with the next layer up the stack in the Layers palette.

Photoshop indicates a clipping group by underlining the name of the base layer, making the line between layers in the group dotted, and indenting the thumbnail of the top layer in the group as shown in Figure 16.3.

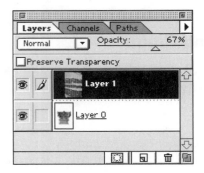

Figure 16.3 When layers are grouped, the base layer appears underlined, the line between grouped layers is dotted, and the top layer's thumbnail is indented.

Layers must be contiguous to be part of a clipping group. A layer can only be part of one clipping group, but there may be more than one clipping group in an image. Also, once you remove a layer from a clipping group it can be used as part of another clipping group.

To remove a layer from a group:

- Select the layer and either choose the **Ungroup** command, **Shift-Command-G** (Macintosh) or **Shift-Ctrl-G** (Windows), from the Layer menu, or open the Layer Options for that layer and deselect the **Group with Previous Layer** check box.

- Hold down the **Option** key (Macintosh) or **Alt** key (Windows) and position the pointer in the Layers palette on the dotted line between two grouped layers. Click to ungroup them.

Ungrouping layers removes all clipping effects without changing any pixels in the layers.

NOTE

If you ungroup a layer with more than one layer above it, all layers above are ungrouped.

Applying a Clipping Effect

Once you have achieved the desired effect of a clipping group, you will probably want to make the changes permanent, which reduces the file size. You must merge the layers in the group to do this. If you think you may want to make changes in the future or create different versions, then save the image both with the clipping group and without.

To apply a clipping effect, choose **Merge Down** from either the Palette menu or the Layer menu, **Command-e** (Macintosh) or **Ctrl-e** (Windows). You will have to Merge Down as many times as there are layers above the base layer, or you can hide all layers that aren't in the group and use the Merge Visible command.

LAYER MASKS

Rather than working with groups of layers, a layer mask affects only a single layer, and every layer can have one. When you paint on the layer mask, pixels in the layer are obscured or revealed, but no pixels in the image are changed until you specifically apply the mask. This lets you experiment and make changes to the mask without tediously saving previous versions and reverting.

The layer mask is actually an 8-bit grayscale channel or alpha channel. The significance of this is explained in more detail in Chapter 17. For now, it's only important to know that you are working in grayscale—white, grays, and black—when you paint on the layer mask.

Also, since this is a mask, effects happen in reverse. Painting in black on the mask makes a hole in the layer, revealing pixels in the underlying layer. Painting with white either has no effect or reverses the effect of painting with black. Painting with gray partially reveals the layers underneath. White reveals pixels on the masked layer; black hides them, making them transparent to the layers below.

A layer mask (Figure 16.4) can be enabled either by using the Mask button in the Layers palette or the commands in the Add Layer Mask submenu in the Layer menu.

Figure 16.4 The effect of a layer mask is only felt on its layer and does not affect any other layers.

To add a layer mask using the Mask button:

1. Click in the Layers palette on the layer you wish to mask. If there is an active selection on the layer, it will be used as the basis for the mask boundaries (see Figure 16.5).

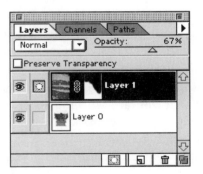

Figure 16.5 A layer mask is indicated in the Layers Palette by the second thumbnail image. The standard layer thumbnail is augmented by a mask thumbnail. The two can be edited separately by clicking on the appropriate thumbnail.

2. Click on the **Mask** button to turn on a white mask, or hold down the **Option** key (Macintosh) or **Alt** key (Windows) and click on the **Mask** button to turn on a black mask.

To add a layer mask using the Add Layer Mask submenu:

1. Click in the Layers palette on the name of the layer you wish to mask.
2. Choose the **Reveal All** command from the Add Layer Mask submenu in the Layer menu to turn on a white mask, or choose the **Hide All** command from the Add Layer Mask submenu in the Layer menu to turn on a black mask.

If there is an active selection on the layer you have selected to mask, then two more commands are available.

- Choose **Reveal Selection** from the Add Layer Mask submenu in the Layer menu to reveal the selection and hide the rest of the image.
- Choose **Hide Selection** from the Add Layer Mask submenu in the Layer menu to hide the selection and reveal the rest of the image.

When a layer mask is added to a layer, there are two thumbnails displayed in the Layers Palette: one for the layer and one for the mask. The mask is automatically activated as indicated by the Mask icon in the second column of the Layers Palette. Any changes you make affect the mask in relation to the image.

Click on the layer thumbnail to activate the layer pixels as indicated by the brush icon in the second column of the Layers Palette. Now you can edit the information in the layer without affecting the mask.

There is also a Chain Link icon between the two thumbnails. This indicates that the mask and layer are linked and can be moved together. Click on the Link icon to break the link and move the two independently.

To turn off or disable a layer mask without removing it, do one of the following:

- Shift-click on the layer mask thumbnail in the Layer palette. Shift-click again to toggle the mask back on.
- Choose **Disable Layer Mask** from the Layer menu. The command changes to Enable Layer Mask so that you can toggle the mask back on.

A red x is added to the mask preview in the Layers palette to indicate that the mask is disabled.

NOTE

You can view just the maskby Option/Alt clicking on the layer mask icon in the Layers palette. This is a shortcut for turning off all channels except the Layer Mask channel.

It's important to realize that to apply the effects of a layer mask, you must remove it.

There are two ways to apply or remove a layer mask:

- Choose **Remove Layer Mask** from the Layer menu.
- With the Layer Mask thumbnail active, click on the **Trash** icon in the Layers palette.

Either method brings up an alert box with three buttons: Discard, Cancel, and Apply. Apply is the default, and it applies the masking changes to the pixels in the layer. No pixels have been altered up to this point. Discard leaves the layer alone and simply discards the mask. Cancel returns you to the image and makes no changes.

ADJUSTMENT LAYERS

An Adjustment layer allows you to try out image commands without changing any pixels in the image. This is a significant new feature of Photoshop 4. Adjustment layers can only be used to view the effects of the Image Adjustment commands. These commands are discussed in Chapter 22, so we won't discuss the effects here, only the use of them with Adjustment layers.

An adjustment layer can only be used for one image effect, but you can have many layers to preview many different image effects simultaneously. Adjustment layers can be edited or moved around in the stack. They can also be used with a selection to mask the image effects.

Adjustment layers are manipulated just like any other layers, as discussed in Chapter 15, except that you use the New Adjustment Layer command to create them. Adjustment layers use all of the layers beneath them in the stack to calculate effects, unless you group them with specific layers using the clipping group commands, described earlier in this chapter.

Because Adjustment layers are masks, none of the effects make any permanent changes to the image until you merge the Adjustment layer with the image layers below it. You cannot merge two **N O T E** Adjustment layers. They must be merged with the image layers beneath them.

To add an Adjustment layer:

1. There always seem to be three ways to do things with layers, and this is no exception.

- Choose the **New Adjustment Layer** command from the Layer palette menu.
- Choose **Adjustment Layer** from the New submenu in the Layer menu.
- **Command-click** (Macintosh) or **Ctrl-click** (Windows) on the New Layer button at the bottom of the Layers Palette.

   The New Adjustment Layer dialog is the same as the New Layer dialog, with one important difference: the Image Adjustment Type dropdown menu.

2. Pick a Type from the dropdown menu shown in Figure 16.6 and click **OK**.

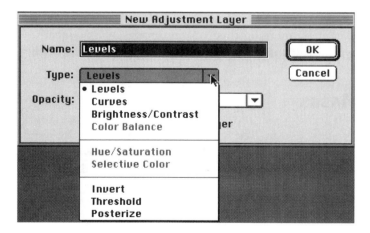

Figure 16.6 The New Adjustment Layer dialog lets you pick the adjustment type from the dropdown menu.

3. All types except Invert have setting dialogs that you must adjust before the effects are applied. The various effects are described in Chapter 22.

4. Click **OK**, and the Adjustment layer is inserted. Adjustment layers can be identified by the mask icon in column two of the Layers palette and a diagonally divided circle icon added to the right side of the layer's name.

You can always go back and readjust the option settings for an adjustment layer by either double-clicking on the adjustment layer in the Layers Palette, or by choosing **Adjustment Options** from the Layer menu.

Painting on the Adjustment Layer Mask

Just like mask layers, adjustment layers are 8-bit grayscale channels. (See Chapter 17.)

To paint on the adjustment layer mask, select an adjustment layer and paint on it in black to obscure all adjustment effects. You can use selections or any other editing tools to paint on the mask.

All areas painted white reveal adjustment effects, and areas painted gray partially reveal adjustment effects.

Merging Adjustment Layer

Use the Merge commands as described in Chapter 15 to make adjustment effects permanent by merging them to the image layers beneath. No pixels in the image layers are changed until the Adjustment layer is merged.

QUICK MASKS

Quick Masks allow you to see both the mask and the image and provide an easy way to edit masks. The Quick Mask is an alternative to display mode for making selections with protected and unprotected areas differentiated by color. Quick Masks are turned on and off from the Toolbox (see Figure 16.7).

Figure 16.7 The Quick Mask is controlled by these two buttons in the Toolbox—the right toggles Quick Mask on, left toggles it off and is the default.

N O T E By default, Photoshop uses a rubylith-like effect to indicate masking. This covers the selection or mask with a semi-transparent color so that you can view the whole image, yet distinguish between areas that can be edited and those that are protected. As the name implies, the default color is red and the default opacity is 50%. But you can change these in the Quick Mask Options dialog. The channel masks, discussed in Chapter 17, use this same rubylith like overlay.

To make a Quick Mask:

1. Make a selection in the image.
2. Click on the **Quick Mask** button in the Toolbox. This covers protected areas outside the selection with a semi-transparent overlay, while unprotected areas are left unchanged, and the selection marquee is hidden (see Figure 16.8).

Figure 16.8 An image with the Quick Mask turned on. Unprotected areas are unchanged, while protected areas are displayed behind a semi-transparent overlay.

NOTE

You can reverse the semi-transparent overlay by **Option-clicking** (Macintosh) or **Alt-clicking** (Windows) on the Quick Mask button. This overlays unprotected areas and leaves protected areas unchanged. You have to Option/Alt click to change the Quick Mask overlay back to its default setting.

3. Select a tool from the toolbox to edit the mask. Painting with black increases the masked area, protecting more of the image. Painting with white has the opposite effect, while painting with anything other than white or black makes areas of the mask semi-transparent in relation to the grayness of the color chosen.

4. To turn off the Quick Mask, click the **Standard Mode** button next to the Quick Mask button in the Toolbox. The selection marquee is redisplayed around the unprotected areas.

To change Quick Mask options:

1. Double-click on the **Quick Mask** button in the Toolbox.

2. The Quick Mask Options dialog has three options:

   • **Color Indicates**: Choose the **Masked Areas** (the default) or **Selected Areas** radio button. These toggle the rubylith-like overlay, between the selection and the mask.

- **Color**: Choose a color for the overlay. Click on the color box to bring up the color palette to change this setting.
- **Opacity**: Set the opacity for the overlay in percents.

Lesson 16: Masking Layers, Over & Under

This lesson is comprised of three exercises: clipping path, mask layer, and adjustment layer. As explained in the chapter, these three techniques, though related by terminology, have very different purposes and uses.

A QUICK CLIPPING PATH

Although we created a clipping path in the previous lesson, it's such a useful technique, it's worth another quick exercise. This time we'll use text as the clipping path.

N O T E

You'll see the words *path* and *group* both connected with clipping. A clipping path is the actual outline mask through which clipping occurs, while the group is the collection of layers grouped to the path that the mask reveals.

1. Open the file **CIRRUS_C.TIFF** from the Lesson16 folder on the CD.
2. Select the **Text** tool (t) from the Toolbox and click in the middle of the image window. This will create a new text layer above the background layer.
3. In the Text Tool dialog, enter the following values:

   Font: Helvetica

   Size: 72 point

   Style: Bold and Anti-aliased

   Alignment: Centered

   Type the words **Sky Writer** in the text box, and click **OK**. See Figure 16.9.

Figure 16.9 Settings for the Text Tool dialog as specified in the lesson—but any big bold typeface will do.

The text appears in the image window filled with the foreground color. But the color is irrelevant, because we will be using this text purely as a clipping path. To do this, the text needs to be under the background, but the background layer always has to be on the bottom. We'll rename the background layer and then change the layer order. Figure 16.10 shows

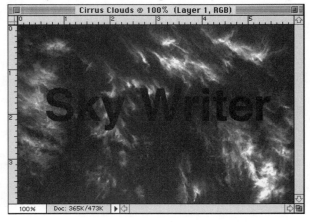

Figure 16.10 The new text layer, black letters over the background.

N O T E Since a clipping path forms a hole through which the layers above are revealed, it is necessary to put the text layer under what will become the fill, whereas one usually puts text or other filled objects on top of the background layers.

4. Make sure the Layers palette is open by selecting **Show Layers** from the Window menu or by clicking on the **Layers** tab in the Layers/Channels/Paths palette group.

5. Double-click on the **Background** layer both to select it and open the Layers Options dialog.

6. Photoshop automatically offers a new name of Layer 0 for the Background (Figure 16.11). Click **OK** without making any other changes.

7. In the Layers palette, drag Layer 0 until it is over Layer 1 in the stack (Figure 16.12). The text is now obscured under the sky.

8. Hold down the **Option** key (Macintosh) or **Alt** key (Windows) and move the pointer to the line between the two layers in the Layers palette. The pointer turns into the clipping path icon of two intersecting circles, shown in Figure 16.13.

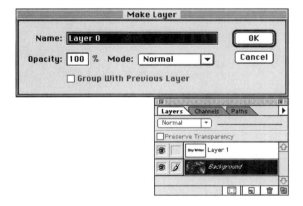

Figure 16.11 Changing the name of the Background layer so that it is no longer restricted to a background function.

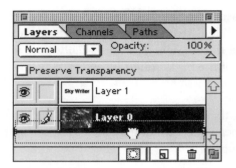

Figure 16.12 Changing the order of the layers by dragging Layer 0 over Layer 1. This effectively hides the text, but puts it into position for use as a clipping path.

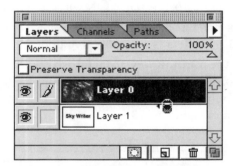

Figure 16.13 The two intersecting circles indicate that by clicking, the layers on either side of the dividing line will be combined into a clipping group.

9. Click the mouse button and the two layers are grouped. The result is shown in Figure 16.14.

Figure 16.14 Creating a clipping group causes the text layer underneath to become a mask for the sky layer so that it is only visible through the letters. Both layers can be moved individually, but the text will clip the sky as long as the two layers are grouped.

The text forms a path or mask through which the sky and clouds are revealed. Everything outside the path is transparent. This group is ready to be used with other layers to create a complete image, but this will not be part of this exercise. You may want to play around with this image before going on to the next exercise in this lesson. With the text layer selected, choose the **Move** tool (v) and move the text around to reveal different areas of sky. Then choose the sky layer and see how you can also move it around independently of the mask.

10. When you have achieved a pleasing fill of sky and clouds for the text, choose the **Flatten Image** command from the palette menu to make the text clipping permanent.

PAINTING ON A LAYER MASK

Photoshop's layer mask is intended for use as a kind of single-layer sketch pad. You can paint and erase without affecting the pixels in the layer or in the rest of the image.

1. Open the file FERN_STR.TIF and then the file **GREEN_TR.TIF** from the Lesson16 folder on the CD.

    We will copy the image of the frog into the stream and hide it under a fern frond. There are several ways to copy the frog, minus its white background, into the stream window. We'll use a little of what we've already covered in previous chapters and touch on paths.

2. The GREEN_TR.TIF image should be active. If not, click on it.

3. Open the Paths palette, either by choosing **Show Paths** from the Window menu or by clicking on the **Paths** tab in the Layers/Channels/Paths palette group.

4. Click on the path labeled **Outline** to select it. Since this image is from PhotoDisc's Object Series, it has a predefined outline path. (Paths are discussed in Chapter 18.)

5. Choose the **Make Selection** command from the palette menu, shown in Figure 16.15.

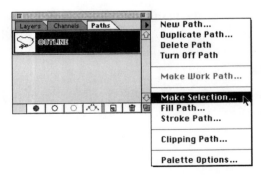

Figure 16.15 Choosing the Make Selection command from the Paths palette menu turns a predefined path into a selection so that we can drag it to another image.

6. In the Make Selection dialog, make sure the Anti-aliased box and the New Selection radio button are chosen. These are the defaults (Figure 16.16). Click **OK**.

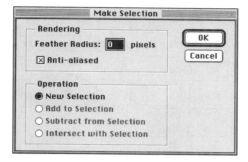

Figure 16.16 The Make Selection dialog has several options, but the defaults will work fine for this example.

7. With the frog selected, choose the **Move** tool (v), and drag the frog into the fern window. Release the mouse button. This creates a new layer, called Layer 1, for the copied frog over the stream.

8. With the Move tool still selected and the stream window active, drag the frog so that it is over the fern frond on the right side of the image, as shown in Figure 16.17.

Figure 16.17 The frog was dragged over from another window and now sits on the fern frond as a new layer.

9. To put the frog under the fern, we'll use a layer mask. Since the last step used the Paths palette, we need to activate the Layers palette by clicking on its tab in the palette group.

10. With the frog layer still active, click on the **Mask** button at the bottom of the Layers palette window. The Mask icon replaces the Brush icon next to Layer 1, and a Mask thumbnail is added to the layer (Figure 16.18).

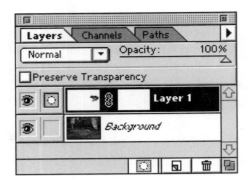

Figure 16.18 The frog layer, Layer 1, with an active layer mask. The Mask Thumbnail is white, because we haven't painted anything on it yet.

With the mask active, we can paint in black over the frog to reveal the fern frond pixels on the layer below. Remember, painting in black on a mask makes the area transparent, white makes it opaque, and gray is semi-transparent.

11. Make sure that black is the foreground color by clicking on the **Reset** button in the Toolbox (d), then choose the **Paint Brush** tool (b).

12. Open the Brushes palette, either by choosing **Show Brushes** from the Window menu or by clicking on the **Brushes** tab in the Color/Swatches/Brushes palette group. Select the largest brush from the second row.

13. Paint over the frog to reveal the fern beneath so that it appears to be on top. Paint carefully to the end of each leaflet. If you obliterate too much of the frog with the black brush, change the foreground color to white and make corrections. This is the beauty of the layer mask. None of the pixels in the image are changed until you apply the mask. You can paint and correct until you get exactly what you want. Figure 16.19 demonstrates this.

Figure 16.19 Painting on the mask with a black brush creates transparency and reveals the fern frond beneath.

14. When you have revealed all the leaflets under the frog, drag the Layer Mask Thumbnail to the Trash icon in the Layers palette (Figure 16.20). A dialog box allows you to discard the mask, cancel, or apply the mask. Click on **Apply** and the changes are made.

Figure 16.20 Dragging the Mask Thumbnail to the trash allows you to apply or discard the mask. Note the black paint on the thumbnail where the transparency was painted.

Once a Layer Mask is applied, the pixels are changed permanently. Try moving the frog out from under the fern frond. You'll see that there is now a big transparent patch across his back. Select **Undo** to put him back in the right spot. He's no longer a mobile frog.

N O T E

To view the completed image, open the file **FROG_FR.PSD** in the Lesson16 folder on the CD.

ADJUSTING WITH ADJUSTMENT LAYERS

This is a powerful new feature added to Photoshop 4. Adjustment layers allow you to experiment with image adjustments, but we haven't discussed what image adjustments are yet. These are covered in Chapter 22. Nonetheless, you can try out a couple and see that the Adjustment layer makes the process of image correction a bit more forgiving.

1. Open the image **DIM_LAKE.TIF** from the Lesson16 folder on the CD. You can see that this photograph is badly in need of some sort of lighting/color/contrast correction.

2. Choose the **New Adjustment Layer** command from the Layers palette menu (see Figure 16.21).

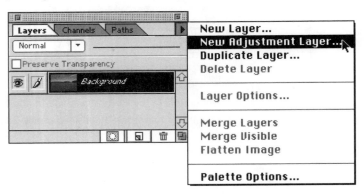

Figure 16.21 The New Adjustment Layer command in the Layers palette menu.

3. In the Adjustment Layer dialog, choose **Levels** from the Type dropdown menu. (You shouldn't have to choose anything, because Levels is the default.) Click **OK**.

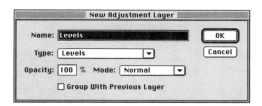

Figure 16.22 The Adjustment Layer dialog default settings.

4. Because we selected Levels, the Levels dialog (Figure 16.23) comes up. Click on the **Auto** button to let Photoshop make its best guess at the proper corrections for this photo, then click **OK**.

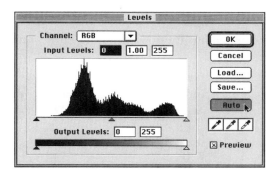

Figure 16.23 The Levels dialog opens automatically when you create a Level Adjustment layer.

The photo looks a lot better, but I think there's still room for improvement. We'll use another Adjustment Layer to refine the image corrections.

4. Choose the **New Adjustment Layer** command again from the Layers palette menu.

5. In the Adjustment Layer dialog (Figure 16.24), choose **Brightness/Contrast** and click **OK**.

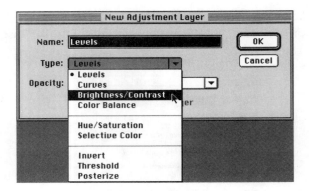

Figure 16.24 Choosing a different adjustment type from the dropdown menu.

6. In the Brightness/Contrast dialog, make sure you have Preview checked, and move the Brightness slider to +10. You can see that the slightly brighter image looks a bit sunnier. Click **OK**.

    Now you have two Adjustment layers, but you still haven't changed any pixels in the original image, so we can continue to refine.

7. In the Layers palette (Figure 16.25), click on the **Eye** icon in the first column of the Brightness/Contrast adjustment layer to Hide this layer. You can toggle back and forth between the image with and without the brightness correction we just made. We can see that it looks good, but might look better still.

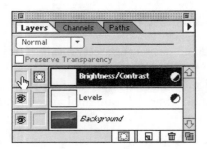

Figure 16.25 Hiding the Brightness/Contrast layer to view the effects of the two layers separately.

8. Make sure all layers are showing, then double-click on the **Brightness/Contrast** layer. This opens the Brightness/Contrast dialog so that we can make further corrections.

9. Move the Contrast slider to +20. Ah, I think this is what we needed. Click **OK**.

N O T E

This is not the exact adjustment methodalogy discussed in Chapter 22, but it is effective for this photograph

Since Adjustment layers are actually masks, you can draw on the mask to make areas transparent or opaque and apply adjustments selectively to layers. This gives a very fine level of control for image correction. We could continue to make fine adjustments by using our Adjustment layers, or by adding more, but for the purposes of this exercise, the corrections are good enough.

10. No permanent changes are made by the Adjustment layers until they are merged into the image layers. Choose the **Merge Visible** command from the palette menu to make the changes to the image and discard the Adjustment layers.

Channels

In this chapter…

- About channels
- The Channels palette
- Alpha channels
- Editing channels

ABOUT CHANNELS

The idea of channels is foreign to most new or inexperienced users of Photoshop, yet they are part of the standard working vocabulary of Photoshop professionals. They are easy to understand and as easy to use as Photoshop's layers described in the previous two chapters.

Every Photoshop image is comprised of color channels—one 8-bit channel per color. When Photoshop displays these in the Channels palette, it adds an additional composite channel, which represents the combined color information. So CMYK images have five color channels, RGB and Lab images have four, and grayscale and bitmap images have one, with no composite necessary. This is how Photoshop keeps track of the color information for each pixel in an image (see Figure 17.1).

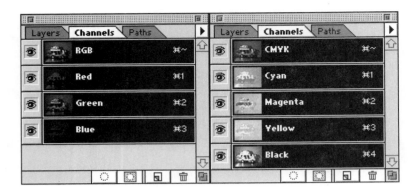

Figure 17.1 An RGB representation of an image with four color channels, versus a CMYK representation with five color channels in the Channels palette.

The color channels are created automatically by Photoshop. They can be edited and manipulated, but their order in the Channels palette is fixed. There can be up to 24 channels per image, including the color channels.

Channels are also used to store selections. When you use the Save Selection command, Photoshop creates a new channel to save the information. These selection channels are also known as Alpha channels, and they can be used to create masks of various sorts for various purposes. An alpha channel can be created from a selection or as a blank new channel that is edited and used for effects or turned into a selection.

 All channel information is discarded if you save a file in other than Photoshop formats, Raw formats, PICT, or TIFF. When channel information is saved, Photoshop automatically compresses it to save space.

THE CHANNELS PALETTE

The Channels palette is part of the Layers/Channels/Paths palette group and works very similarly to the Layers palette. Each channel is displayed on a line in the palette with a Hide/Show box, an optional Thumbnail, and the channel name. See Figure 17.2.

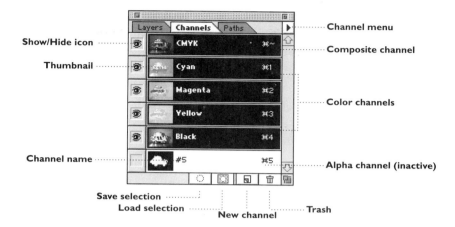

Figure 17.2 A diagram of the Channels palette.

To show the Channels palette:

- Select **Show Channels** from the Window menu.
- Click on the **Channels** tab in the Layers/Channels/Paths palette group.

Channels are listed with color channels at the top and alpha channels beneath them. Channels can be activated/deactivated and hidden/shown using the palette.

To activate/deactivate a channel:

- Click on a channel name or thumbnail in the Channels palette. This highlights the channel and makes it active. All other channels are inactive, except when you select the composite color layer, which makes all color channels simultaneously active.
- Hold down the **Shift** key and click on a channel name to activate more than one channel at a time.
- Hold down the **Command** key (Macintosh) or **Ctrl** key (Windows) and then press a number key. For the composite channel, press the **Tilde** key without Command/Ctrl. This is a shortcut method for activating single channels without using the mouse.

Each channel is automatically assigned a number key from 1 to 9, depending on its order in the stack. (The composite channel, which is always first, is assigned the Tilde key.) Only the first ten channels are numbered this way.

To hide/show a channel, click in the column to the left of the channel name and thumbnail. This toggles the channel visibility on and off. When the channel is visible, a small hand icon appears in the show/hide box.

Drag the pointer through the show/hide column to show or hide several channels simultaneously.

Moving Channels in the Palette

As with the Layers palette, you can drag channels in the Channels palette to change their order. However, this is only for convenience and it does not affect the display of the image at all.

You can only move alpha channels. Color channels are always in their fixed order at the top of the channel stack.

To create a new blank channel, either:

Click on the **New Channel** button at the bottom of the Channels palette and a new blank channel is added and given a default ordinal name.

Or choose the **New Channel** command from the palette menu. This allows you to set a few options before creating a new channel and means that each channel can have different display options:

Name: Type in a name or leave the default name, which is always the number of the channel.

Color Indicates: Choose the Masked Areas (the default) or Selected Areas radio button. These toggle the rubylith-like overlay (explained in Chapter 16) between the selection and the mask.

Color: Choose a color for the overlay. Click on the color box to bring up the color palette to change this setting. The default is red.

Opacity: Set the opacity for the overlay in percent. The default is 50%.

Figure 17.3 shows the Channel Options dialog.

Figure 17.3 The Channel Optionsl dialog lets you name the channel and set the display options.

Copying Channels

This is also similar to working with layers in that you can copy within the Channels palette, to another image, or to a new image. It's not something you'll do often, but copying channels is useful when you want to save a channel backup before you make changes that might be difficult to undo. You can also decrease the size of an image to make it easier to manipulate by copying channels to another document and deleting them. You can then load the channels back in later if you need them. Converting channels to paths also saves space, but you have to make sure there are no semi-transparent areas in the channel mask.

When copying channels from one image to another, the images must be identical in size and resolution.

N O T E

To duplicate a channel:

- Drag the channel to the New Channels icon at the bottom of the palette window.
- Drag the channel from the palette window to the image window.
- Select the channel and choose **Duplicate Channel** from the palette menu. There are several options that are identical to the New Channel options listed previously.

To delete a channel:

- Drag a channel to the Trash icon at the bottom of the Channels palette.
- Select a channel and click on the **Trash** icon. This will ask you to confirm the deletion.
- Select a channel and choose the **Delete Channel** command from the palette menu.

You cannot delete the composite color channel, and you cannot delete more than one channel at a time.

N O T E

To change channel options:

- Double-click on a channel name to open the Channel Options dialog.
- Select a channel and choose Channel Options from the palette menu.

The Channel Options are identical to the New Channel dialog, described previously.

Splitting and Merging Channels

There are two commands in the palette menu that allow you to Split Channels into separate grayscale images or Merge Channels into a single image. The use of these commands is straightforward, but their purpose is relatively esoteric.

Changing Thumbnail Size

Channel thumbnails provide a convenient means to identify channels in the palette. Smaller thumbnails use less space in the palette, and turning off thumbnails can improve performance. To change the thumbnail size:

1. Choose **Palette Options** from the Channels palette menu. Thumbnail size is the only palette option.
2. Click on a thumbnail size or choose none, then click **OK**.

View Color Channels in Color

By default, all channels, except composite, are displayed in grayscale, but it's possible to view color channels in their colors:

1. Choose **General** from the Preferences submenu in the File menu.
2. Click the **Color Channels** in Color Option in the General Preferences dialog.

ALPHA CHANNELS

As mentioned earlier in this chapter, there are two types of channels: the color channels that Photoshop creates automatically and the channels you create, which are called *alpha channels*. Alpha channels were Photoshop's original masking method, but are now only one of three, including Quick Masks and Layer Masks. You may want to read the section "About Masks" in Chapter 16.

Alpha channels are used to store and edit selections, which can be used as masks. Masks can be edited directly or used to limit the application of effects on the image. In fact, selections and masks provide two means to achieve the same ends. The pixels within a selection or outside a mask are unprotected and can be edited, while the pixels outside a selection or within a mask are protected and cannot be edited.

The tools used to edit selections and masks are different, but with both you can expand, contract, or make intersections. Both allow you to copy or move unprotected areas. But the capabilities of masking go beyond those of selections.

Masks can be semi-transparent, which allows you to select pixels partially. With the ability to save selections as channels, you can manipulate multiple selections simultaneously to create overlay and transparent effects. Channel masks take selections beyond what you can do with the selection tools. While the two Selection commands—Save Selection and Load Selection—work with channels, they don't necessitate working with the Channels palette.

To save a selection in a new alpha channel:

1. Make a selection using any of the selection tools.
2. Click on the **Save Selection** button at the bottom of the Channels palette. This does the same thing as the Save Selection command in the Select menu, but there are no options when you use the button (see Figure 17.4).

Figure 17.4 Clicking on the **Save Selection** button at the bottom of the Channels palette creates a new channel using the selection in the active window.

A new channel is created using the active selection as a mask. If you save the image now, it will include this new alpha channel with its selection mask, as shown in Figure 17.5.

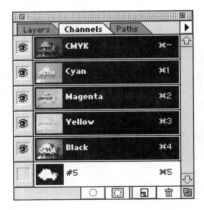

Figure 17.5 The Channels palette with an alpha channel added beneath the color channels. The mask in the alpha channel matches the selection in Figure 17.4.

Loading an Alpha Channel as a Selection

By saving selections as channels, you can reload them into the image at any time. To load an alpha channel as a selection in an image, use the Load Selection command or work with the shortcuts in the Channels Palette.

- Click on the **Load Selection** button at the bottom of the Channels palette to load the active channel. If more than one channel is active, the topmost active mask is loaded.

- **Command-click** (Macintosh) or **Ctrl-click** (Windows) on the channel you want to load. The icon changes to a hand with a selection marquee when you hold down the Command/Ctrl key.

- Use **Shift-Command-click** (Macintosh) or **Shift-Ctrl-click** (Windows) to add to a current selection. The Load Selection icon has a plus sign in it.

- Use **Option-Command-click** (Macintosh) or Alt-Ctrl-click (Windows) to subtract from a current selection. The Load Selection icon has a minus sign in it.

- Use **Shift-Option-Command-click** (Macintosh) or **Shift-Alt-Ctrl-click** (Windows) to make an intersection with a current selection. The Load Selection icon has an x in it.

N O T E

Instead of clicking, you can also use the number key for a channel in combination with the above shortcut key combinations to execute any of the load options.

Editing Channels

When we speak of editing a channel, this means editing the actual mask and not the image. Editing the mask in an alpha channel is no different from editing a Layer Mask or Quick Mask, and these are both described in detail in Chapter 16. Briefly, painting on a mask with black adds to the mask (Figure 17.6), white subtracts and gray partially adds or subtracts.

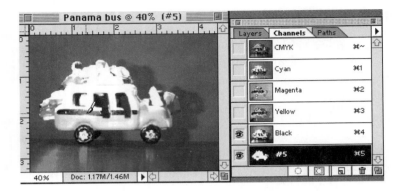

Figure 17.6 Adding to the Black channel mask by painting on it with black. This makes the area of the image covered by the mask larger, and therefore makes the unprotected editable area smaller.

To edit a channel mask:

1. Click on a channel in the Channels palette. This will be the target channel.

> If more than one channel is selected, editing occurs on all target layers simultaneously.

NOTE

2. Set the foreground color in the Toolbox. Since you are editing an 8-bit grayscale channel, choose white, any gray, or black. Only the composite color channel displays colors.

3. Paint on the image.

When the composite color channel is not selected (in other words, when you select a channel or channels other than the topmost channel), all editing occurs directly to the mask. When you select an alpha channel containing a selection, the image shows a black mask. This display mode makes it evident that painting in black will add to the mask and painting in white will subtract.

You can click in the hide/show column of any channel so that you can see the image under the mask of the target channel. If any of the color channels is showing, the image displays as a rubylith-like overlay instead of a black mask.

This is similar to Quick Mask mode described in Chapter 16.

When you are editing a channel, click on the show/hide box for the composite channel to preview the effects of the edited channel (Figure 17.7). Sometimes it's easier to edit a target channel with all channels showing. It's a matter of personal preference or the particular image.

Figure 17.7 The alpha channel, #5, is selected as the target channel, but by clicking on the Show/Hide box for the CMYK composite channel, the entire image is visible behind the rubylith overlay. This can make it easier to edit the mask when the image details can be seen.

The edited mask is saved with the image and can be loaded into the image as a selection at any time.

Lesson 17: Making Friends with Channels

We've already practiced some channel-like exercises in previous lessons—creating and editing masks, saving and loading selections, and a brief visit with semi-transparent selections/masks. In this lesson, we'll do some of the same things, but using the Channels palette. We'll start by using the color channels and then create an alpha channel to mask a cast shadow.

COLOR CHANNELS CAN BE FUN

As you might have guessed, we'll be using the Channels palette in this lesson. So if it isn't open, choose **Show Channels** from the Window menu or click on the **Channels** tab in the Layers/Channels/Paths palette group. Also, I like to see the color channel thumbnails in color rather than the default, gray. Choose **General** from the Preferences submenu in the File menu, and click on the **Color Channels** in Color option in the General Preferences dialog.

1. Open the file PANAMA_B.TIF from the Lesson17 folder on the CD.

    You'll notice that this is a CMYK image and that there is already an alpha channel, #5, defined. This photograph was taken using Apple's QuickTake 150 digital camera's close-up lens, and the reflection from the flash has completely washed out some of the areas of color. We will touch these up using the color channels.

2. Click on the channel name **Black** in the Channels palette, or press **Command-4** (Macintosh) or **Ctrl-4** (Windows). This leaves the one channel active and deactivates all others (Figure 17.8). This also changes the image window so that only the pixels from the Black channel are visible.

Figure 17.8 Clicking on the Black channel activates it and deactivates and hides all other channels.

What you see is one fourth of the pixels that make up this image—an 8-bit grayscale channel or mask. We will edit this mask so that the black stripe down the side of the bus is continuous.

3. Choose the **Airbrush** (a) without changing the default options. (If you've changed these, select **Reset Tool** from the Options Palette Menu.)

4. Open the Brushes palette by clicking on the **Brushes** tab in the Brushes/Options palette group, or choose **Show Brushes** from the Window menu.

5. Choose the hard-edged 9-pixel brush, fourth from the left on the top row.

6. Paint over the black stripe in the image. (If you have set the foreground/background colors to something other than black and white, click on the **Restore** button (d) in the Toolbox.)

   We'll paint right into the black channel as if it were a mask. This will eliminate the white glare of the camera's flash. Work in short strokes over the white areas. If you make a mistake, either choose **Undo** or use the **x** key to switch the foreground and background colors so that you are painting with white. When painting in a channel, white erases the mask. Since we are using this color channel as a semi-transparent mask, any gray areas you paint over with white will also be erased. See Figure 17.9.

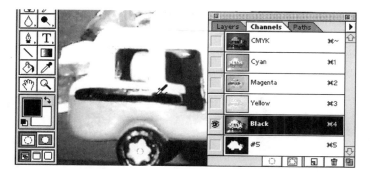

Figure 17.9 Painting a mask over the black stripe of the bus so that the white reflection of the flash will be blocked.

Now do the same thing for each of the other three color channels with one additional step.

7. Before you paint in each of the CMY channels, hold down the **Option** key (Macintosh) or **Alt** key (Windows) to turn the pointer into the eyedropper icon. Click on the color in an area that isn't washed out by the flash, and then release the Option/Alt key to start painting. This allows you to paint in the correct shade of gray to match the semi-transparent mask. See Figure 17.10.

Figure 17.10 In the Magenta channel (as illustrated here), there are areas outside the red of the bus that are washed out. By sampling with the eyedropper tool you can edit the channel mask using the correct shade of gray.

8. When you've masked each of the four channels individually, click on the **CMYK** composite channel to view the image with its masks. You can also click on the **Show/Hide** box for the CMYK channel to show all the color channels without activating them at any time during the masking process. See Figure 17.11.

Figure 17.11 Before and after views of the bus. On the left with no masking, and on the right with four channel masks to edit out the reflection of the camera's built-in flash.

9. Save your edited bus if you wish. There is also an edited version on the CD, saved as the file **PANAMA_B.PSD** in the Lesson17 folder.

It just so happens that this Panamanian bus is painted in shades very close to cyan, magenta, yellow, and black, so masking each channel gives a fairly close match without having to touch up the same areas in every channel. You may be wondering why we didn't just sample and paint right on the image instead of using masks. Go ahead and try it and the reason should become evident fairly quickly.

The advantages of painting on a mask are twofold. First, it's easy to adjust the mask by painting over it with white or a shade of gray to match the original background. Second, if you use a semi-transparent mask in one channel while leaving the others unedited, much of the original information and texture of the area is preserved, so changes blend in better. When you paint directly on the image, all the pixels are replaced and you lose all texture and subtle shadings.

Alpha Magic

Many of Photoshop's neatest tricks are accomplished through the use of alpha channels. We'll create a cast shadow using the mysterious fifth channel from the previous exercise's image. We'll also be using layers, selections, and something not yet covered, image adjustments.

1. Open the file **DESOLATE.TIF** from the Lesson17 folder on the CD. This is from Image Club's *Mountainscapes* collection.

2. If you closed or discarded your work from the previous exercise, open the file **PANAMA_B.PSD**. We will use the saved alpha channel to select the bus and copy it to another image. (I made this alpha channel using repeated selecting with the Magic Wand tool and then saved the selection as a channel.) Make sure the Channels palette is open.

    I happen to know that the resolution of the image we are copying from is not the same as the image we are copying to. We'll resize the first.

3. Choose **Image Size** from the Image menu and change the resolution to 72 dots per inch, then click **OK**. This does not affect the channel information. Leave the circle boxes at their defaults with constained proportions and Resample Image checked.

4. Hold down the **Command** key (Macintosh) or **Ctrl** key (Windows) and move the pointer over the **#5** channel in the Channels Palette. The pointer turns into a hand icon with a selection marquee (Figure 17.12). This is the short cut to load a selection without activating a channel. By saving this channel in advance, I have saved you the trouble of making a clean selection around the bus.

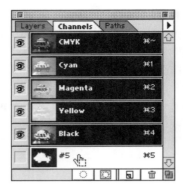

Figure 17.12 Command/Ctrl clicking on an alpha channel loads the channel as a selection marquee in the image window.

5. Hold down the **Command/Ctrl** key and move the pointer inside the selection marquee in the image. The pointer turns into a scissors icon. Click and drag the selection to the Desolate Plain image window.

6. Hold down the **Shift** key before you release the mouse button to center the copy of the bus in the image window. A new layer is created.

   We will create a cast shadow of the bus, so that it appears to be a more natural element in this unnatural-looking landscape.

7. Switch to the Layers palette by clicking on the **Layers** tab in the Layers/Channels/Paths palette group.

8. Hold down the **Command/Ctrl** key once again, and click on the words **Layer 1** in the Layers palette. The pointer turns into the same Load Selection icon we saw in Step 4, and even though there is no selection here to load, this creates a selection out of the non-transparent pixels in the layer. You have just created what is called a transparency mask in the form of a selection marquee around the bus. See Figure 17.13.

9. Switch back to the Channels palette by clicking on the **Channels** tab in the Layers/Channels/Paths palette group, and click on the **Save Selection** as channel button at the bottom of the palette. This creates a new channel from the selection, as shown in Figure 17.14. We could also have used the Save Selection command from the Select menu to do the same thing.

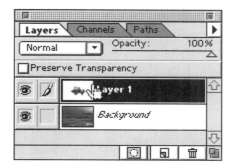

Figure 17.13 This special hand with selection marquee icon appears when you hold down the Command/Ctrl keys over a layer or channel. In this case, clicking creates a transparency mask selecting the non-transparent object in the layer.

Figure 17.14 Clicking on the **Load Selection** button in the Channels palette turns the transparency mask we made using the Layers palette into an alpha channel.

By working with an alpha channel instead of a layer, we are able to edit the selection as a mask rather than editing the image directly.

10. Click on channel #4 in the Channels palette or press **Command/Ctrl-4** to activate the alpha channel. This activates the channel mask and deactivates all other channels (see Figure 17.15).

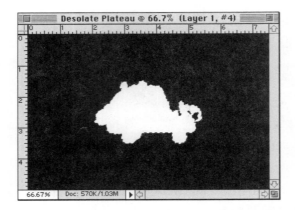

Figure 17.15 With the alpha channel active and all color channels deactivated, the image window shows a mask around the bus along with a selection marquee.

11. Click in the **Show/Hide** box next to the RGB channel to make the entire image visible. This turns the black mask into a rubylith covering everything in the image except the bus (Figure 17.16).

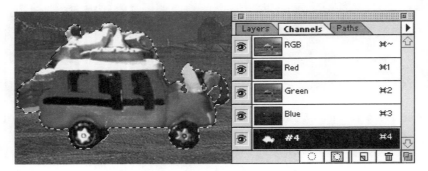

Figure 17.16 Showing all color channels with an active alpha channel makes the image window look the same as if you had used a Quick Mask, except that the selection marquee is still visible.

12. Choose the **Distort** command from the Layer Transform submenu. This surrounds the selection marquee with an eight-handled distortion rectangle.

13. Move the pointer over the top-center handle, press the mouse button, and drag so that the rectangle lies to the side and behind the bus (see Figure 17.17.) Press **Return** to complete the distortion. This distorts the

selection marquee, allowing us to cast the shape of the bus across the desolate plain, marking the area that we will turn into a shadow.

Figure 17.17 Dragging the distortion rectangle in the alpha channel repositions the selection marquee, but does not affect the image.

14. We're done with the channel, so click on the **Show/Hide** box next to alpha channel #4 in the Channels palette. The selection marquee remains, while the rubylith mask is gone.

15. Show the Layers palette. The distorted selection has been turned into a floating selection (Figure 17.18), but since a floating selection contains no pixels, we can't cast a shadow with it.

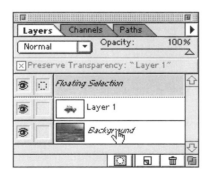

Figure 17.18 After distorting this selection, it became a floating selection in the Layers palette, but a floating selection is useless for our purposes. Another layer must be activated, and the floating selection automatically attaches itself to the active layer.

16. Click on the **Background** layer to make it active. The floating selection sinks onto the background and we have something to apply effects to.

17. Make sure that the foreground color in the Toolbox is black, then choose the **Gradient** tool (g). In the Gradient Options palette, click on the **Edit** button.

18. In the Gradient Editor (Figure 17.19), create a shadow that will fade into the background by doing the following:

    * select **Foreground to Transparent** from the scrolling Gradient list,
    * click on the **Transparency** radio button,
    * click on the left slider box and type **90%** into the Opacity box,
    * click on the right slider box and type **50%** into the Opacity box,
    * click **OK**.

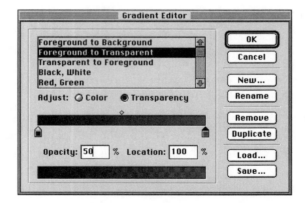

Figure 17.19 Transparency options set in the Gradient Editor for the cast shadow.

19. Move the pointer to the top edge of the selection in the image window, click and drag the gradient to the bottom edge at an angle equal to the angle of the shadow cast, then release the mouse button (Figure 17.20). The gradient fills the selection. Since the gradient is partially transparent, the background is still visible under the cast shadow.

Figure 17.20 Dragging out the guide line for a gradient fill. The gradient becomes more transparent the farther the shadow is cast.

20. Drop the selection by pressing **Command-d** (Macintosh) or **Ctrl-d** (Windows).

If you wish, open the file **WRONG_TU.PSD** from the Lesson 17 folder to view a version of the finished image.

CHAPTER

Paths

In this chapter...

- About paths
- The Paths palette
- Editing paths
- Manipulating paths
- Filling and stroking paths
- Paths into selections

ABOUT PATHS

Paths are used to define smooth anti-aliased selection borders that can be used like any other selection for painting, image adjustments, or masking. Paths are defined by using the Pen tool and stored in the Paths palette. (The Pen tool is discussed in Chapter 7.) Just as the Pen tool provides an alternative to the Lasso tool for making selections, the Paths palette provides an alternative to the Channels palette for storing them.

The path came to Photoshop by way of Adobe Illustrator in company with the Pen tool. A path is a vector; it has length and direction and is controlled by anchor points. It has nothing to do with pixels. The Pen tool draws paths; more precisely, it is used to place the anchor points between which path segments are drawn.

Because they are vector-based (as opposed to the rest of Photoshop, which is pixel-based), Paths and the Pen tool are unlike anything else in Photoshop. Yet the Pen is a powerful addition to Photoshop, because it allows you to draw smooth, even lines of remarkable complexity with relative ease.

Paths do not affect the image in any direct way. They are visible in the image and are stored with the image, but they cannot be printed. They can be cut, copied, pasted, moved, and manipulated in several ways, but the image does not change as paths are edited. In fact, it is their editability that make paths so useful. Paths must be converted into fills, strokes, or selections before they can affect the pixels in the image. You can also convert selections directly into Paths for editing.

In Chapter 7, the details of placing anchor points and adjusting direction lines to create straight and curved path segments were discussed. This chapter discusses the use of the Paths palette to save and load paths and the conversion of vector information into pixels.

THE PATHS PALETTE

While the Paths palette (Figure 18.1) makes it possible to save and manipulate paths, you don't need to use the Paths palette every time you create a path. As we saw in Chapter 7, you can select the Pen tool and draw a path on the image at any time. This creates a temporary path or what Photoshop calls a *Work Path*. All of the examples in Lesson 7 used Work Paths.

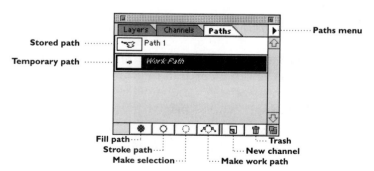

Figure 18.1 A diagram of the Paths palette.

NOTE Any time you use the Pen tool without activating a path first, a Work Path is created in the Paths palette. Work Paths are saved along with all other paths when you save the image, but they are temporary in that a new Work Path is created and the old one erased if you start drawing with the Pen tool again when no paths are active.

Work Paths behave like a clipboard for storing your most recently created path. A Work Path can hold only a single path (or group of subpaths) at a time and is replaced as soon as a new one is created. If you do not save a Work Path by turning it into a named path, your original work is likely to disappear.

To convert a Work Path into a named path:

- Double click on the **Work Path** in the Paths palette and name the path in the Save Path dialog.
- Drag the Work Path to the New Path button at the bottom of the Paths Palette. Like channels, paths are named sequentially.

The Paths palette is very similar to the Layers and Channels palettes. Paths are stacked in order and may be rearranged within the palette by dragging. Click on a path to make it active. Double-clicking on a path name allows you to rename the path. There are buttons across the bottom of the palette and commands that do the same things in the Palette menu (Figure 18.2).

Figure 18.2 The Paths palette menu commands.

Paths are saved with files in Photoshop, JPEG, and TIFF formats. However, no paths are active when you open a file that has paths. You must specifically activate a path in the Paths palette to use it.

NOTE Photoshop is ambiguous about what it calls a path. The path is what you draw with the Pen tool, but it is also a named entity in the Paths palette. As a named entity, a path can consist of numerous disconnected subpaths. As long as a single path remains active in the Paths palette, every collection of anchor points and segments you draw becomes part of that named entity or path.

Adding a New Path to the Path Palette

With the Paths palette open (either choose **Show Paths** from the Window menu or click on the **Paths** tab in the Layers/Channels/Paths palette group), there are two ways to add a new path:

- Click on the **New Paths** button at the bottom of the Paths palette. A new Path is added with a numerical name.
- Either choose **New Path** from the palette menu or hold down the **Option** key (Macintosh) or **Alt** key (Windows) and click on the **New Paths** button. In the New Paths dialog, type in a name.

Adding a new path to the palette does not create a path. You have to select the **Pen** tool and lay down anchor points on the image, just as you would for a Work Path.

To copy a path:

- Drag a path to the New Paths button at the bottom of the Paths palette. A duplicate path is added to the stack with *copy* appended to its name.
- Activate a path in the Paths palette, and click on the **Duplicate Path** command in the palette menu. Name the duplicate in the Duplicate Path dialog.

To delete a path:

- Drag a path to the Trash button at the bottom of the Paths palette. The path is deleted.
- Select a path and either click on the **Trash** button or choose the **Delete Path** command from the palette menu. Confirm the deletion.

To activate/deactivate a path:

- Clicking on a path in the Paths palette activates that path and deactivates all others. Only one path can be active at a time, including the Work Path.
- Choose the **Turn Off Path** command to deactivate all paths, including the Work Path.

There are two commands in the palette menu that are not dependent on any selections in the image or palette: Clipping Path and Palette Options.

The Clipping Path command allows you to specify a path as a clipping path for export in EPS format. This allows you to import the file in another program with a clipped image.

A clipping path defines an outlinearound an image. All pixels outside the path are treated as transparent. This can be used to create text runarounds in page layout programs that conform to the shape of the image rather than to a rectangular shape. To create a clipping path for export:

1. Choose the **Clipping Path** command from the palette menu.
2. Choose a path from the Paths dropdown menu.
3. Specify a Flatness setting from 0.2 to 100. Flatness is a measure of detail used by PostScript to create curved lines out of straight line segments. Lower flatness settings are more detailed. Pixel-based programs like Photoshop do not use flatness, but object-based programs do.
4. Save the file in EPS format. When you import the file into another program, the clipping path is automatically applied so that any pixels outside the path are transparent.

As with the Layers and Channels palettes, there is only one palette option for the Paths palette and it allows you to set the thumbnail size.

EDITING PATHS

The power of paths lies in their editability. Paths are represented in memory by mathematical relationships that are easily changed without affecting any of the pixels in the image. Paths are edited using the Pen tool and the hidden Pen tools in the Toolbox. There are also many editing shortcuts.

NOTE For the purposes of this book, we will speak of editing paths as distinct from manipulating paths. Editing concerns the physical shape of the path in the image—the placement of anchor points and adjustment of direction lines. Manipulating is what you do with paths in the Paths Palette or with the Path commands and buttons.

To select and adjust path segments and/or anchor points:

- Choose the Direct-Selection tool from the hidden Pen tools in the Toolbox. The Direct-Selection tool is also active in the following situations:
- When the Pen tool is chosen, hold down the **Command** key (Macintosh) or **Ctrl** key (Windows) to activate the Direct-Selection tool.
- When the Add Anchor Point tool is chosen, move the pointer over any anchor point to activate the direct-selection tool.
- When either the Delete Anchor Point or Convert Anchor Point tool is active, move the pointer over a path segment to activate the Direct-Selection tool.
- Click on any anchor point or path segment to select it (Figure 18.3).
- Click and drag around a group of segments and anchors within a path to select any part of a path.
- Hold down the **Option** key (Macintosh) or **Alt** key (Windows) and click on any anchor point or segment to select the entire path.
- Hold down the **Shift** key and click on an anchor point or segment to add to a selection.

Once selected, any portion of a path may be adjusted.

Figure 18.3 Selecting an anchor point with the Direct-Selection tool.

- Dragging a segment moves or adjusts it (Figure 18.4). Straight line segments move with their anchor points, while the anchor points for curved line segments remain fixed and the direction lines are adjusted.

Figure 18.4 Moving a curved segment with the Direct-Selection tool adjusts the direction lines.

- Dragging an anchor point moves it (Figure 18.5). The segments on either side are adjusted accordingly.

Figure 18.5 Moving a straight segment with the Direct-Selection tool moves the anchor points with the segment.

- When an anchor point is selected, drag on the endpoints of either direction line to adjust the associated curved line segment.
- Press the **Delete** key to delete any selected anchor points or segments. After deletion, the remaining path is selected.

To add or subtract anchor points, select either the Add Anchor Point tool to add anchor points or the Subtract Anchor-Point tool to subtract anchor points. Both are hidden Pen tools in the Toolbox.

 You can add/subtract anchor points while the direct-selection tool is active by holding down the **Command-Option** keys (Macintosh) or **Ctrl-Alt** keys (Windows). When the pointer is over a segment, you can add an anchor point, and when the pointer is over an anchor point, you can subtract that anchor point.

• Click on a segment with the Add Anchor Point tool (Figure 18.6) to add an anchor point without changing the path. Click and drag to add an anchor point and adjust direction lines that change the path.

Figure 18.6 Adding a smooth anchor point by clicking and dragging with the Add Anchor Point tool.

• Click on an anchor point with the delete-anchor-point tool (Figure 18.7) to delete an anchor point and reshape the path to fit the remaining anchor points. Click and drag to delete the anchor point and adjust the shape of the path.

Figure 18.7 Subtracting an anchor point and reshaping the segment by clicking and dragging.

To convert anchor points between smooth and corner point:,

- Choose the convert-anchor-point tool from the hidden Pen tools in the Toolbox.

NOTE You can activate the convert-anchor-point tool while the Pen tool is selected by holding down the **Control-Command** keys (Macintosh). There is no Windows shortcut.

- Click on a smooth point to convert it to a corner point (Figure 18.8). The segments are redrawn.

Figure 18.8 A smooth point becomes a corner point when clicked by the Convert Anchor Point tool.

- Click and drag on a corner point to convert it to a smooth point and create direction lines (Figure 18.9). The segments are redrawn according to the direction lines.

Figure 18.9 A corner point becomes a smooth point when clicked by the Convert Anchor Point tool.

MANIPULATING PATHS

As already mentioned, paths can be copied, cut, pasted, and moved like any object or selection. However, no pixels are changed when you manipulate a path.

Using the Edit commands to manipulate paths:

1. Select a path or part of a path as described above.
2. Use the Cut, Copy, or Paste command from the Edit menu.

Cutting removes a path from an image but does not remove the path from the Paths palette. The Cut and Copy commands both put a copy of the path on the Clipboard so that you can Paste it back into the image or into any other open image or open document in any application that supports Cut and Paste.

To move or copy a path:

1. Select a path as described above.
2. Choose the Direct-Selection tool and drag the path anywhere in the image (Figure 18.10).

Figure 18.10 Dragging an entire path with the Direct-Selection tool to move it.

You can also drag the path from the image window or from the Paths palette into any other open image window to copy the path to another document.

If you hold down the **Option** key (Macintosh) or **Alt** key (Windows) while you move a path, a copy is made. This is not the same as duplicating a path as described above, because it does not create a new path in the Paths palette.

You can move a path so that it is off the boundary of the image window. This is okay and does not cut off the path for future uses.

N O T E

FILLING AND STROKING PATHS

When you create objects in a drawing program like Adobe Illustrator, you define an outline, a stroke for the outline, and a fill. Paths in Photoshop behave the same way. A stroke applies colored pixels to the path border itself, while a fill applies color to the pixels surrounded by the path.

There are two ways to fill or stroke: using either the Fill Path or Stroke Path commands in the Palette menu or the buttons at the bottom of the Paths palette. If only a subpath is selected, the palette menu commands change to Fill Subpath and Stroke Subpath, and only the subpath is affected.

The Fill and Stroke commands add pixels to the active layer. Make sure that the layer you want to add pixels to is active in the Layers palette before executing these commands.

N O T E

To stroke a path:

1. Select a path in the Paths palette or a subpath in the image.
2. Select a painting or editing tool from the Toolbox. The options for this tool will be used to create the stroke. Set options in the Options palette and pick a brush from the Brushes palette to determine the size of the stroke. You can use any brush, including custom brushes.
3. Do one of the following:

   • Click on the **Stroke Path** button at the bottom of the Paths palette, or drag any path in the Paths palette to the Stroke Path button. This immediately applies a stroke using the tool, options, and brush you specified in Step 2.

   • Choose the **Stroke (Sub)Path** command in the palette menu or hold down the **Option** key (Macintosh) or **Alt** key (Windows) and click on the **Stroke Path** button at the bottom of the Paths palette. This brings up the Stroke Path dialog with a single option that lets you choose from the Tool dropdown menu if you didn't already pick a tool in step 2.

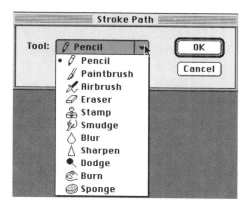

Figure 18.11 The Stroke Path dialog lets you select only one of the painting or editing tools from the Tool dropdown menu. Options and size must be specified before invoking the Stroke command.

The actual options and brush used to create a stroke cannot be set in the Stroke Path dialog. You must anticipate and pick a tool, set options, and choose a brush before stroking a path. This is neither intuitive nor convenient, but it does work.

Unlike the Stroke command, the Fill dialog is full of options. To fill a path, select a path in the Paths palette or a subpath in the image, and do one of the following:

- Either click on the **Fill Path** button at the bottom of the Paths palette, or you can drag any path in the Paths palette to the Fill Path button without selecting it. This fills the path using the default or previous settings in the Fill Path dialog.

- Choose the **Fill (Sub)Path** command in the Palette menu or hold down the **Option** key (Macintosh) or **Alt** key (Windows) and click on the **Fill Path** button at the bottom of the Paths palette. This brings up the Fill Path dialog (Figure 18.12) with three option groups.

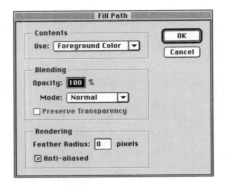

Figure 18.12 The Fill Path dialog with three option groups.

The three option groups are as follows:

- **Contents**—The Use dropdown menu (Figure 18.13) lets you select a fill option. These are the same as those offered by the Fill command described in Chapter 13.

- **Blending**—Set an opacity from 0-100%. Choose one of the blending modes from the Mode dropdown menu. These are described in Chapter 3. Check the Preserve Transparency box to leave transparent pixels unfilled.

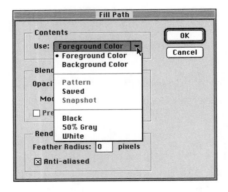

Figure 18.13 The Use dropdown menu is identical to the Fill command in the Edit menu. You can specify a fill color or use a fill pattern.

- **Rendering**—Fill in a Feather Radius amount from 0 to 250.0 to set the distance from the path that a feathered edge extends. Check the Anti-aliased box to smooth the transition of the fill border by anti-aliasing pixels.

Click **OK** to accept the Fill Path options and apply the fill to the active layer.

TURNING PATHS INTO SELECTIONS

Aside from stroking and filling, the main use for paths is as selections. When paths are converted, they can be used with other selections to create larger or smaller selections. Paths or subpaths can be turned into selections, and if you convert an open path, by necessity it becomes a closed selection since there is no such animal as an open selection.

To turn a path into a selection:

1. Select a path in the Paths palette or a subpath in the image, and do one of the following:

- Click on the **Make Selection** button at the bottom of the Paths palette or drag any path in the Paths palette to the Make Selection button. This will convert the path into a selection using the default or previously set options.

- Either choose the **Make Selection** command from the palette menu or hold down the **Option** key (Macintosh) or **Alt** key (Windows) and click on the **Make Selection** button at the bottom of the Paths palette. This brings up the Make Selection dialog with two option groups (see Figure 18.14).

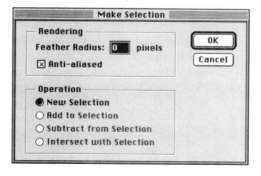

Figure 18.14 The Make Selection dialog with two option groups. The Operation radio buttons are only active if there is an active selection in the image.

- **Rendering**—As in the Fill Path dialog above, you can specify a Feather Radius and turn on anti-aliasing.

- **Operation**—This controls the interaction of the path with any active selections in the image. Check the appropriate radio button to create a New Selection, Add to Selection, Subtract from Selection, or Intersect with Selection. If there is no active selection, New Selection is the only choice.

2. Click **OK** to convert the path into a selection on the active layer.

There is another shortcut method to turn paths into selections, and it uses the selection modifier keys and icons. Click on any path in the Paths palette while holding down the following keys:

- To convert a path using the default or previous options, hold down the **Command** key (Macintosh) or **Ctrl** key (Windows).
- To convert a path by adding it to an active selection, hold down the **Command-Shift/Ctrl-Shift** keys.
- To convert a path by subtracting it from an active selection, hold down the **Command-Option/Ctrl-Alt** keys.
- To convert a path by creating an intersection with an active selection, hold down the **Command-Option-Shift/Ctrl-Alt-Shift** keys. See Figure 18.15.

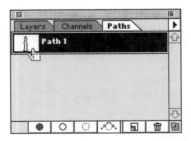

Figure 18.15 Converting a path into a selection using the command key shortcut. The icon is the same, the hand with selection marquee, used when converting Channels to selections.

Even though the goal of most paths is to become selections, you can convert in the other direction when you want to use the Pen tools to edit a selection. In many cases, this is easier than using the Lasso tool to add to and subtract from a selection.

With any selection active either click on the **Make Work Path** button or choose the **Make Work Path** command from the palette menu. The selection is converted into a Work Path replacing any other Work Path. The button uses whatever Tolerance setting was last used. The command brings up the Make Work Path dialog and lets you set the Tolerance from 0.5 to 10.0. You can also **Option/Alt-click** on the Work Path button to set the Tolerance before conversion (see Figure 18.16).

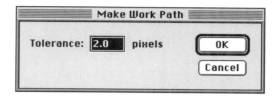

Figure 18.16 The Make Work Path dialog has only a single option to allow you to set the tolerance for the conversion.

The Tolerance setting determines how closely the path will approximate the selection. A higher Tolerance creates a smoother path with fewer anchor points, while a lower Tolerance creates a path that is closer to the original.

The process of converting from a selection to a path is an approximation, and so some of the detail of a selection is lost.

NOTE

Lesson 18: Path Practice

Since Lesson 7 dealt with the Pen tool in some detail, we'll concentrate on editing and manipulating paths in this lesson.

Make sure the Paths palette is open for this lesson. Either choose **Show Paths** from the Window menu, or click on the **Paths** tab in the Layers/Channels/Paths palette group.

First, lasso a bird with a path.

1. Open the file **NUT_BIRD.TIF** from the Lesson18 folder on the CD. You'll notice that there's already a path saved with this image. We'll look at this later by way of comparison with the work we're about to do.

This is another Panamanian artifact—a bird carved from a single nut of the ivory palm tree and then handpainted. The background of this photograph isn't very useful, in fact, it's a downright nuisance. We can't use the Magic Wand tool to select and delete it, because it has too much texture and too many shadows.

Our options are to outline the entire bird painstakingly using the Lasso tool, adding and subtracting selections to make up for our rather unsteady plying of the mouse, or creating a nice smooth path. Do my adjectives betray the answer? See for yourself.

2. Choose the **Lasso** tool(l) and trace the outline of the bird.

3. Since this is a lesson about paths and all we have so far is a selection, click on the **Make Work Path** button at the bottom of the Paths palette. You could also choose **Make Work Path** from the palette menu and specify a Tolerance, but since the default is fine, we'll use the shortcut.

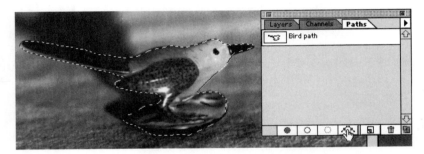

Figure 18.17 Our poor lassoed bird about to be turned into a path by clicking on the Make Work Path button. This selection is mostly okay, but it's got some distinct wobbles and could use touching up in a number of places.

4. Choose the direct-selection tool by moving the mouse over the Pen tool in the Toolbox, holding down the mouse button, and sliding to choose the tool from the pop-up window.

5. Move the pointer over the path in the image window, hold down the **Option/Alt** key, and click to select the entire path. This shows all of the anchor points.

This is not an elegant path. There are too many anchor points, and we still don't have a clean outline (Figure 18.18). But there's a trick here.

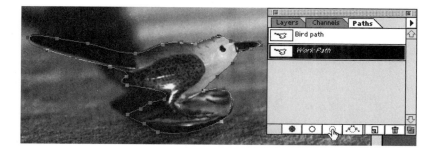

Figure 18.18 What used to be a selection marquee is now a path that has been selected to show the anchor points. It's about to be turned back into a selection by clicking on the Load Selection button.

6. Click on the **Load Selection** button to turn the path back into a selection. The process of converting between selections and paths loses information but helps our cause.

Loading a selection does not actually convert the path—path and selection are both active.

NOTE

7. Click on the **Make Work Path** button again. This converts the new selection and overwrites the previous Work Path. There can only be one Work Path.

8. Hold down the **Option/Alt** key and select the path again. You can see in Figure 18.19 that this process of multiple conversions has given us a better path with fewer anchor points.

Figure 18.19 The path of a twice-selected bird is smoother, with fewer anchor points. It won't be difficult to edit this path to make a nice smooth selection.

9. Drag the Work Path in the Paths palette to the New Path button. This gives you the opportunity to name a path, just as you would a layer, and makes our path permanent so that we don't inadvertently write over it.

Adjusting for Inaccuracy

Your original lasso selection will have been different from mine, so your anchor points will not be the same as those in the screen shots. If you'd like an exact match, click on the Channels palette and load channel #4 as a selection. Then repeat steps 3-9, and you should be exactly where I am.

1. Choose the direct/selection tool from the Pen's hidden tools in the Toolbox.

    I like to make adjustments by moving anchor points with the direct-selection tool and holding down the **Command-Option/Ctrl-Alt** keys to add or subtract anchor points. In this case, we'll mostly be subtracting.

2. Move the pointer over the anchor point that is close to its neighbors and click to delete it. You rarely need more than one or two anchor points on any given curve.

3. Drag the remaining anchor points to place them where they do the most good. You can also drag segments to change their curve slightly.

4. To adjust curves more precisely, click on an anchor point to select it and then drag the direction lines to adjust the curve, as shown in Figure 18.20.

Figure 18.20 Adjusting the direction line of the selected anchor point. All the extraneous anchor points have already been deleted.

You should not need to add or convert any anchor points for this exercise, but you can try these tools out if you wish. It's easy to make adjustments.

5. Once you have a nice smooth path without extra anchor points, convert the path back into a selection by clicking on the **Load Selection** button again.

6. Choose the **Turn Off Path** command from the Palette menu to hide the path. Now you can see that the loaded selection is very smooth and precise—a selection to be proud of (Figure 18.21).

Figure 18.21 Loading the path one more time as a selection. You can see that this selection very accurately separates the bird from its background.

7. Save your changes if you wish.

Creating Paths from Scratch

We've used a kind of shortcut to create a path and avoid using the Pen tool. It's very convenient to start a path as a selection and then convert it. But one can very quickly draw a path around this bird with just the Pen tool.

1. Choose **Revert** from the File menu to go back to the saved version of the Nut Bird file.

2. Choose the **Pen** tool (p) from the Toolbox. If you wish, click on the **Rubber Band** check box in the Pen Options palette so that you can preview curves before you set the anchor point.

3. Start placing anchor points as indicated in Figure 18.22. For the first anchor point, just click to make it a corner point. For all other points, drag to create smooth points.

Figure 18.22 A few anchor points placed with the Pen tool. The first point is a corner point, and the others were dragged to create smooth points.

4. Continue dragging anchor points. Remember to take advantage of the natural back-and-forth s-shaped curve of the Pen tool as you draw. See Figure 18.23.

Figure 18.23 Back at the starting point, and the Pen icon has a small circle next to it to indicate that clicking will close the path.

5. Once the path is closed, choose the direct-select tool from the Toolbox, or hold down the **Command/Ctrl** key.

6. Since it's very difficult without a lot of practice to draw a line with the Pen tool exactly where you want it, adjust the points and lines of the path to fit the outline of the bird more precisely.

   There are lots of ways to use the Pen tool to trace an outline. As you get more efficient at it, you'll find that it takes fewer anchor points to create a complex path.

7. Click on the path **Bird Path** in the Paths palette. This is one that I tried to make with as few anchor points as possible. You'll notice that it is more efficient than the path shown in the screen shots. Is it more accurate? You can decide for yourself.

Getting Around
in an Image

In this chapter…

- Basic navigation & viewing
- The Navigator palette
- The Info palette

The Navigator and Info palettes are part of the same default palette group as the Options palette. (The Options palette in all its various permutations is explained in the various chapters discussing each of Photoshop's tools.) The Navigator palette, which is new to Photoshop 4, lets you control the image view more interactively, and it extends the capabilities of the Hand and Magnifier tools. The Info palette is strictly for informational feedback. Neither of the palettes or tools discussed in this chapter affects the image directly.

BASIC NAVIGATION & VIEWING

While other programs have implemented unlimited zooming and panning, it's taken Photoshop until Version 4 to update its image-viewing capabilities. At last, we can zoom in any percentage increment to any area of the picture. We can see exactly what we want to see, provided that it's actually there.

Before Photoshop 4, there were only the Hand and Magnifier tools, along with a few commands in the View menu that allowed us to control the view of an image. We'll discuss these first before going on to discuss the additional control provided by the Navigator Palette.

Using the Zoom Tool

Select the **Zoom** tool (z) from the Toolbox. 100% zoom is based on actual pixels, not image size. In other words, 1 image pixel for every screen pixel equals 100% enlargement.

- Click on the image to zoom in, enlarging the image view.
- Hold down the **Option** key (Macintosh) or **Alt** key (Windows) and click on the image to zoom out, reducing the image view.

You can zoom without the Zoom tool. **Command-Option-[=]** (Macintosh) or **Ctrl-Alt-[=]** (Windows) zooms in, and **Command-Option-[-]** (Macintosh) or **Ctrl-Alt-[-]** (Windows) zooms out.

- With the Zoom tool selected, click and drag over the area of an image you wish to enlarge. Photoshop magnifies that area to fill the window.

You can magnify by dragging without selecting the Zoom tool, by holding down **Space-Command** (Macintosh) or **Space-Ctrl** (Windows) and dragging. Option/Alt-Space allows you to zoom out.

- Double-click the **Zoom** tool to change the magnification to 100%, or press **Command-Option-0** (Macintosh) or **Ctrl-Alt-0** (Windows).

Using the Hand Tool

The Hand tool is used to reposition an image within its display window.

- Select the **Hand** tool (h) from the Toolbox and drag the image to reposition.
- To reposition an image without changing tools, hold down the **Space** key and drag.
- Double-click the **Hand** tool in the Tool palette to make the image and its window as large as will fit on your display. This is the same as the View Fit on Screen command.

Using the View Commands

The View Menu includes five commands that duplicate functions of the Zoom and Hand tools.

- **Zoom In**, **Command-[=]** (Macintosh) or **Ctrl-[=]** (Windows), reduces the image.
- **Zoom Out**, **Command-[-]** (Macintosh) or **Ctrl-[-]** (Windows), reduces the image.
- **Fit on Screen**, **Command-0** (Macintosh) or **Ctrl-0** (Windows), magnifies the image to the maximum size that will fit on your display.
- **Actual Pixels**, **Option-Command-0** (Macintosh) or **Alt-Ctrl-0** (Windows), changes the magnification to 100%.
- **Print Size** (there are no shortcuts for this command) shows the image at its actual print size regardless of resolution.

You can also change the magnification of an image by typing a number into the magnification display at the bottom-left corner of the window frame.

THE NAVIGATOR PALETTE

To open the Navigator Palette:

- Choose **Show Navigator** from the Window menu.
- Click on the **Navigator** tab in the Navigator/Info/Options palette group.

The Navigator Palette (Figure 19.1) presents a thumbnail view of the image and a highlighted box that indicates the size of the image window. Across the bottom of the Navigator Palette are the image magnification, the zoom buttons and slider, and the resize box or corner.

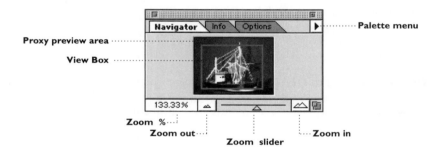

Figure 19.1 Diagram of the Navigator palette, one of Photoshop 4's new features.

To resize the Navigator Palette, click and drag on the bottom-right corner of the palette. As you drag the palette larger, the preview image is resized to fill the space. It is in fact possible to make the Navigator image larger than the actual image window, but what's the point?

To change the image magnification using percents:

1. Type any number between .16% and 1600 % in the magnification box in the lower-left corner of the palette.
2. Press **Return** (Macintosh) or **Enter** (Windows) and the image is zoomed to the magnification you entered.

Photoshop will zoom to the centerpoint of the current view when changing the image magnification this way.

There are two buttons on either side of the magnification slider. The smaller mountains on the left represent the Zoom Out button, while the larger mountains on the right represent the Zoom In button.

To change the image magnification using the zoom buttons:

- Click on the **Zoom In** button to magnify in preset increments.
- Click on the **Zoom Out** button to reduce the magnification in preset increments.

The increments of magnification are very roughly logarithmic—finer at smaller magnifications and coarser at larger magnifications.

To change the image magnification using the Zoom slider, drag the triangle under the slider to increase or decrease the magnification. The image is zoomed interactively. The interactivity of the slider is more effective on faster machines.

To change the image magnification by dragging a new View Box:

1. Hold down the **Command** key (Macintosh) or **Ctrl** key (Windows).
2. Drag a rectangle around the area you wish to magnify in the preview area of the Navigator Palette.
3. Release the mouse button, and the image magnification is adjusted to match the rectangle you just drew.

The View Box

The View Box is a rectangle superimposed on the proxy preview area that indicates the size of the active window. Areas of the image outside the View Box are also outside the view of the active window.

To move the View Box:

- Move the pointer inside the View Box in the Navigator palette. The icon turns into a hand. Click and drag the View Box. As you move the View Box, the image moves in the active window.

- Move the pointer outside the View Box in the Navigator palette. The icon turns into a pointing hand. Click on the image preview and the View Box moves so that the point clicked is the center of the view in the active window, or as close to being centered as the edges and size of the window allow.

NOTE

If you hold down the **Shift** key while dragging, the move is constrained to either horizontal or vertical.

To change the View Box highlight color:

1. Choose the **Palette Options** command from the palette menu. The Palette Options dialog has only a single View Box option.

2. Choose a color from the Color dropdown menu, click on the color square to select any color from Photoshop's Color Picker, or sample a color from any image window by moving the pointer outside the dialog box.

3. Click **OK** to change the color of the View Box. See Figure 19.2.

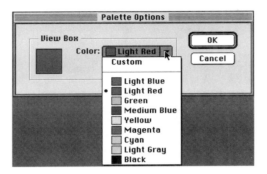

Figure 19.2 The View Box Color in the Palette Options dialog allows you to change the color of the View Box to suit your fancy.

THE INFO PALETTE

The Info palette is like Photoshop's time and temperature display. It shows pointer coordinates and color information for whatever pixel is under the pointer. You can see what it's like anywhere in the image, but you can't do anything about it. (At least, not from the Info palette.)

The display in the Info palette changes depending on the tool you're using. You can also alter the scale or mode of the display from the palette menu commands or the tool dropdown menu within the palette. The Info Palette, shown in Figure 19.3, cannot be resized.

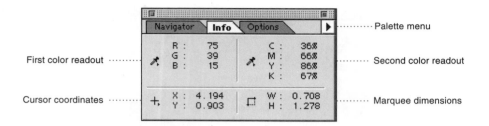

First color readout ······

Cursor coordinates ······

Palette menu

Second color readout

Marquee dimensions

Figure 19.3 A diagram of the Info Palette.

As you move the pointer across an image, the information in the Info Palette is updated. It displays the color in the two-color systems of your choice and the coordinates of the pointer in relation to the upper-left corner of the window.

- When using the Marquee (m), Crop (c), or Zoom (z) tool, the Info palette also displays the width (W) and height (H) of the marquee as you drag. The angle of rotation (A) for the Crop tool is also displayed.

- When using the Line (n), Pen (p), or Gradient (g) tool, the Info Palette displays the change in X (Δx), the change in Y (Δy), the angle (A), and the distance (D) as you drag.

NOTE

You can use the Line tool (n) to measure distances by setting the line width in the Line Options palette to 0.

- When using the Free Transform, Scale, Rotate, Skew, Distort, or Perspective command, the Info palette displays the percentage change in width (W) and height (H), the angle (A), the horizontal skew (H), and the vertical skew (V).

- When moving the pointer over pixels in an image while using any of the color adjustment dialogs, the Info palette displays the before and after color values of the pixels.

To Change the Info Palette Readouts

There are two ways to change the readouts in the Info Palette: either by using the Palette Option command from the Palette menu or by clicking and dragging on the icons in the palette.

1.   Choose the **Palette Option** command from the Palette menu (see Figure 19.4).

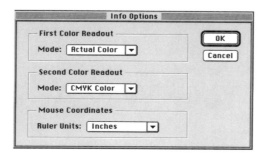

Figure 19.4 The Info Options dialog with three dropdown menus to set the readouts in the Info palette. The same options are available by clicking and dragging on the icons in the Info palette.

There are three options in the Info Options dialog: First Color Readout, Second Color Readout, and Ruler Units. The two color readouts allow you to compare actual color levels to printed equivalents, or one color scale to another.

The choices for color readout include: Actual Color, RGB, HSB, Lab, CMYK, Total Ink, and Opacity. Total Ink refers to the amount of CMYK inks in percent, and Opacity refers to the current layer and cannot be used with the background layer, which can have no transparency.

- First Color Readout defaults to Actual Color, which shows colors in the mode of the image.
- Second Color Readout defaults to CMYK, which is the standard mode for color printing.
- Ruler Units defaults to Inches. It can also be set to Pixels, Centimeters, Points, or Picas.

The same choices as those stated above are available from the icon dropdown menus in the Info palette.

NOTE

2. Hold down the mouse button when the pointer is over the eyedropper or cross-hairs icon and drag to select an option.

Lesson 19: Finding Your Way Around an Image

Using the Navigator and Info palettes is as straightforward as can be. I'll just guide you through some of the things that you can do, and most of the exploration will be up to you. We'll also pay a quick visit to some of the related View commands and tools.

Because there's really no sequence to this lesson, I've simply bulleted the steps instead of enumerating them.

- Open the file **ROWBOATS.PSD** from the Lesson19 folder on the CD. This file is big. This means that it has lots of pixels to look at.

  The first thing to notice is that Photoshop opens this file at 50% magnification so that it can fit the entire image on your display. (This may vary depending on the size of your monitor.)

- Make sure the Info palette is open, and then watch what happens as you move the pointer over the image. Move the pointer into the darkest areas of shadow and then into the lightest areas of the boat (Figure 19.5). You'll see that as the RGB values in the First Color Readout approach 0, the CMYK values in the Second Color Readout approach their maximum values, and vice versa.

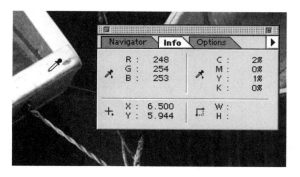

Figure 19.5 As you move any tool over the image, the Eyedropper tool in this screen shot, the Info palette reports the position and color. Here the color is very close to white.

- Hold down the mouse button while the pointer is over one of the palette icons, eyedropper or plus sign, and change the measurement scale for one of the fields.

- Make a selection using the Marquee tool (m), and watch the Info palette as you drag. Do the same with the Crop tool (c) and then rotate the crop. Choose the Line tool (n) and set the Line Width in the Line Options palette to 0. Measure the sterns of the two rowboats.

- Click on the **Navigator** tab in the palette group window.

- Choose the **Actual Pixels** command from the View menu. This changes the magnification to 100%. Look at the Navigator palette. The View Box displays the area of the image that is showing in the image window. Notice that it's centered.

- Click on the **Zoom Out** button. This changes the magnification to 66.67%. Click on the **Zoom Out** button again and we're back at 50%.

- Choose the **Zoom** tool (z) from the Toolbox. Click near the bottom right of the image on the knots of the lines. This increases the magnification in the same size steps as the Zoom buttons. But notice that Photoshop has centered the display as close to where you click as possible, rather than on the center of the image.

- Move the pointer into the Navigator palette and drag the View Box around. Click outside the View Box to move without dragging (Figure 19.6).

Figure 19.6 Dragging the View Box around in the Navigator palette.

- With the Zoom tool still selected, drag around the bow of the rowboat. Photoshop enlarges the area you select to fill the image window. It uses exactly the magnification necessary to do this.

- Drag an area in the Navigator palette's Proxy Preview Area. This has the same effect as dragging in the image with the Zoom tool.

- Grab the Zoom slider and drag it slowly to the right, toward the Zoom In button. Watch as Photoshop changes the zoom. When you get up to the maximum zoom ratio, 1600%, you can see every square pixel. The Navigator palette is especially useful at higher magnifications, because you can keep track of the entire image while working on a very small area. See Figure 19.7.

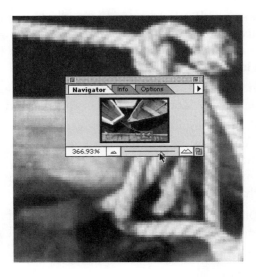

Figure 19.7 Dragging the Zoom slider so that the details of the pixels are revealed, but the image remains completely visible in the Navigator Palette.

CHAPTER 20

Automating Photoshop

In this chapter...

- The Actions palette
- Actions in action
- Creating and editing Actions
- Batching Actions
- Manipulating Action sets

THE ACTIONS PALETTE

The Actions palette is perhaps the neatest new feature of Photoshop 4, or is it really so new? In a sense, the Actions palette represents an expansion and renaming of the former Commands palette, which allowed you to list Photoshop commands as buttons and click on them to execute or invoke them through function key assignments. With the Actions palette, you can go further to create your own commands.

The Actions palette allows you to script groups of Photoshop actions into a single button in the Actions palette and play them repeatedly with a single mouse click. Scripting is not for everyone, but for a dedicated group of Photoshop users, the capabilities of the Actions palette and the ability to run the same actions on a batch of files is a long-awaited feature.

There are certainly those who would like more robust scripting capabilities and full AppleScript support or interfaces to programming languages, but this first (second?) incarnation of the Actions palette is aimed at the more typical Photoshop user, emphasizing ease-of-use over a complex feature set. (See Figure 20.1.)

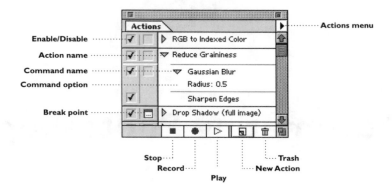

Figure 20.1 Actions Palette diagram.

The Actions palette makes it easy to reproduce frequently used multi-step processes and techniques. For example, you can combine a series of filters to reproduce a favorite effect or run a sequence of commands to prepare files for on line publishing.

You will use the Actions palette in two ways: to execute actions and to create or edit them. There are many options for Actions, and as a result of this, the Actions palette menu is easily the longest of all Photoshop's palette menus (Figure 20.2).

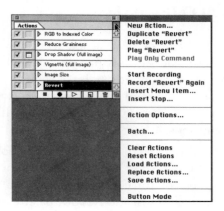

Figure 20.2 The Action palette menu. It takes a lot of extra commands to create, manipulate, and execute even a simple scripting system.

ACTIONS IN ACTION

The Actions palette lists all actions available so that you can select, edit, rearrange, and execute actions. It shares the basic properties of all other palettes, and many features, like the palette menu and the New and Trash buttons are familiar. You select actions by clicking on them and rearrange them by dragging in the palette.

Choose **Show Actions** from the Window menu to open the Actions palette. The Actions palette toggles between two display modes: Button Mode displays only Action names in button bars, like the former Commands palette, while List Mode allows you to see and edit the steps of an Action.

To toggle Button Mode, choose **Button Mode** from the Actions palette menu. Button Mode is either checked (on), or unchecked (off). (See Figure 20.3.)

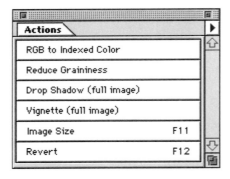

Figure 20.3 The Actions palette with Button Mode on. You can only execute, change the options, or change the order of Actions in Button Mode.

Actions are made up of steps of commands, and each step may have substeps or settings. In Button Mode the steps are hidden, but in List Mode, the steps can be expanded and edited. In List Mode, each Action is listed with a small right-pointing triangle before it.

To view Action steps:

- Click on the triangle to open an Action and reveal its contents. The steps of the Action are listed beneath it. Steps can also be listed with expansion triangles.

- Click on the triangle again to collapse an Action or step. (See Figure 20.4.)

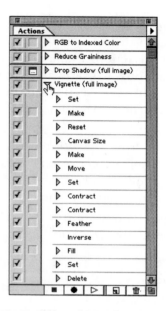

Figure 20.4 Click on the right-facing triangle to expand the Action and reveal its steps.
You can do the same with a step.

The first column of the Action list displays a check mark to show that Actions or steps are included and usable. Click in the column next to any Action or command to exclude it (Figure 20.5). Click again to redisplay the check mark and include the Action or command. Excluding steps is a convenient way to alter Actions temporarily without rewriting them.

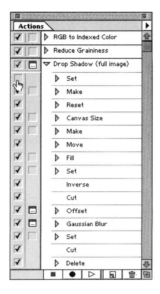

Figure 20.5 Click in the first column to exclude or include an Action or step. The absence of a checkmark in this column indicates that the item cannot be executed and will be skipped.

Setting Break Points

Break points within an Action pause action execution to wait for user intervention. This may be used to fill in options for a command, make a selection, or supply some other variable form of input. The second column in the Actions palette toggles break points on or off for an entire Action or single step. To set a break point in an Action, click in the second column next to an Action name or step to turn on the dialog box icon. Click again to remove the break point (see Figure 20.6).

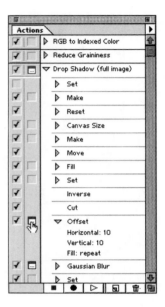

Figure 20.6 Click in the second column to toggle break points on and off. With the dialog icon showing, the Action breaks to let you fill in the dialog options. With the box empty, the Action uses the default option settings without pausing.

Photoshop will not let you turn on a break point for a step with no options. Also, if a break point is not turned on, the Action will execute without pausing, using the option values recorded.

NOTE

Executing Actions

To execute an Action in either Button Mode or List Mode, click on an Action to select it, and then click on the **Play** button at the bottom of the Actions palette, or choose the **Play** command from the palette menu.

This will execute all steps of an Action in order. Actions will pause when a break point is reached. Enter new values and click **OK**, or click **Cancel** to accept the default values. Any excluded steps are skipped. Execution continues until all steps are executed.

Sometimes, an Action will only work if the image is in the correct state before initiating execution. For instance, you may record an Action that only works if a selection is active or requires multiple layers or channels. The results of executing an Action may not turn out as you wish if the initial state of the image is not what the Action is expecting.

To execute a single step:

1. Select a single command within an Action.
2. **Option-click** (Macintosh) or **Alt-click** (Windows) on the Play button, or choose the **Play Only** command from the palette menu. No other commands within the Action will be executed.

CREATING AND EDITING ACTIONS

The simplest way to create an Action is to record a series of steps as a script.

Photoshop executes commands as they are recorded, so you may want to work on a copy of your image when recording Actions.

To record an Action:

1. Click on the **New Action** button at the bottom of the Actions palette, or choose **New Action** from the palette menu.
2. There are three options in the New Actions dialog. Set the options or leave the defaults.

- **Name** lets you name the Action. It will appear with this name in the Actions palette.
- **Function Key** is a dropdown menu that lets you assign function keys from 1-15 to an Action. Any keys already assigned are grayed and cannot be reassigned. Click the **Shift** check box to assign the Shift modifier key with a function key.

You can't assign command keys, because they are used in the Channels palette.

- **Color** defaults to none, or choose one of the seven colors from the drop-down menu. The Action will be displayed in the palette using the color you assign.

3. Click **OK** in the dialog. The Record button is red to indicate that recording is on (Figure 20.7).

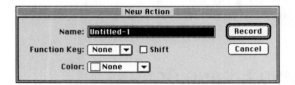

Figure 20.7 The New Actions dialog lets you label an Action and assign a function key as an execution shortcut.

Any of the options set in the New Action dialog can be changed by choosing the **Action Options** command from the palette menu or by double-clicking on an Action name.

4. Execute the commands that you wish to be a part of the recorded action.

Responses to dialogs are recorded along with the commands. Clicking **Cancel** in a dialog is not recorded. Some commands cannot be recorded and must be inserted manually.

5. Click the **Stop** button at the bottom of the Actions palette to stop recording.

When you choose an Action and click the **Record** button, recorded actions are appended to the bottom of the list. You can drag the appended commands to insert them in a different place in the Action.

To Duplicate an Action or step:

- Select either an Action or single step in the Actions palette and choose the **Duplicate** command from the palette menu.
- Drag either an Action or step to the New Actions button in the Actions palette.

  Duplicated Actions are added to the bottom of the Actions list with the word *copy* appended to the name.

  Duplicated steps are added below the current selected step. The name is not changed.

To Delete an Action or step:

- Select either an Action or single step in the Actions Palette and choose the **Delete** command from the Palette menu. Confirm the deletion.
- Drag either an Action or step to the Trash button in the Actions Palette. No confirmation is requested.

To append steps to an Action:

- Select an Action and either choose the **Start Recording** command or
- Click on the **Record** button at the bottom of the Actions palette. Any commands executed will be appended to the bottom of the Action as additional steps.

  Press the **Stop** button to finish.

Appended steps can be moved by dragging in the Actions palette to insert them in a different order.

NOTE If a step is selected rather than the Action title, any recorded commands are inserted rather than appended.

Recording New Action Values

The Record Again command lets you change the values for dialogs in an Action without changing the steps.

To record new Action values:

1. Select an Action in the Actions palette.
2. Choose **Record Again** from the palette menu. The Action executes until it reaches a dialog, where it stops and waits for new input.
3. Change the values in the dialog and click **OK** to record them and continue execution, or click **Cancel** to retain the values and continue execution.

You can Record Again the values for a single step by double-clicking on it and entering new values in the dialog.

NOTE

Depending on the mode of an image, there are some commands that won't be available when you're recording. You can easily insert a command after recording an Action, but any value for inserted commands is not recorded.

To insert a menu item into an Action:

1. Select an item in an Action. The insertion will be made before this item.
2. Choose the **Insert Menu Item** command from the Palette menu. This displays a dialog.
3. Either choose a command from the menus, type a name into the field, or type a partial name and click on the **Find** button, then click **OK**.

A stop is different from a check point described above. Both cause the Action to pause, but while check points concern dialogs, stops show user-specified alerts. In either case, user response is required when an Action is interrupted

To insert a stop into an Action:

1. Select a step in an Action. The stop will be inserted after the selected step.
2. Choose the **Insert Stop** command from the palette menu.
3. In the Stop dialog (Figure 20.8), type in the message you wish to appear on screen as an alert when execution of the Action pauses. This will usually include instructions as to what to do at this point.

Figure 20.8 The Stop dialog lets you insert a message into an Action.

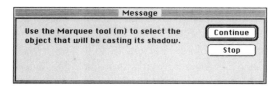

Figure 20.9 During execution, the Action pauses to display stop messages as alerts. Click **OK** and do as directed, then Click the **Play** button to continue execution.

4. Check the **Allow Continue** box to include a Continue button in the Stop dialog. This allows you to continue execution of the Action after a pause, essentially ignoring the stop alert, without the need to reclick the Play button.

5. Click **OK**.

NOTE If you select an Action title and insert a stop, it is appended to the bottom of the step stack. Drag the stop to insert it where it is needed.

BATCHING ACTIONS

One of the most useful time-saving features of Actions is that they can be executed on a batch of files with a single command (see Figure 20.10). If you know that every file you've created needs to be converted to CMYK mode for printing, execute the RGB to CMYK Action for the entire batch.

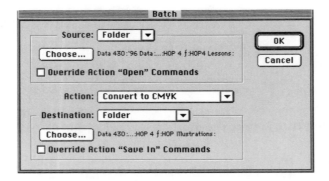

Figure 20.10 The Batch dialog has several options so that you can choose the source, pick an Action, and designate the output destination of a batched Action.

1. Choose the **Batch** command from the palette menu. All batch actions are executed from the Batch dialog. There are three sections:

   • **Source**—Choose either **Folder** or **Import** from the Source dropdown menu. For Folder, click on the **Choose** button and point to the folder containing the files to be batched. If the Action you are using contains Open commands, click on the **Override** check box to ignore them.

NOTE It may be necessary to move or copy files to a single folder before using the Batch dialog.

   If you choose **Import for the Source**, select an Input option from the dropdown box. These are the same as those listed in the Import submenu in the File menu.

   • **Action**—Choose the desired Action to be executed from the dropdown menu.

   • **Destination**—From the dropdown menu, choose **None**, **Save and Close**, or **Folder**. None leaves the images open. Save and Close writes the images back to their previous location. Folder allows you to save the changed images to a new location. Click the **Choose** button to specify a folder. Click in the check box to override any Save commands in the chosen Action.

2. Click **OK**. Photoshop opens each file in sequence and executes the chosen Action.

MANIPULATING ACTION SETS

The Actions listed in the palette are collectively known as an Action set. Sets can be saved and reloaded. It's possible to store sets for different purposes or to share Actions between machines and with other users. All commands for working with sets are in the Palette menu.

To clear the Actions palette:

1. Choose the **Clear Actions** command and confirm by clicking **OK** in the dialog. All actions are deleted and the Actions Palette is left empty.

To reset the Actions palette:

1. Choose the **Reset Actions** command.
2. Click **Confirm** in the dialog to restore the default list and delete all other Actions, or click **Append** to add the default list to the bottom of the current list.

To load an Action set:

1. Choose the **Load Actions** command from the palette menu.
2. Locate the file and click **Open**. The Actions in the set replace the current list of Actions in the palette.

To append an Action set:

1. Choose the **Append Actions** command from the Palette menu.
2. Locate the file and click **Open**. The Actions in the set are appended to the current list of Actions.

To save an Action set:

1. Choose the **Save Actions** command from the Palette menu
2. Give the set a name, pick a location, and click **Save**. All Actions in the current Palette are saved as a file.

 As with all Photoshop palettes and options, the current Action list is saved when you quit Photoshop and restored when you next launch.

N O T E

Lesson 20: Actions Explored

We'll exercise some of the options in the Actions palette and create an action to use for ourselves. Make sure the Actions palette is open before proceeding.

ACTION IN THE ACTIONS PALETTE

1. Choose **Load Actions** from the Actions Palette menu.

2. In the file dialog, find the Lesson20 folder on the CD and open the file **MOREACTI.ATN**.

3. Click **OK** and the actions are added to the bottom of the Actions palette. These actions, shown in Figure 20.11, have been furnished by Adobe and are also available from Adobe's Web site.

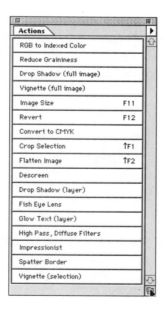

Figure 20.11 A lot of actions displayed in the default Button Mode. You can see that a couple of actions have been assigned Function and Shift-Function execution shortcuts.

The default display for the Actions palette is Button Mode. You can change the order of actions and the Action Options in this mode, but you can't see or edit the steps.

4. Click the **Button Mode** command in the palette menu to deselect it and toggle to List Mode.

5. Click on the **Size** box (the upper-right corner of the palette frame) to enlarge the Palette so that all the actions are visible.

    There is no way to sort actions except by dragging them around within the palette. We can try and put the list into some logical order.

6. Drag the Drop Shadow (layer) action so that it is just after the Drop Shadow (full image) Action (Figure 20.12). You can do the same with the Vignette (selection) and Vignette (full image) actions, but it should quickly become apparent that there really is no logical order to actions.

Figure 20.12 Dragging an Action to a new location is the only way to reorder the Action list.

For some, putting the most-used actions at the top will be most helpful. For others, alphabetical order will work, and there are always those who live best in the unordered world.

Let's take a closer look at a simple action.

7. Click on the triangle next to the Reduce Graininess action. This expands the action, and you can see that there are two steps.

8. Click on the triangle next to the Gaussian Blur step to expand it and reveal the option settings used for this command.

    We can see quite readily that executing this action applies two filters: a fairly small Gaussian Blur with a Radius of 0.5 and the Sharpen Edges filter. We'll change this action to allow manual setting of the Gaussian Blur filter.

9. Click in the second column of the Gaussian Blur step to toggle on the dialog switch. (Notice how the dialog icon also shows next to the action name. You can turn off all dialogs for an action from this box.) Now when you execute this action, the Gaussian Blur dialog is displayed and the action pauses so that you can change the options. Click **OK** in the dialog and the action proceeds.

AN ACTION OF OUR OWN

Remember the cast shadow we created in Lesson 17? We can turn the steps into an Action, and then we won't have to remember them all the next time we want to cast a shadow. I should warn you that this is a non-trivial action to record and requires a couple of manual insertions. But it points out both the strengths and shortcomings of this new feature.

If you'd like, try creating a trivial action first. For instance, I created an RGB to Grayscale action, because every screenshot in this book needed to be converted to grayscale for printing. It's a one-step action, but it allows me to skip the Flatten Image dialog every time.

1. Open the file **SNOW_DON.PSD** from the Lesson20 folder on the CD. We need to work from an image, and this one is fairly similar to the one we used in Lesson 17.

2. Click on the **New Action** button in the Actions palette.

3. Name the action **Cast Shadow (layer)**. Adobe has used the convention of putting action conditions in parentheses as part of the name. Since our action works on layers, we will follow Adobe's lead and say so in the name.

4. You don't need to set any other options, but I find it useful to use a color for all the actions I create. Then they stand out better in the palette.

5. Click **Record**. The new action is added to the bottom of the Actions palette, and the Record button is red to indicate that any commands we execute will be recorded. See Figure 20.13.

Figure 20.13 Naming an action according to Adobe's convention and choosing a color so that the action stands out in the palette.

Next, create an Action.

With the Record botton, follow these steps to create a cast shadow. You may find it helpful to watch what happens in the Actions palette as you execute each step. You may also want to refer to Lesson 17 if you have any trouble here.

To Create an Action:

1. Hold down the **Command/Ctrl** key and click on the **Donkey** layer in the Layers palette. This creates a transparency mask.

2. Click on the **Channels** tab, then click on the **Make Mask** button to create a new channel from the transparency mask.

3. Click on channel **#4** to select it, then click in the first column of the RGB channel to reveal the image beneath a rubylith mask.

4. Choose the **Distort** command from the Free Transform submenu in the Layers menu.

5. Adjust the distortion handles to cast a shadow away from the sun, then press the **Return/Enter** key.

6. Click in the first column next to channel #4 to deselect it.

7. Click on the **Layers** tab, then click on the Background layer to select it and cause the floating selection to become a part of the background.

8. Choose the **Gradient** tool (g), then click on the **Edit** button in the Options palette.

9. Set the gradient to **Foreground to Transparent**. Click on the **Transparency** radio button and set the left box to 90% and the right box to 50%. Click **OK**.

10. Drag a gradient from the forehoof of the donkey's shadow to the tip of his ear.

11. Press **Command/Ctrl-d** to drop the selection.

12. Click on the **Stop** button to end the recording in the Actions palette. Figure 20.14 shows the Action.

Figure 20.14 The Cast Shadow action as recorded in the Actions palette. You can see that all the steps were not recorded.

Editing an Action

Now we have to edit our Action, because, as you may have noticed, not all of the steps were recorded as we executed them. The twelve steps outlined above are only five steps in the recorded action.

To edit an Action:

1. Find the Revert action in the Actions palette, select it, and press the **Play** button to revert the Snow Donkey to its former pristine state. You can even drag the Revert action so that it's just above the Cast Shadow action, because we may need to use it again.

2. Select our new action by clicking on it, then click the **Play** button. Photoshop pauses so that you can confirm the creation of a new channel. This isn't necessary, so we'll turn off the dialog for this command later. For now, click **OK** and let the action continue.

    Unfortunately, our Distort and Gradient actions were not recorded, so our action does nothing but create a new channel. We have some manual editing to do to make this action work as we wish.

3. Click in the second column of the Duplicate step to turn off the dialog display (Figure 20.15).

Figure 20.15 Click in the second column to toggle off the dialog display for this step.

Now we need to add the Distort command, but where does it go?

4. Click on the triangles next to both Select steps. The first selects channel #4 and the second selects the Background layer. We want to insert the Distort command between these two.

5. Click on the first **Select** command, then choose the **Insert Menu Item** command from the palette menu, as shown in Figure 20.16.

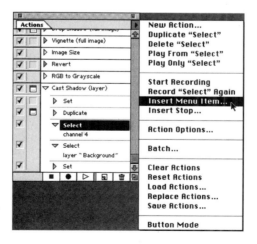

Figure 20.16 The two Select steps expanded to show what they are selecting. We can see that the missing Distort command should be between them, and we will add it by using the Insert Menu Item command.

6. You can either type the name of the command into the Insert Menu Item dialog (Figure 20.17) or choose the command directly from the Layer menu using the mouse, then click **OK**.

Figure 20.17 The Insert Menu Item dialog can either find and expand a name you type in or fill in the name if you make a choice using the mouse as we did here.

Since the Distort command requires user intervention to distort the selection, we need to add a stop.

7. Choose the **Insert Stop** command from the palette menu. Type instructions into the Stop dialog as indicated in Figure 20.18. Click **OK**. Notice that the show dialog icon is toggled on for the Stop step.

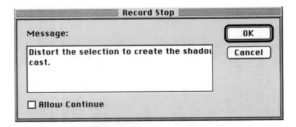

Figure 20.18 Type instructions into the Stop dialog so that you'll know what to do when execution of the action pauses.

Now we need to add another Stop after the Background selection step to allow for the gradient.

8. Click on the Select, layer Background, step, then choose the **Insert Stop** command, just as you did in the previous step of this lesson. Type in the message as indicated in Figure 20.19, then click **OK**.

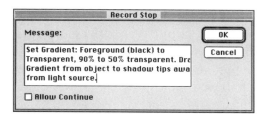

Figure 20.19 Another Stop step with very specific instructions to add a gradient.

This should do it. If you've made any changes to the image, choose the Revert action again and execute it.

9. Highlight the **Cast Shadow** action and click on the **Play** button. It should no longer stop to ask if we want to create a new channel. The Action will pause and display the first message we entered.

10. Click on the **Stop** button. The action increments to the next step and halts so that you can drag the handles of the distortion rectangle into place (Figure 20.20). You'll notice that the rubylith mask did not record as part of the action. It's a convenience, but not necessary. Don't forget to click **Return/Enter** to finish the distortion.

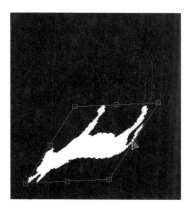

Figure 20.20 Dragging the distortion handles to cast the shadow. Since every cast shadow is different, it's impossible to automate this step.

11. Click on the **Play** button and the action resumes, then pauses again for the gradient.

12. Click the **Stop** button, then select the **Gradient** tool (g) and set the options. (The options are probably still set from before.) Drag to make the gradient in the selection.

13. Click on the **Play** button again, and the action finishes.

The Donkey and his shadow are saved in the Lesson20 folder as **SHADOW_D.PSD**. The Cast Shadow action, along with the RGB to Grayscale Action, are saved in the same folder as **L20ACTIO.ATN**.

Image Commands

In this section...

- Editing images
- Color and tonal correction
- Filters

MENU COMMANDS

Photoshop is extremely screen-oriented. It's not just the images you work on, but also its Toolbox and palettes that make the Photoshop experience more visual than other computer programs. Yet its computer heritage from the early days of the Macintosh is still evident and important. To be sure, many of the commands in the menus have palette-based equivalents, but there are still commands that are most easily accessed in the place we expect to find them—the menus.

Menu-based commands remain an important part of Photoshop. Everyday computing operations, like file commands for input and output, the standard Cut, Copy, and Paste editing commands, and program controls like preferences, have all remained menu-bound, and we'll discuss these in the next section. Some of the features that first made Photoshop so popular—the image commands and filters—are still fixed to the menu bar, as are the new Transform commands.

Editing Images

In this chapter...

- Cut, Copy, and Paste
- Buffers: Clipboard, Pattern, and Snapshot
- Rulers, Guides, and Grids
- Image/Canvas Size
- Image/Layer Transformations
- Edit Text

Everything you do in Photoshop can be summed up as editing images. But for the sake of simplicity, we gather a few specific commands under the editing rubric: those that are in the Edit menu, those that bear any similarity to editing in a word processing program, and a few others that don't fall conveniently elsewhere. It's not particularly scientific, but it has a certain undeniable logic to it.

CUT, COPY, AND PASTE

The classic Edit commands are Cut, Copy, and Paste—Command-x (Macintosh) or Ctrl-x (Windows), Command-c (Macintosh) or Ctrl-c (Windows), and Command-v (Macintosh) or Ctrl-v (Windows) respectively. These work about as you would expect. Cut and Copy require a selection to be active, while Paste requires a loaded Clipboard. These commands work with the actual pixels of the image and cannot be used to alter selection marquees, as explained in Chapter 12.

To cut a selection from an image:

1. Make a selection.

2. Choose **Cut**, **Command-x** (Macintosh) or **Ctrl-x** (Windows), from the Edit menu.

3. The selection is removed from the image and placed on the Clipboard. If the selection is cut from a Background layer, the void is filled with the current background color. If the selection is cut from another layer, the void is left transparent.

To cut without copying to the Clipboard, use the **Edit Clear** command, or press the **Delete** key (Macintosh) or **Backspace** key (Windows).

To copy a selection from an image:

1. Make a selection.

2. Choose **Copy**, **Command/Ctrl-c**, from the Edit menu.

3. The selection is copied to the Clipboard, and the image and selection are left unchanged.

To copy everything selected through all layers, use the **Edit Copy Merged** command, **Shift-Command/Ctrl-c**. There must be something on the Clipboard for the Paste command to be available.

To copy a selection into an image using paste:

1. Choose the image you want to paste into.

2. Choose **Paste**, **Command/Ctrl-v**, from the Edit menu.

Photoshop either copies the contents of the Clipboard into another part of the image or pastes the contents into the center of another image as a new layer.

Choose **Paste Into** from the Edit menu to copy into another selection. This turns the destination selection into a layer mask for the copied source. Layer masks are discussed in Chapter 16. Figures 21.1–21.4 show a sequence of screen shots demonstrating the steps of the Paste Into command.

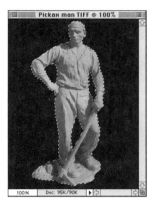

Figure 21.1 The target selection.

Figure 21.2 The copy source.

Figure 21.3 The image after executing
the Paste Into command.

Figure 21.4 The Layers palette for the finished
image with the resulting Layer mask.

NOTE The resolution of the pasted image is maintained. This means that if the source and target have different resolutions, the pasted image may appear larger or smaller than expected. Use the Image Size command, discussed later in this chapter, to match resolutions.

Copying from Another Application into Photoshop

As discussed in the next section, Photoshop shares the Clipboard with all other applications running on your system. It's possible to copy images from other applications and paste them into Photoshop and vice versa. Artwork can be rasterized or turned into Paths if the source is a vector-based program like Illustrator.

The Paste dialog will automatically open if the contents of the Clipboard is vector data. Choose either **Paste As Pixels** or **Paste As Paths**. The former is rasterized by Photoshop and will be anti-aliased if the check box is selected (see Figure 21.5).

Figure 21.5 The Paste dialog pops up automatically when you try to paste from a vector-based program into a Photoshop image. You can convert the contents of the Clipboard to pixels, anti-aliased pixels, or paths.

Pasting between applications is a function of the operating system in use. When exporting Clipboard data, Photoshop automatically converts information to bitmap format so that other applications can use it. This can be turned off using the preferences discussed in Chapter 27.

It's also possible to move or copy selections by dragging (This is described in Chapter 12). Dragging between applications is a function of the operating system and depends on application compliance to Macintosh Drag and Drop or Windows OLE support.

Matting a Moved or Pasted Selection

It is the nature of anti-aliased selections, or selections of irregularly-shaped objects on textured backgrounds, that some extra pixels will be picked up along the way. To hide these pixels, Photoshop includes the Matting submenu of three commands at the bottom of the Layer menu. (It's in the Layer menu, because when you copy or paste, it usually ends up in a new layer.)

To matte a moved or pasted section, select the layer with the floating selection that contains the offending copy.

If the pasted image includes a sort of halo of its old background, choose the **Defringe** command. This replaces the color of any "fringe" pixels with a color from an inner neighbor. A Defringe value of 1 or 2 pixels is sufficient for most images.

If the pasted image was an anti-aliased selection made from a black or white background, choose either the **Remove White** or **Remove Black** command. These locate any fringe pixels that are white or black and remove any ghosting effect. See Figures 21.6 and 21.7.

Figures 21.6 and 21.7 In Figure 21.6 (left), an anti-aliased selection has been pasted, and bits of the white background have come along for the ride. In 21.7 (right), the layer matting, Remove White Matte command has been used to remove the unwanted white border around the duck.

BUFFERS: CLIPBOARD, PATTERNS, AND SNAPSHOT

When you cut or copy, or when you create a pattern or Snapshot, Photoshop needs to store the information somewhere. There are three separate buffers set aside for this purpose. While these buffers behave similarly, their purposes remain distinct.

There is also a fourth buffer maintained for the Edit Undo command, Command/Ctrl-z. Almost any Photoshop command can be reversed by using the Undo command, but only the last operation is saved in the Undo buffer.

What about Clipboards?

You'll probably find that drag and drop techniques have gained ascendancy over the use of the Cut, Copy, and Paste commands. But there are still times when it's most convenient to use the Clipboard. This is especially true when working with other programs to make copies or when image windows become hidden one under another.

The Clipboard is a function of the operating system. Unless you have installed a utility to expand the built-in Clipboard functionality of your system, Photoshop has access to a single Clipboard. Anything you copy to the Clipboard replaces any contents that was there before it.

Since system memory is allotted to store the contents of the Clipboard, the size of the clipboard is limited. But this varies according to your system. Be aware that it is possible to copy an area that is too large for the Clipboard and that there are occasions when the Clipboard is unable to convert its contents when switching between applications. In situations like these, use a workaround to either reduce the size of the selection or to use the file system instead of the Clipboard.

Whence Patterns?

You use patterns with the Rubber Stamp tool (s) (discussed in Chapter 6) or the Edit Fill command. But where do patterns come from?

When you invoke the Define Pattern command from the Edit menu, Photoshop makes a copy of the current rectangular selection and saves it in the pattern buffer (one of two internal clipboards maintained by Photoshop). Information in the Pattern buffer can be used only by the Rubber Stamp Tool and with the Edit Fill command. Like a clipboard, the copied selection remains in the buffer until you define another Pattern or until you quit Photoshop. There is only one pattern buffer.

Why Snapshots?

Photoshop's Snapshot feature provides a kind of selective undo. Unlike the Pattern buffer, every open image has its own Snapshot buffer. But you can't use the Snapshot from one image for another image.

Snapshopts are only used with the Rubber Stamp tool discussed in Chapter 6. You can save a single layer by using the Edit Take Snapshot command or an entire image by using the Edit Take Merged Snapshot command. Then after you change the image, you can selectively restore the saved copy by painting it back in with the Rubber Stamp tool.

When to Purge?

It's sometimes possible to use up so much memory with one of these buffers that Photoshop cannot execute any further commands. To free up buffer memory so that Photoshop can proceed, there is a Purge command; choose **Purge** from the Edit menu and slide the mouse to select one of four buffers from the Purge submenu.

You can selectively Purge the Undo, Clipboard, Pattern, or Snapshot buffer this way. There is no Undo for the Purge command, shown in Figure 21.8.

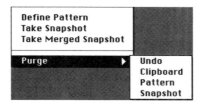

Figure 21.8 You can selectively empty the Undo, Clipboard, Pattern, or Snapshot buffer by choosing one of the Purge commands to free up memory. This bottom end of the Edit menu also includes the Pattern and Snapshot commands.

Rulers, Guides, and Grids

Guides and grids are new features in Photoshop 4 that extend the capabilities of rulers. These features are used to help guide your work and in no way affect the pixels of an image. Rulers, Guides, and Grids are controlled from the View menu. They are maintained separately for every image window and are saved with the image.

Using Rulers

When you turn on rulers for an image, a scale is placed on the top and left sides of the window. You can change the units and zero point of the rulers.

To hide/show rulers, choose **Hide/Show Rulers** from the View menu. As the default, both vertical and horizontal rulers begin in the upper-left corner of the window at zero.

This can be changed for each image window individually.

To change the zero origin:

- Move the pointer into the upper left corner at the intersection of the ruler scales. Click and drag into the image. Guidelines follow the pointer as you drag to indicate the new origin. Release the mouse button and the zero point on the rulers is moved.
- Hold down the **Shift** key as you drag to snap the zero origin to ruler ticks.
- Choose **Snap to Guides** or **Snap to Grid** in the View menu to have the zero origin snap to the Guide or Grid as you drag.

To reset the zero origin to its default:

- Move the pointer into the upper-left corner at the intersection of the ruler scales and double-click. The zero origins are reset.

To change ruler settings:

- Double-click on a ruler to open the Units & Rulers Preferences dialog or choose **Preferences** from the File menu. The Preferences dialog lets you change the units, column size, and point/pica size and is discussed in Chapter 27.

Changing the units in the Info palette also changes the ruler units.

NOTE

Using Guides and Creating Grids

Many programs include guide and grid features. Version 4 introduces these features to Photoshop. Guides are lines that float above the image and are used to align objects (or in any way you may find a guide helpful). Guidelines are not printable. Grids, when showing, display a regular array of guidelines that can be used for numerous layout functions.

You can use guides and grids for visual alignment, or you can turn on a snap feature for either or both. Selections, selection borders, and tools snap to a guide or grid when dragged within eight screen pixels of a visible guideline.

Like rulers, the setting of guides is image-specific. Grids are set in the Preferences dialog and while their function is image-specific, their specifications are global. Preferences are set in the Guides & Grid Preferences dialog discussed in Chapter 27.

Rulers must be showing to place a guide. To place the guide, drag from either ruler into the image. A vertical or horizontal guideline, depending on which ruler you dragged from, follows the pointer until you release the mouse button to set the guide. Hold down the **Shift** key while dragging to snap guides to ruler ticks or a visible grid line (see Figure 21.9).

Figure 21.9 Creating or moving a guide amounts to the same thing. To create a new guide, drag from the ruler. To move a guide, use the Move tool (v) and drag. To delete a guide, drag it off the image.

To move a guide:

1. Choose the **Move** tool (v) from the Toolbox.
2. Put the pointer over a guideline. The pointer turns into a double-headed arrow.
3. Click and drag to a new position. Hold down the **Shift** key while dragging to snap guides to ruler ticks or a visible grid line.

By holding down **Option/Alt** and clicking or dragging on a guide, it is converted from a horizontal to vertical guide or vice versa. You can also Option/Alt double-click on a guide to open the Guide and Grids preferences dialog.

N O T E

To remove guides:

*   Drag a guide completely off the image to remove it, or
*   Choose **Clear Guides** from the View menu to remove all guides from an image.

There are four Guide commands in the View menu:

- **Show/Hide Guides** (Command/Ctrl-;) makes guides visible or invisible.
- **Snap To Guides** (Shift-Command/Ctrl-;) turns snapping on or off.
- **Lock/Unlock Guides** (Option/Alt-Command/Ctrl-;) locks or unlocks all guides so that they cannot or can be moved.
- **Clear Guides** removes all guides from the active image window.

The Grid

While grid specifications are set in the Guides & Grid Preferences dialog, they are controlled for each image from the View menu. Only a regularly-spaced rectangular grid can be defined.

- Choose **Show Grid** from the View menu to turn the grid on by making the grid guidelines visible, as shown in Figure 21.10.

Figure 21.10 The default grid with major grid lines every inch and minor lines every quarter inch.

- Choose **Snap to Grid** to turn the snap feature on.

Both commands toggle between on and off—Show changes to Hide, and Snap is either checked or unchecked.

IMAGE AND CANVAS SIZE

As discussed in Chapter 2, the "size" of an image is determined by three dimensions: height, width, and pixel depth or resolution. The product of these three measurements equals the image or file size in bits. The physical size of the canvas is determined by the first two dimensions alone. Image and canvas size can be adjusted at any time using the Image Size and Canvas Size commands in the Image menu.

The Image Size Command

Choose **Image Size** from the Image menu to open the Image Size dialog. There are two dimension areas, Pixel Dimensions and Print Size, and two check boxes. You can type a new value into any dimension field to change the image size. Sizes can be measured in units or percentages. Percentages make it easy to cut the size of an image in half rather than specifying an exact dimension.

The two Pixel Dimensions fields, Width and Height, show the number of pixels in the image. The product of Width and Height is the total image size in pixels. Multiply this by the number of channels and divide by 1024 to calculate file size.

Pixel dimensions can be adjusted by typing in a new value in pixels or percents. Hold down the dropdown box next to the value field to set the units.

As mentioned before, there are three dimensions to Print Size. Width and Height can be set by percent, inches, cm, points, picas, and columns as determined by the dropdown box next to each value field. Resolution can be set to pixels/inch or pixels/cm. The product of Width, Height, and Resolution squared is approximately equal to the total print file size in pixels (approximate, because Photoshop rounds off dimensions in the value fields to thousandths). Figure 21.11 shows the Image Size dialog.

Use either area to change the dimensions of an image. Changes in one area are updated in the other. You can also assure that changes in one dimension are reflected in every dimension so that the image aspect ratio is maintained.

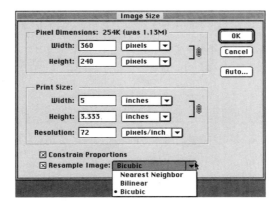

Figure 21.11 An image that is being sampled down: the file size will be reduced to 254K from 1.13M. The Resample Image dropdown menu is open, showing the choice of three interpolation algorithms (bicubic is the default and generally the best choice).

To maintain image proportions, click on the **Constrain Proportions** check box to maintain the aspect ratio of the image dimensions. This is the default. With the box checked, link icons appear next to both Width and Height fields to indicate that changing one changes the other proportionally.

When Constrain Proportions is not checked, no dimensions are linked. This will cause image distortion, because one dimension must be stretched or squeezed when the aspect ratio is changed.

To change dimensions without changing file size, click on the **Resample Image** check box to allow resampling. This is the default. Resampling results when the file size on disk is altered because pixels are either being lost or gained.

There are three resampling methods: Nearest Neighbor (the fastest but lowest quality), Bilinear (a compromise for speed and quality), and Bicubic (the most sophisticated and the default). Choose a method from the dropdown menu next to the Resample check box.

When the Resample Image box is not checked, the Resolution field is linked along with all other dimension fields. Changing one value changes all values to preserve file size and prevent resampling.

The current file size and resampled file size are displayed next to the Pixel Dimensions title.

To have Photoshop resample for you, click on the **Auto** button in the Image Size dialog. Fill in the Screen Frequency you intend to use for printing the image. Click on one of the Quality radio buttons: Draft, Good, or Best. Photoshop resamples without changing the physical dimensions of the image (Figure 21.12).

Figure 21.12 If you know the print specifications you'll be using for an image, you can enter the information yourself. Photoshop picks the appropriate resolution for the job and resamples the image accordingly.

It is generally not a good idea to sample up. It's better to rescan the image at a higher resolution. I often use the New File dialog to calculate the required file size, then set the scan accordingly.

If you hold down the **Option/Alt** key, the Cancel button changes to Reset. Click on the **Reset** button to set the image size back to its original dimensions while keeping the dialog open.

The Canvas Size Command

As explained above, *Canvas Size* refers to the physical dimensions of the image, regardless of resolution—the size at which it will be printed. You can expand or contract the dimensions without changing the pixels in the image or the resolution. This is useful if you want to add an extra background around an image or combine two images into one larger image.

The Canvas Size command does not resample the image. It will crop the image if the new size is smaller than the old, and it will fill any additional canvas area with the background color. You can specify how to center or justify the existing image within the new canvas area (Figure 21.13), but, except for cropping, the size of the image within the new canvas area is unchanged.

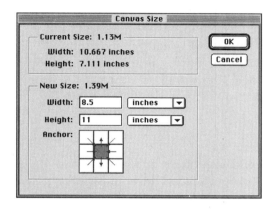

Figure 21.13 The Canvas Size dialog. In this instance, the new canvas is larger in one dimension and smaller in the other. The arrows in the Anchor diagram indicate where the image will be cropped and where there will be extra space around it.

To change the Canvas Size:

1. Choose **Canvas Size** from the Image menu. There are two areas in the dialog, Current Size and New Size. Both show the size and dimensions before and after.

2. Enter the new dimensions for Width and Height, setting the units as necessary.

3. The Anchor diagram lets you set the orientation of the old image within the new canvas size. You can justify to either side or center, horizontally or vertically. This results in a nine-position matrix. Click on one of the matrix squares to set the position of the image within the new canvas. Outward pointing arrows indicate that the canvas has expanded in this direction, while inward facing arrows indicate where cropping will occur.

4. Click **OK**. Confirm any crops.

IMAGE/LAYER TRANSFORMATION

Doesn't the idea of transformation sound wonderful? You can just imagine that this new command in version 4 is the answer to all your image needs. But what's being transformed here? Transform lets you change the shape and orientation of an image instead of the color value of pixels as do the Image commands discussed in Chapter 22.

The process of transforming images requires a lot of algorithmic image processing and can involve pixel interpolation to resample areas where pixels have been transformed. Photoshop uses the default resampling method set in the Preferences dialog. This is discussed earlier in this chapter and in Chapter 27.

As you work with layers and transformations, it's possible to have pixels that extend beyond the boundaries of the visible image window. This makes it possible to make adjustments that fall outside the canvas without losing information. However, any pixels beyond the canvas border are out of reach of any image or filter modifications that you make, and they are lost completely if you collapse layers. Use the Canvas Size command to alter the canvas border to include these "invisible" pixels.

There are three ways to transform an image: the Rotate Canvas submenu in the Image menu works on the whole image, and the Free Transform command and Transform submenu in the Layer menu that work on single layers. We'll start with the Image command, which is not a new feature.

Transformations cannot be made to the Background layer, but they can be used on selections in the Background layer. They can also be used with alpha channels and layer masks.

Rotating or Flipping an Entire Image

The Rotate Canvas submenu in the Image menu contains four rotation commands and two flip commands. Each of them affects the entire image.

- 180° rotates the canvas halfway around a circle, head-over-heels.
- **90° CW** rotates the image a quarter turn clockwise.
- **90° CCW** rotates the image a quarter turn counterclockwise.
- **Arbitrary** lets you enter any value in degrees and choose to rotate clockwise or counterclockwise.
- **Flip Horizontal** flips the image across the vertical axis.
- **Flip Vertical** flips the image across the horizontal axis.

Figures 21.14–21.16 show an image in various stages of rotation and/or flipping.

Figure 21.14 The original image.

Figure 21.15 The image flipped horizontally.

Figure 21.16 The image flipped vertically.

Using the Transform Commands

The Layer Transform submenu contains 11 commands in four groups. The bottom five (Rotate 180°, Rotate 90° CW, Rotate 90° CCW, Flip Horizontal, and Flip Vertical) are identical to the commands in the Image Rotate Canvas command, except that they affect layers or selections rather than the entire image. The first six commands involve some serious transformations.

The first group of five (Scale, Rotate, Skew, Distort, and Perspective) share the same controls. Invoking any of these commands surrounds the layer or selection with an eight-handled distortion marquee. Moving the pointer over one of the handles turns the icon into a two-headed arrow that indicates that you can move the handle in or out. Or the pointer turns into a white-headed arrow to indicate that the handle can be dragged linearly. Move the pointer inside the marquee, and you can drag the selection with its contents. Move the pointer outside the marquee, and it turns into a curved, two-headed arrow that indicates that you can freely rotate the selection. The exact distortion movements of the control points and marquee depends on the command chosen.

- **Scale** (Figure 21.17) allows you to move side control points in two directions and corner control points in any direction. Hold down the **Shift** key to maintain the aspect ratio of the selection as you drag corner points. Hold down the **Option/Alt** key and the opposite control moves simultaneously in the opposite direction of the point you're dragging. You can use this to flip an image arbitrarily. You cannot rotate while scaling.

Figure 21.17 Scale allows you to change the size of a selection or layer proportionally.

- **Rotate** (Figure 21.18) allows selection rotation, but not scaling. Move the pointer anywhere outside the marquee and rotate in a clockwise or counterclockwise direction. You can also move the marquee by putting the pointer inside it and dragging. Hold down the **Shift** key while rotating to constrain rotations to 15° increments.

Figure 21.18 Rotate allows you to rotate a selection or layer freely by dragging.

- **Skew** (Figure 21.19) moves handles in the axis of the line they are a part of. For corners, you can move the direction of one line or the other, but not both. The pointer turns to a white-headed pointer over corner handles and to a white-headed pointer with a double-headed arrow on side handles. Where the Scale command allows handles to be dragged perpendicular to the direction of the line, Skew moves handles in the same axis as the line. This changes the corner angles as you drag and thus skews the selection. Holding down the **Option/Alt** key while skewing switches to Perspective instead of Skew.

Figure 21.19 Skew allows you to pull or push a handle in one direction as if you were leaning against the marquee.

- **Distort** (Figure 21.20) uses only white-headed pointers and lets you move handles at any angle. This is the least constrained and most distorting of all the Transform commands. Holding down the **Shift** key while dragging a corner handle constrains the drag to the Skew angle. Holding down the **Option/Alt** key while dragging a side handle moves the opposite handle simultaneously.

Figure 21.20 Distort lets you move any handle in any direction. It's the most distorting of the Transform commands.

- **Perspective** (Figure 21.21) skews while keeping lines parallel. The corner angles change, but opposite angles remain congruent. Holding down the **Option/Alt** key while dragging a side handle causes the opposite handle to move simultaneously in the opposite direction.

Figure 21.21 Perspective lets you drag parallel handles, creating a forced perspective-like effect.

With this first group of Transform commands you can switch from one to another while executing the transformation. While the eight-handled marquee is active, select another of this group from the Transform submenu and continue transforming. The transformation is not executed until you press the **Return** key (Macintosh) or **Enter** key (Windows).

Numerical Transformations

To make numerical transformations, choose the **Numeric** command, **Shift-Command/Ctrl-t**, from the Transform submenu.

You can Scale, Skew, Rotate, and move a selection all at once using numerical values entered in the Numeric Transformation dialog.

Each of the four functions has a check box. Click to turn the function on or off.

- **Position**—Enter values for the X and Y coordinates. Choose the scale from the dropdown box next to the value field. Click in the **Relative** check box to move relative to the current position. Deselect the check box to enter absolute coordinates for the move.

- **Scale**—Enter a Width and Height value in units or percents. Click in the **Constrain Proportions** check box to link the width and height and maintain the selection aspect ratio.

- **Skew**—Enter an amount in degrees for Horizontal and Vertical skew.

- **Rotate**—Enter an Angle amount in degrees or drag the circle around to choose a rotation.

As with all dialogs, click **OK** to execute the transformations (see Figure 21.22).

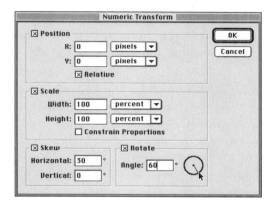

Figure 21.22 The Numerical Transform dialog lets you enter values for three simultaneous transformations and move the selection marquee with its contents.

EDITING TEXT SPACING

Once text has left the Text dialog and is entered as a layer or type mask, it is still possible to edit the letter spacing and leading. However, this has nothing to do with any special text handling capabilities on Photoshop's part. You use the standard selection tools and drag the letters around like any other selection.

Select characters using the **Lasso** tool (l) or **Magic Wand** tool (w). Make sure you get the whole character. Subtract from or add to the selection by holding down the **Shift** or **Option/Alt** keys while selecting. Use the **Move** tool (v) or hold down the **Command/Ctrl** key to move letters around. Use the **Move** tool in combination with the **Arrow** or **Shift-Arrow** keys to move text selections in 1 or 10 pixel increments in any direction.

Lesson 21: The Big Top

I have an assignment to create a circus logo for my sons' school. My wife has supplied me with an elephant drawing, and I have put together some text in Adobe Illustrator. Let's put drawing and text together and see what we get.

1. Open the file **BIGTOPO.AI** from the Lesson21 folder on the CD. The format for opening this file is Generic EPS, which Photoshop should recognize automatically. This text was converted to outlines within Illustrator, because Photoshop's rasterizer has a hard time with the text on curves I used in this sample.

    In case you're interested, the typeface used here is Adobe's Multiple Master face, Jimbo. It seemed only appropriate for use with Jumbo, as you'll see.

2. In the Generic EPS Rasterizer dialog used to import Illustrator files (see Figure 21.23), set the resolution to 200 pixels/inch, because I'll be sending this file to an imagesetter for separations. Leave the other settings where they are and click **OK**. The file opens as a single layer of anti-aliased text with a transparent background.

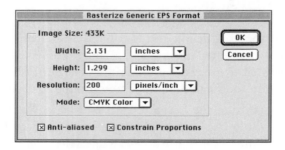

Figure 21.23 Since Illustrator files specifically and EPS files in general are resolution-independent, you have the option of telling Photoshop what size to make the image. This does not affect the clarity of the image.

3. Open the file **ELEPHANT.TIF** from the Lesson21 folder on the CD. This is a scan I made of the original drawing. Since I can never remember which way to put the original in the scanner, we'll need to flip this one over.

4. Choose **180°** from the Rotate Canvas submenu of the Image menu to put this elephant on its feet.

I happen to know that this elephant was scanned at 200 pixels/inch, and so it matches the text image. But it's too big to fit with the text, so we'll have to resample it.

5. Choose **Image Size** from the Image menu (Figure 21.24). The default settings in the Image Size dialog, with the two check boxes selected, is what we want. Set the Width to 3 inches and the Height is adjusted proportionally. Click **OK** and the image is resampled downward.Information is discarded and the file shrinks.

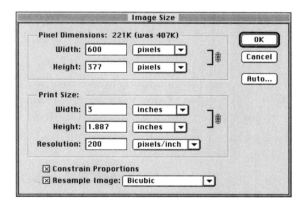

Figure 21.24 The Image Size dialog lets you change the size of the image. Here, the Width and Height are linked by selecting the Constrain Proportions check box. Resampling is also checked, so making the width smaller will resample the image downward.

Now we need to combine the two images into a single image, but neither is large enough to hold the other, so we need to enlarge the canvas size. But how much bigger?

6. Click on the **Big Top Outlines** window to select it. (Choose the image name from the Window menu if it isn't visible.) Hold down the **Option** key (Macintosh) or **Alt** key (Windows) and click on the file information area in the lower left side of the window frame. This tells us that we'll need at least another 1.3 inches to fit the text under the elephant (see Figure 21.25). We'll add a little extra to make sure we have room to play.

Figure 21.25 Option/Alt click on the info area of the window to show the size statistics for the image.

7. While we're in the Big Top window, choose **All** from the Select menu, **Command/Ctrl-a**, then choose **Copy** from the Edit menu, **Command/Ctrl-c**. We'll just leave this copy on the Clipboard until we need it.

8. Click on the **Elephant Scan** window to select it, and choose the **Canvas Size** command from the Image menu.

9. In the Canvas Size dialog shown in Figure 21.26, change the Height to 3.25 (1.885+1.3+a margin of error), and click to move the anchor to the top middle square. Click **OK**.

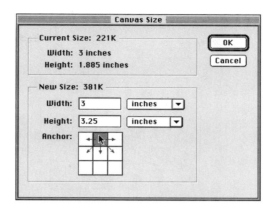

Figure 21.26 We're using the Canvas Size dialog to enlarge the image window and put the Elephant scan at the top, so that there is room to copy the text into the bottom.

10. Choose **Paste** from the Edit menu, **Command/Ctrl-v**. This copies our text into the middle of the Elephant window, but horrors! Everything is grayscale. We forgot that both images need to be in CMYK mode.

11. Choose **Undo** from the Edit menu, **Command/Ctrl-z**, then choose **CMYK Color** from the Mode submenu of the Image menu. Notice that this quadruples the image size. (The saved size is a bit smaller due to Photoshop's compression scheme.)

12. Now repeat step 10 to paste the text into the Elephant window. The text is still on the Clipboard and in comes in as a new layer.

13. Select the **Move** tool (v) or hold down the **Command/Ctrl** key and drag the text layer so that it fits neatly under the elephant. Make sure that layer 1 is the target layer and that you hold down the **Shift** key as you drag to constrain the move and center the text in the image.

Figure 21.27 Dragging the text under the dainty foot of the elephant, while holding down the Shift key to keep the text centered.

Even though this text came from Illustrator, we can edit it like any other text in Photoshop. But first, we'll rotate this pachyderm a little less precariously onto his perch.

14. Click on the Background layer in the Layers Palette to make it the target. If the Layers palette isn't visible, choose **Show Layers** in the Window menu. Unfortunately, we can't transform a Background layer.

15. Double-click on the Background layer or choose **Layer Options** from the Palette menu. Changing the name to the default suggestion, Layer 0, is all we need to do, so click **OK**.

16. Choose **Rotate** from the Transform submenu of the Layer menu. The Transform marquee surrounds the entire layer. Move the pointer near to one of the corners and rotate clockwise until the elephant's back foot rests comfortably on the E, as shown in Figure 21.28. Wait a moment for the calculations to finish and the preview to draw, then make finer adjustments or click the **Return** key (Macintosh) or **Enter** key (Windows) to accept the rotation.

Figure 21.28 Using the Transform command to rotate the elephant layer so that the elephant's feet balance on the text. The checkerboard pattern revealed by the rotation indicates transparent pixels under Layer 0, the layer we're rotating.

You'll notice that we've chopped the elephant's head off. This is one of those occasions when a layer contains more information than the image can show. It's still there, it's just not visible.

17. In the Layers palette, click on the link box for **Layer 1** (Figure 21.29). Now the two layers are linked and we can move them together.

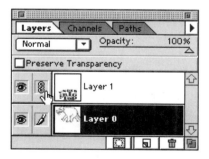

Figure 21.29 Linking the two layers in the Layers palette so that they can be moved together.

18. The Move tool (v) should still be chosen from Step 13. Put the pointer in the image, press the mouse button, and drag so that the elephant's head and tail are back on the canvas. That extra space we left at the bottom of the canvas has come in handy.

Now we will transform the type one letter at a time. We'll use the Magic

Wand to make selections. It's a good idea to save your image before we start transforming the text.

19. Click on **Layer 1** in the Layers palette to make it the target layer, then double-click on the Magic Wand tool to select it and open its Options palette. Make sure that the Anti-aliased box is not checked.

20. Click on the **G** in BIG to select it, then choose **Distort** from the Transform submenu in the Layer menu. Drag as indicated in Figure 21.30 to distort the G. Wait a moment to give Photoshop time to calculate the preview. Continue distorting or click **Return** (Macintosh) or **Enter** (Windows) to finish the distortion.

21. Repeat step 20 for the B.

22. Click on the **I** to select it, then choose **Perspective** from the Transform submenu in the Layer menu. Drag one of the bottom corner handles inward to make the base of the I smaller. Drag one of the top corner handles outward to make the cap of the I larger. Drag the bottom center handle to the right and the top center handle to the left to skew the I. Press **Return/Enter** to complete the transformation, as shown in Figure 21.31.

Figure 21.30 Distorting the G by dragging one of the handles.

Figure 21.31 Applying perspective to the I. First make the base smaller, the top larger, and here drag the center handle to the side to skew the perspective.

This does not complete my project. This elephant is more of a sketch than a final drawing, and I might use some patterns in the letters. But it does complete the lesson. Open the file **BIG_TOPL.PSD** from the Lesson21 folder on disk to see a completed version of this lesson.

CHAPTER

Color and Tonal Correction

In this chapter…

- The correction process
- Introduction to Levels and Curves
- Levels
- Curves
- More general color correction tools
- Special-purpose image commands

Photoshop's image tricks and special effects are great fun, but the hard work of making tonal and color corrections is equally important. Most of this work is accomplished from the Adjust submenu of the Image menu. The commands and dialogs used to make these corrections may at first appear daunting—so full of variables that it's hard to know where to begin, how to proceed, or where it ever ends.

Fear not! The apparent complexity is a natural byproduct of the inherent inaccuracies of color reproduction. The result is a multiplicity of systems to achieve the unachievable: perfect color. The Adjust submenu includes commands for making very fine color corrections; Levels and Curves; and others for making more general corrections; Color Balance; Brightness/Contrast; and Hue/Saturation. The latter rely on eyeballing, while the former give precise control and remove much of the guesswork of color correction.

NOTE Any of the commands in the Adjust submenu can be used with an Adjustment layer (discussed in Chapter 15) to try them out before applying the changes.

THE CORRECTION PROCESS

Color correction used to be a high-end art that only those with access to drum scanners or familiar with the intricacies of the printing process ventured into. Photoshop has made us all high-end artisans. In order to apply these formerly esoteric procedures to our own artwork, we need to have an orderly approach. Fortunately, Adobe has given it to us.

One of the best new features of Photoshop 4 isn't listed on any of the product sheets. It is a completely new chapter called "Making Color and Tonal Adjustments," Chapter 6 in the *User Guide*. It's as important that you read through this chapter as it is the previous chapter on calibration. In fact, the first step in the process is calibration.

I'll summarize the steps here for those who have already read the chapter in the Photoshop *User Guide* and are just looking for a refresher.

Step 1: Calibration

Before you start working on any images, you must calibrate your monitor. Without this, the possibility of reproducing accurate color is near nil. If you don't care about accurate color, then step blindly forward into the abyss.

Follow the instructions in Chapter 5 of the Photoshop *User Guide* to set up your monitor and the File Color Settings parameters in Photoshop. You'll also need to print a CMYK calibration image on the color printer you'll be using to make the final monitor adjustments. If you work with a printer or prepress house, take the test image to them and have them print it.

Remember, changing a variable in the color balance requires recalibration. Monitors and printers are only part of the color picture. Room light, the background pattern on your monitor, even reflected color from the clothes you wear can affect the way colors look.

Step 2: Checking Scan Quality—Histogram

Whether you make the scan yourself or acquire the image from an outside source, it's important that the image have sufficient pixel detail to work with. Photoshop's Histogram command gives you a quantitative evaluation of scan quality.

With any image, choose the **Histogram** command in the Image menu. The Histogram window (it's not a dialog, because it accepts no user input) graphs the number of pixels of each value for each channel in your image, plus a count for luminosity (see Figure 22.1). You can view each histogram by selecting it from the Channel dropdown menu. The histogram can show you at a glance where the pixel values are skewed and give you some idea of how much work it will be to bring them into reasonable balance.

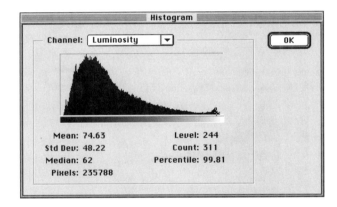

Figure 22.1 The Histogram shows the number of pixels for each color or luminosity value. There are also statistics for the overall image or any level you point to in the Histogram.

 When used with an active selection, the Histogram gives statistics only for the selected area.

N O T E

Of course, you can tell by looking at an image if it "looks good" or not. But the histogram gives you graphic evidence. It also supplies statistics on the mean and median pixel values and the standard deviation. If you move the pointer into the histogram, it also gives you a read-out of how many pixels there are at the level you're pointing to.

From the Histogram, you can determine the "key type" of the image. If the histogram shows that detail is concentrated in the shadows or darker end of the scale, the type is said to be "low-key." With pixels concentrated at the lighter, highlight end, the type is "high-key." You can use this information to guide later color corrections.

Step 3: Setting Highlight and Shadow Values—Levels

The object of this step is to find the areas of the image that are representative highlights and shadows, not the blackest or whitest spots, and to set target values for these. You use the eyedroppers to sample the image and set the target values. By looking at the readouts in the Info Palette, you can find the best areas and even get some quantitative feedback on setting the target values. See Figure 22.2.

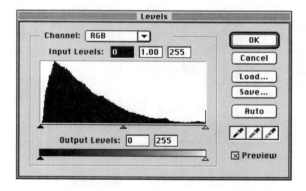

Figure 22.2 The Levels dialog, showing the composite channel for a high-key image. While the histogram pictured in the Levels dialog is for the same image as for that in Figure 22.1, the composite channel values are not the same as the Luminance values in the previous figure.

For instance, if you move the eyedropper over an area of the image that should be white, and the Info Palette shows that instead it is 255 red, 240 green, and 225 blue, you average the values and set the target to 240, 240, 240, instead of the 244 recommended as the standard highlight value.

If you're wondering why we don't just use the Auto Levels command every time instead of fiddling with these details, it's because the assumptions this command makes only work well on average-key images. Setting the Auto Levels options can help, but in most cases, this is a manual process.

Eliminating unwanted color casts is a separate task from setting the highlight and shadow levels. This step uses only the composite channel.

You can set the midtones, also known as *gamma*, using the Levels dialog, but it's more difficult to pinpoint a midpoint than the highlights or shadows. So this becomes the next step.

Step 4: Adjusting Midtones—Curves

You may find that this step isn't needed for average-key images. Adjusting the shadows and highlights often adjusts the midtones as much as is needed. But how often do you get perfect input? As mentioned above, you can use the Midtone slider and the input and output levels to improve the midtones and contrast, but the Curves dialog gives much more precise control.

The key to successful use of the Curves dialog (Figure 22.3) is, again, sampling. The advantage of Curves over Levels is that you are not limited to three sampling points (highlights, midtones, and shadows). You can adjust at any level with up to 16 adjustment points for each channel.

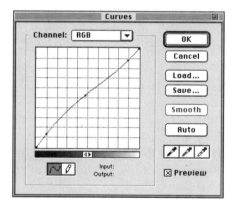

Figure 22.3 The Curves dialog facilitates very fine-grained adjustments, because you can have up to 16 adjustment points for each channel.

With the Curves dialog open, move the Eyedropper over the area of the image you'd like to correct. Hold down the mouse button, and a circle on the curve indicates what level you are pointing to. Now you know where to adjust the curve; drag to adjust. As you add points to the curve, the adjustments become finer, because the curve adjusts only between two points.

You can tell when you've gone too far adjusting a point on the curve, because you begin to lose levels, and the image starts to look posterized.

NOTE

Just as in the previous step, the adjustments for midtones are made on the composite channel to avoid introducing unwanted color casts.

Step 5: Finding Balanced Color—Take Your Pick

As with all these adjustments, it's possible to look at an image, scratch your head and say: "There's too much yellow here." But often enough, the necessary corrections are so subtle that you can't trust your own judgment. This is where the Info Palette is so useful.

As described in Step 3, you can move the Eyedropper over what should be a neutral area of color to see if it's really neutral. If one of the color values is out of line with the others, then you'll probably need to correct the color balance.

There are many situations when color casts are not unwanted. For instance, sunsets cast a distinctive red that may be the whole point of the image.

NOTE

The operative word here is balance—more of one color means less of another. This is the nature of the color wheel. It means that every balance adjustment has side effects, but it also means that you can achieve the same effect in different ways. For instance, you can increase the balance of red by adding red or by subtracting green and blue.

You can adjust the individual channels in the Levels or Curves dialog using the readouts from the Eyedropper and Info palette to guide you. If the histograms in the Levels dialog show missing pixels at either end of the scale, you can drag the input values to eliminate these and remove some color casts. For finer adjustments, pick the channel you wish to correct in the Curves dialog and use the pointer to find the level that needs adjusting. It's best to use a very gentle hand when adjusting the curves, because often a small nudge to the curve can yield less than subtle results.

But why are we using the same dialogs when there are other dialogs seemingly made for this task? Indeed, the Color Balance and Hue/Saturation commands can be used for setting overall image colors. The Color Balance command, like the Levels command, can set balance for shadows, highlights, and midtones. The Hue/Saturation command can adjust the hue, saturation, and lightness for each of the six additive and subtractive colors, plus a master setting.

Sometimes, when I have a clear idea of what correction needs to be made, it's easy to open one of these dialogs, make the change, and be done. Using them with Adjustment layers helps, too. But usually I need extra guidance, and there's more feedback available and less eyeballing necessary with the Levels and Curves dialogs.

Step 6: Sharpen the Image

We haven't discussed filters yet, but the Sharpen filter is the last step for almost every "realistic" image that you're going to print. It compensates for the imprecisions of scanning and other data acquisition methods by making the borders between adjacent color areas more distinct. The Sharpen filter is fully described in Chapter 23.

MORE ABOUT LEVELS AND CURVES

The Levels command and its associated dialog is a powerful image correction tool, providing both instant feedback and numerous adjustments. Its only limitation is that adjustments can be applied only to highlights, shadows, and midtones.

The Curves command is equally powerful—more flexible than the Levels command, but without any direct quantitative image feedback. It does, however, provide a mechanism for locating the value of image pixels on the Curves display.

There are several properties that these dialogs share.

To select a channel:

- Choose a channel from the Channel dropdown menu. There is a listing for each color channel, including the composite channel, which is the default display.

- To work on a combination of channels, select them in the Channels Palette first, then open the Levels or Curves dialog. The combination channel will be displayed by first letter abbreviation, CM for Cyan and Magenta, and so on. The single channels you've selected along with their composite are available from the Channel dropdown menu.

If you have a source of images that needs the same corrections every time, or if you have created an effect that you would like to reuse, it's possible to save all the current settings of the Levels or Curves dialog as a file and reload them into other images.

To save and load Levels or Curves settings:

- Click on the **Save** button, choose a location in the standard file dialog, name the file, and click **Save**.
- Click on the **Load** button. Find the setting file using the standard file dialog and click **OK**. The file values are loaded into the dialog. Any previously set values are overwritten.

To Auto Adjust levels:

- Choose **Auto Adjust** from the Image Adjust submenu, or
- Click on the **Auto** button in the Levels or Curves dialog.

Photoshop will redistribute the pixel values so that they fall within the default clipping range of .05% black and .05% white. Pixels with values outside this range are adjusted inward on the histogram. This is referred to as clipping, because the extreme values are lost.

To change the Auto Adjust range:

1. Hold down the **Option** key (Macintosh) or **Alt** key (Windows) while the Levels or Curves dialog is open. The Auto button changes to Options.
2. Click the **Options** button.
3. Change the Black Clip and White Clip values (see Figure 22.4), then click **OK**. These values will be used the next time you choose Auto Levels.

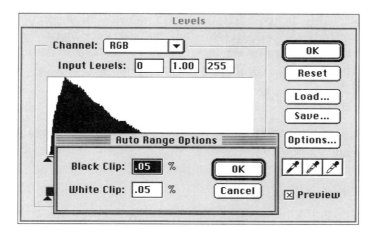

Figure 22.4 The Auto Adjust Range dialog. These variables determine the percent of values that the Auto Levels command will remap inwards on the Levels scale.

As an alternative to the Auto Adjust command, you can set the range of clipping as target values instead of as a percent of pixels.

To use the Eyedroppers to set target values:

1. Double-click on the **Eyedropper** tool (i) in the Toolbox. From the Sample Size pop-up menu in the Options Palette, select the **3 x 3 Average**. This will allow you to set target values from a true sample rather than a single pixel value.

2. Open either the Levels or Curves dialog from the Image Adjust submenu or the Adjustment layers dialog.

3. Double-click on one of the three Eyedroppers—white to set highlights, black to set shadows, or gray to set midtones.

4. In the Color Picker, enter the target values. The *Photoshop User Guide* recommends 4% gray for white and 96% gray for black, but this value will vary depending on the image, as described above.

5. With the targets set, click in the area of the image you want to map to the target. Pixels in the area are mapped to the new value, and other pixels are redistributed proportionally.

To preview adjustments, click on the **Preview** check box to preview adjustments as they are made.

LEVELS

The Levels dialog displays histograms for each color channel and lets you adjust the brightness, contrast, and gamma, using sliders or by setting target values. The plot of pixels by values in the histogram gives a quantitative view of the image—the number of pixels for each of the 256 values (0-255) for each 8-bit channel.

To use the Levels dialog:

- Choose the **Levels** command from the Image Adjust submenu, or
- Choose the **New Adjustment Layer** command in the Layers palette menu, and select **Levels** from the Type dropdown menu. (Adjustment layers are described in Chapter 15.)

If there are not enough pixels at either end of the histogram, or the distribution of pixels is too heavily weighted to one side, then the image is likely to need color or tonal adjustment.

To make tonal adjustments using the Levels sliders, use the two adjustment areas in the Levels dialog, shown in Figure 22.5.

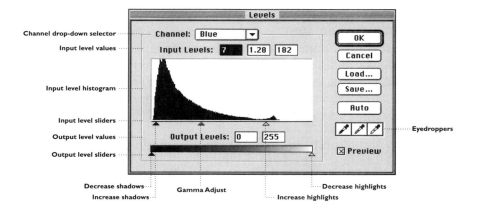

Figure 22.5 A diagram of the Levels dialog.

The top portion contains a histogram of Input Levels with three sliders to adjust contrast—black for shadows, gray for midtones, and white for highlights. There are corresponding input boxes that give the position of the sliders on the scale, or where you can enter values to adjust the sliders.

On the bottom is an Output Levels slider with two adjustment handles and two corresponding data boxes. There is no midtone adjustment. The Output slider is the inverse of the Input slider.

Changing the position of a slider remaps the pixels that fall outside the range of the new position. For instance, to increase image contrast, drag the black input slider to a value higher than 0, say 20. All pixels with values less than 20 are remapped to 0. This deepens the shadows. Increasing the black output slider lightens shadows. Decreasing the white input slider lightens highlights, while decreasing the white output slider deepens the highlights.

Identifying tonal extremes using Threshold Mode

Threshold mode lets you identify the areas of an image that are out of the range of the current settings and will be clipped to pure white or pure black. Why this feature is hidden so that you need to read the manual to find it, I cannot tell. It doesn't seem dangerous in any way, yet there is no Threshold button or command. Threshold mode is only available by holding down the **Option/Alt** key while you adjust the Levels sliders.

1. With the Levels dialog open, pick a channel or use the composite channel.
2. Hold down the **Option** key (Macintosh) or **Alt** key (Windows).
3. Drag either the white or black input levels triangle.

As you drag, the image changes to a high-contrast preview with clipped areas in white or black. As you drag to the center of the levels scale, more areas will be clipped. When you release the mouse button, the image reverts to normal mode.

 The Preview check box must be deselected before using Threshold mode, and Threshold mode can only be used with RGB images.

N O T E

CURVES

To use the Curves dialog:

- Choose the **Curves** command from the Image Adjust submenu.
- Choose the **New Adjustment Layer** command in the Layers Palette menu, and select **Curves** from the Type dropdown menu. (Adjustment Layers are described in Chapter 15.)

Figure 22.6 shows the Curves dialog.

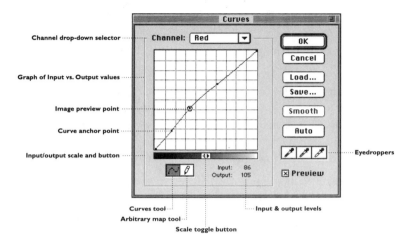

Figure 22.6 The Curves dialog with the finer grid chosen and several anchor points in use. The circled point corresponds to the value of the pixel you have selected with the eyedropper.

The Curves dialog charts the change in input versus output pixel values. Input values are those of the image upon opening the Curves dialog. Output values are those that will become effective after closing the Curves dialog. Since no values are changed when the dialog is open, input and output values are equal and the curve is a diagonal line.

The x-axis of the graph is for input levels—the original brightness values of the image pixels. The y-axis is for output levels—the changed brightness values. Shadows are represented at the lower-left side of the line, midtones in the middle, and highlights to the upper right. The values for RGB images range from 0, black, to 255, white, while for CMYK the values range from 0, black, to 100%, white. However, you can toggle between values and percents by clicking on the center of the input/output scale beneath the graph.

Making adjustment Curves

The curve is a terribly abstract representation of your image. How do the two relate?

To make adjustments using anchored Curves:

1. With the Curves dialog open and the correct channel selected, move the pointer into the image and hold down the mouse button. The value of the pixel you have selected is highlighted on the curve by a circle (see Figure 22.6). This way you can identify areas of the image that need adjusting and locate the point on the curve to adjust.

2. Click on the curve at the point identified in the previous step. This creates an anchor point on the curve.

3. Drag the anchor point to adjust the image. The curve bends to make the adjustment a gradual change across the image. Make sure the Preview box is checked so that you can check the adjustment visually. If you drag too much, the image takes on a posterized look as the blends become too harsh.

You can limit the range of your adjustment by clicking to place anchor points on either side of an area you wish to adjust. As you drag, the curve is only adjusted between two anchor points.

As you make adjustments, other areas of the image may need to be refined. Click in the image to locate the correct point on the curve and then adjust as described above.

The most common tonal adjustment increases contrast and results in an S- or inverted S-curve.

To make adjustments using the Arbitrary map option:

1. Click on the **Arbitrary Map** tool at the bottom of the Curves dialog (the Pencil icon).

2. Click and drag in the graph to draw a curve. Hold down the **Shift** key to constrain the curve to a straight line between the points you click.

3. If you wish, click on the **Smooth** button to smooth the curve.

You can estimate a curve very quickly using the Arbitrary Map tool and then fine tune the curve by dragging the anchor points. You can also create discontinuous curves for very striking effects. But don't create any striking effects unless you have a good reason. The glut of images trying to wow the senses makes them all look rather dull.

MORE GENERAL COLOR CORRECTION TOOLS

There are other tone and color correction commands. As mentioned above, it's not that the Color Balance, Hue/Saturation, and Brightness/Contrast dialogs aren't useful, it's just that they are for the most part superseded by the Levels and Curves dialogs. All five dialogs are available from the Levels Adjust sub-menu or as Adjustment Layers. There is also one more adjustment tool discussed in this section, Variations. It can not be used as an adjustment layer.

The Color Balance Dialog

Color balance can be adjusted for shadows, midtones, or highlights by clicking on one of the radio buttons. There are three sliders that are the same for both RGB and CMYK images, (see Figure 22.7). Lab images use a and b sliders.

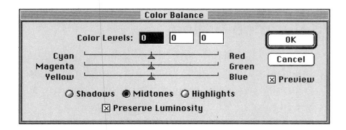

Figure 22.7 The Color Balance dialog adjusts between complimentary colors for shadows, midtones, and highlights.

The sliders use complementary colors, so that increasing the Red level decreases Magenta, and so on. The scales range from -100% to +100% and can be entered directly in the Color Levels boxes, one for each slider.

Click the **Preserve Luminosity** box to maintain the brightness values of the pixels so that adjusting color balance does not change tonal balance.

The Brightness/Contrast Dialog

This is the most general of the commands discussed in this chapter, because it affects all pixels in an image equally. You can make very quick tonal adjustments, but it is not recommended for high-resolution output. The dialog is shown in Figure 22.8.

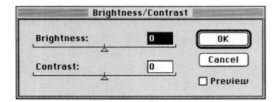

Figure 22.8 The Brightness/Contrast dialog is the most general color correction tool, since it adjusts all pixels at once.

There are two sliders, Brightness and Contrast. The dialog opens with the sliders in the middle, 0. To increase brightness or contrast, slide to the right, to decrease slide to the left. The scale is measured from -100 to +100.

The Hue/Saturation Dialog

You can adjust the color balance indirectly by adjusting the hue, saturation, and lightness. The Hue/Saturation dialog, like the Color Balance dialog, is based on the color wheel and provides somewhat more control for achieving correct color balance. See Figure 22.9.

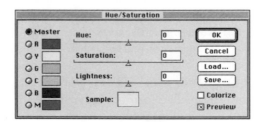

Figure 22.9 The Hue/Saturation dialog offers plenty of variation and overlap so that you can get the same result from different directions.

There are three sliders, one each for Hue, Saturation, and Lightness. Adjusting hue moves around the color wheel, while saturation adjustments move diagonally across the wheel. Lightness effects the range of the color wheel between white and black. All sliders default to 0. Hue ranges from -180 to +180 for the Master selection and from -60 to +60 for colors, while Saturation and Lightness range from -100 to +100. Why 60? Because there are 60° between each of the additive and subtractive colors on the color wheel.

The Hue/Saturation dialog gives you lots of flexibility, because you can choose from six different hues plus a Master setting to adjust all colors at once. Lab mode uses four color sliders instead of six.

1. Click on one of the radio button colors. When you pick a color, the Hue slider indicates the color at each end with a letter. So the Red slider is adjusted between M (magenta) and Y (yellow).

2. Drag the Hue slider to adjust the color component. Sliding all the way to the end brings you to the next color, so red slides to yellow or magenta. You can see that each slider overlaps the values of the next. The color swatches adjust to reflect the shade as you change sliders.

3. Drag the Saturation slider to shift the color value in or out from the center of the color wheel.

4. Drag the Lightness slider to add black or white to the color value.

If there is a particular area of the image you want to adjust, click on it and the Sample swatch in the Hue/Saturation dialog changes to the color you clicked on. This sample adjusts as you change the sliders so that you can check your progress more closely.

The Hue/Saturation dialog has an additional feature that lets you colorize grayscale images or turn color images into colorized grayscale images.

1. Click on the **Colorize** button. This converts the image to shades of red which happens to be hue 0.

2. Drag the Hue slider to the shade you want or type a number into the Hue value box.

Outside of the Hue/Saturation dialog, you can select the Desaturate command from the Image Adjust submenu, which has the same effect as setting the

Saturation slider to -100. This is like removing all color or creating a grayscale image without converting to Grayscale mode.

The Variations Dialog

The Variations dialog (Figure 22.10) is nice, because it is completely visual. There are no numeric values and no odd vocabulary to ponder. However, its strength is also its weakness. Relying on visual feedback does not guarantee the most consistent results and is less useful where precise adjustments are needed.

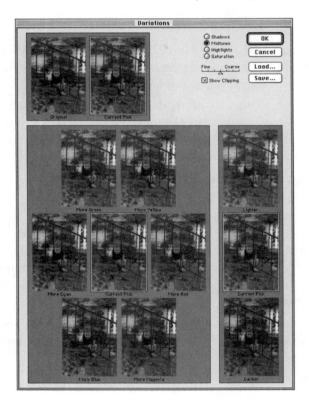

Figure 22.10 The Variations dialog: lots of choices, lots of eyeballing, but little precision.

1. Choose the **Variations** command from the Image Adjust submenu. The dialog shows a whole bunch of thumbnail variations of the original image.

- At the top are before (Original) and after (Current Pick) thumbnails, which will be identical when you first open the image.

- The largest portion of the window shows another thumbnail of the Current Pick surrounded by six thumbnail previews, one for each of the additive and subtractive colors—More Green, More Yellow, More Red, and so on.

- To the right are three thumbnails arranged vertically: Lighter, Current Pick, and Darker.

- In the upper-right corner are the dialog controls: four radio buttons for Shadows, Midtones, Highlights, and Saturation, a slider to adjust the range of variations from Fine to Coarse, and a check box to turn clipping on or off.

2. Click on one of the previews to make it the Current Pick. All the thumbnails update except the Original, which is your reference point.

3. Drag the slider to adjust the granularity of the variations in seven levels from Fine to Coarse.

4. Adjust the Midtones first, then click on the radio buttons to adjust the Shadows, Highlights, and Saturation. Saturation has only two variations, More and Less.

5. Click **OK** and the image is updated.

SPECIAL PURPOSE IMAGE COMMANDS

There are a couple of very special purpose image dialogs, Replace Color and Selective Color, plus a group of one-shot commands with few options, including Invert, Equalize, Threshold, and Posterize.

The Replace Color Dialog

The Replace Color dialog (Figure 22.11) does just what it says—replace selected colors with a new color. The replacement is subtle and can be used for some startling effects. This command is also useful if you want to change the color of an object or element within an image. It works as a kind of cross between the Color Range selection command and the Hue/Saturation dialog to make a selection mask that can be adjusted for color.

1. Choose **Replace Color** from the Levels Adjust submenu. The dialog is divided into two sections, Selection and Transform.

2. The top of the dialog lets you select the source mask and is just like the Color Range command, see Chapter 13. Sample the image using the eyedropper tools and adjust the selection mask using the Fuzziness slider.

3. The bottom of the dialog lets you set the transformation by adjusting Hue, Saturation, and Lightness sliders. There is also a Sample swatch just like the Hue/Saturation dialog discussed earlier in this chapter. Drag the sliders to set the transformation color.

4. Click **OK** to apply the color correction to the selection mask.

Figure 22.11 The Replace Color dialog is an ingenious hybrid of the Color Range command and the Hue/Saturation dialog.

The Selective Color Command

This command is a way to second guess your printer by adjusting the percentage of color and therefore the amount of ink in each of the four color separations. This is not something I have ever wanted to do, but high-end scanners and separation programs use this technique. If you know enough to know that you want to use this command, the dialog should be fairly self-explanatory.

The Invert Command

Choose **Invert** from the Image Adjust submenu and your positive image becomes a negative. This is useful if you scan a negative that you'd like to turn into a positive, or to print a negative on acetate or paper to make contact prints..The process of inversion converts the brightness value of each pixel to its inverse.

The Equalize Command

Equalize does to images what Muzak does to music; it makes it all sound the same. Specifically, the Equalize command takes the brightest and darkest pixels in the image and averages the rest of them to make an even distribution from light to dark.

The Threshold Command

Threshold in Photoshop refers to the point at which everything on one side goes to white, while everything on the other side becomes black. When converting to bitmap or high-contrast images, Photoshop uses the threshold setting to determine which pixels become black and which white.

1. Choose **Threshold** from the Image Adjust submenu. The Threshold dialog shows a histogram of pixel luminance.

2. Drag the slider to set the threshold or type a number into the Threshold Level box. You can use the Threshold command in conjunction with the Histogram to find the mean luminance value of the image.

3. Click **OK**.

The Posterize Command

Posterizing is usually used with grayscale images to reduce the number of brightness values and create high-contrast effects. It can also be used with color images to create more interesting effects or to reduce the size of an image by reducing the number of colors for creating Web-based images.

1. Choose the **Posterize** command from the Image Adjust submenu. The Posterize dialog has only a single option.
2. Type in a number of levels. This determines how many levels of gray will be included in the image.
3. Click **OK**.

Lesson 22: The Eye of the Beholder

Making tonal and color corrections requires shrewdness and patience. It also requires experience to be able to judge the suitability of an on-screen image for four-color printing or other output processes. This is true even when you have a perfectly calibrated and synchronized monitor and printer. There is no substitute for a thorough knowledge of the variability of your system environment.

With these sobering thoughts in mind, we will dash headlong into the Image menu. We will use the measurable qualities of the image as much as possible to "improve" the way our picture looks. As you follow along in this lesson, realize that your image ideals may be, and probably should be, different from mine. So use this lesson as a starting point, as a way to gain familiarity with Photoshop's Image controls so that you can apply them to achieve your own standards.

A JAUNDICED SCAN

I doesn't matter how it happens—a poorly exposed photograph, a careless one-hour processor, or an old, poorly maintained scanner. There are lots of ways to acquire a badly balanced image. I just happen to have one for us to practice with.

NOTE

While Photoshop can rescue many substandard images, its best to start with a high-quality photograph or scan.

1. Open the file **GUTHRIEO.PSD** from the Lesson22 folder on the CD. It's a nicely composed photograph of Guthrie when he was a plump toddler. Too bad it's so dark and jaundiced (see Figure 22.12). The yellow cast alone spoils this snapshot. Where do we begin? We should already have calibrated our system. Step 2 is to check the scan.

Figure 22.12 Even though the yellow cast is not discernible in this screen shot, the overly dark tonal range is evident.

2. Choose **Histogram** from the Image menu. The histogram (Figure 22.13) for Luminosity shows a distinct tilt towards the black end of the spectrum. This confirms our first visual impression—this is a low-key image.

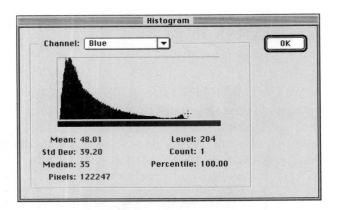

Figure 22.13 A Histogram for the Blue channel of our photograph. There is no blue information beyond level 204, where the pointer shows the last blue pixel, and most of the blue pixels are concentrated at the other end.

We'll adjust the highlights and shadows using the Levels sliders. Instead of invoking the Levels command from the Image menu, we'll use Adjustment layers so that we can review our steps and fine tune them.

We'll also want to gather as much quantitative information from the image as we can, so get ready by double-clicking on the Eyedropper tool to open the Options palette. Set the Sample Size to 3 by 3 Average in the dropdown box. Then make sure that the Info palette is open with its default options set to actual color on the left and CMYK on the right.

3. Open the Layers palette and choose **New Adjustment Layer** from the palette menu. Choose **Levels** from the Type dropdown menu, then click **OK**.

4. In the Levels dialog (Figure 22.14), click on the **Auto** button to see what it does. A visual inspection of Guthrie shows that he is much less jaundiced, but still drearily dark. See Figure 22.15.

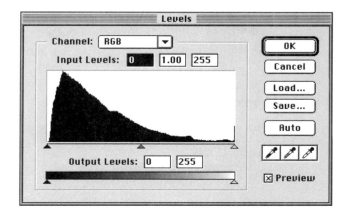

Figure 22.14 The histogram in the Levels dialog for the composite channel of our jaundiced image is not close to being evenly distributed.

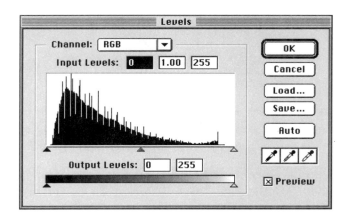

Figure 22.15 The same histogram after clicking on the **Auto** button. Photoshop has redistributed the curve.

5. Move the pointer into the image over the decorative window grating. These are supposed to be white. This is an RGB image and a quick examination of the RGB values shows that what was skewed away from blue (toward its opposite yellow, as evidenced in the CMYK values) is now more evenly distributed. But instead of a strong white, Auto Levels has produced a murtky gray. See Figure 22.

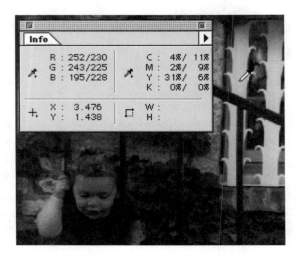

Figure 22.16 The Info palette showing information before and after invoking the Auto Levels command. With the pointer over an area that should be white, it's evident that what used to be heavily yellow is now perhaps lacking yellow.

The Auto Levels command is clearly not up to the task. It's possible that we could adjust the Auto Range options to do a much better job, but we would have to guess the correct values. We'll be better off letting Photoshop help us find the correct target values.

We know from sampling a representative white area that what should have been CMYK values very close to zero showed Yellow around 30% (see Figure 22.16.) This would make an average of the three values of 10%.

To calculate this in the RGB space, add the three original RGB values from Figure 22.16, divide by three to find the average, and then by 255 to find the percent correction. $252+243+195=690/3=230/255=.901$. We'll use 90% for our highlights correction.

When you sample in black areas, the unbalance is closer to three percent, so we'll use this amount for our shadows correction.

6. Double-click on the white Eyedropper in the Levels dialog. Set the brightness value (B) to 90% in the Color Picker, then click **OK**. See Figure 22.17.

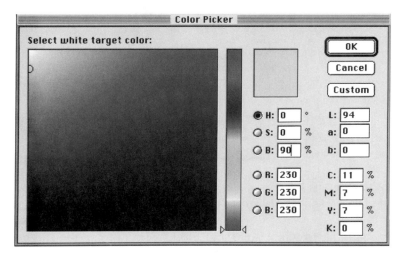

Figure 22.17 Double-click on an Eyedropper in the Levels dialog to set a target value. Here, the target highlight value is being set to a brightness setting of 90%.

7. Select the white Eyedropper in the Levels dialog, move the pointer over the decorative white window grating, and click. Photoshop proportionally adjusts the pixel values throughout the image to match the new highlight value.

8. Do the same for the shadow values. Double-click on the black Eyedropper in the Levels dialog. Set the brightness value (B) to 3% in the Color Picker, then click **OK**. The easiest black area to click on in the image is the black stripe on Guthrie's sneaker. Click on it to tell Photoshop what values to use as representative black and let Photoshop adjust all the shadow values according to the target value we set in the Color Picker. See Figure 22.18.

Figure 22.18 Sampling in the black after setting both highlight and shadow targets, we can see from the Info palette's RGB values of 4 that we are very close to achieving a good balance.

By sampling in white areas and black areas, we can see the before and after color values in the Info palette. We can also see that the image looks a lot better. The yellow cast is gone, but the contrast is still murky.

9. Drag the white triangle on the Input Levels slider to the left to lighten the highlights further. You don't want to go too far, because then you are left with large areas of "spectral white"—areas with no color information. 232 should be about the right value.

10. Examine the color channels by choosing each from the Channel dropdown box. The Red and Green histograms look pretty good, but the Blue channel looks weak. Drag the Input Levels highlight slider to the left until its at 200 (Figure 22.19). This should completely obliterate all traces of the yellow cast.

Now we can go to work on the all important midtones. We could adjust the midtone sliders, but we have no quantitative information to guide us because it's hard to know where to sample a target midtone value.

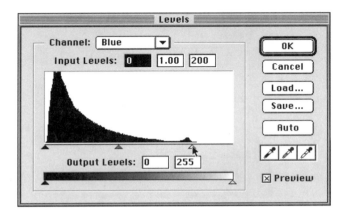

Figure 22.19 Sliding the highlight value to 200 in the Blue channel to stomp out any vestiges of the dreaded yellow cast.

11. Click **OK** to the Layers dialog to create the Adjustment layer.

12. Choose **New Adjustment Layer** from the Layers palette menu again, but this time select **Curves** from the Type dropdown.

     The Curves dialog plots the difference in pixels values before and after making curve adjustments. Since we have made none, the curve is a perfectly straight diagonal.

13. Move the pointer over Guthrie's face and hold down the mouse button to find the corresponding position on the Curves graph. As you drag the pointer around, the readout circle on the graph moves to reflect the value of the pixels you're pointing to. We can see from this that the face values lie between about 88 and 128, slightly higher in highlights and lower in shadows.

14. Move the pointer over the curve at about the 108 point for Input and Output. Drag upward to increase Midtone output values to about 128 (Figure 22.20). You can see that the image brightness perks up quite a bit with this small change.

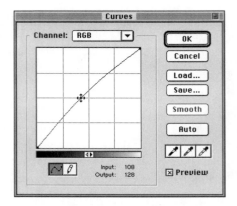

Figure 22.20 Dragging the midtone values in the Curves dialog to lighten the image overall.

Now we can increase the contrast a bit by turning this bulging curving into an s-shaped curve. First, since I like to use the finer grid in the Curves dialog, hold down the **Option/Alt** key and click on the graph.

15. Sample the stair risers which should be in shadow. The input values are around 26.

16. Move the pointer over the curve until it's at Input value 26. Drag down so the output value is back to 26. See Figure 22.21.

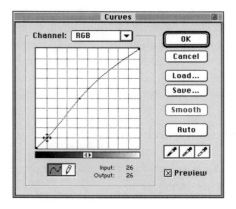

Figure 22.21 Lowering the curve values at the darker end to accentuate shadows.

17. Sample some of the worn, white-washed wall. The values average around 203. We'll lighten these pixels to help improve the overall contrast.

18. Move the pointer over the curve until it's at Input value 203. Drag the curve up to Output value 225, as shown in Figure 22.22.

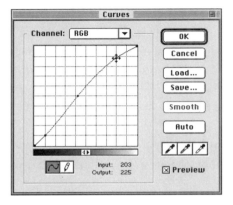

Figure 22.22 Raising the curve values in the lighter range to accentuate highlights. This completes a classic s-shaped curve that is used frequently to improve image contrast.

19. Click **OK** in the Curves dialog.

    We've lightened the midtone values overall and improved the contrast by creating and s-shaped correction curve.

20. The final adjustment we'll make is to color balance. Create a third New Adjustment Layer and choose **Color Balance** from the Type dropdown menu.

21. Sample some of the black railings. This is about as neutral as any of the colors in the image. You can see that we are still low in the blue range.

22. With Midtones selected in the Color Balance dialog, drag the Blue slider up to 20 (see Figure 22.23). The image looks distinctly cooler. We could continue adjusting the color balance for the shadows and highlights, but I'm satisfied with the image where it is. At some point, one has to trust one's visual judgment.

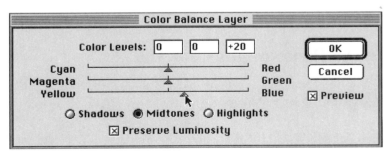

Figure 22.23 A quick fix for color balance, raising the blue values slightly in the Color Balance dialog.

We've created three adjustment layers. You can click on these layers to show and hide them and view the changes we've made from the original.

The final step for this image is to apply the Unsharp mask. We haven't discussed this filter yet, but it can be used with almost every photograph that comes out of Photoshop.

23. Click on the **Background layer** in the Layers palette. We can't apply filters to the Adjustment layers.

24. Choose **Unsharp Mask** from the Sharpen submenu in the Filters menu.

25. Specify an Amount of 150% and a Radius of 1 pixel (see Figure 22.24), then click **OK**.

Figure 22.24 These settings in the Unsharp Mask Filter dialog are pretty standard for a photograph.

At this point, our corrections are done. You can flatten the Adjustment Layers and/or save the image if you wish.

There's also a copy of the finished exercise saved in the Lesson22 folder called **GUTHERIEC.PSD**.

Making Old Photographs Look Old

We'll try one more specialized image effect, that is colorizing a black-and-white photo. This will be a quickie.

1. Open the file **GUTHERIES.PSD** from the Lesson22 folder on the CD. Here is another toddler circa 1925. Do you think we could get away with dressing Guthrie in his Grandfather's clothes?

Ignore the folds and scratches in this old photo—we're going to make it look really old by turning it into a sepiatone image. This means we have to turn this into a color image.

2. Select **RGB Color** from the Mode submenu of the Image menu. (You could also convert to CMYK if you knew the image was going to be printed using process colors.)

3. Choose **Hue/Saturation** from the Adjust submenu of the Image menu. No need to fool around with Adjustment layers this time.

4. Click in the **Colorize** check box to select it.

5. Drag the Hue slider to 20 to give the image a orangish-brown cast.

6. Drag the Saturation slider to 67 to achieve the worn sepia look. See Figure 22.25.

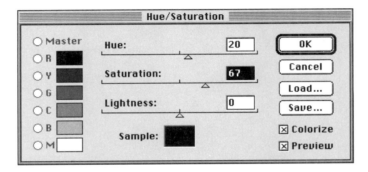

Figure 22.25 These settings in the Hue/Saturation dialog will turn pretty much any black-and-white photo into a sepiatone print. Make sure you click the **Colorize** box.

7. Click **OK**.

Save the image if you wish. There's still a lot that could be done to this photograph to remove those telltale age marks. We could also have used the Image mode command to convert this image to Duotone mode and color it that way.

CHAPTER 23

Aflutter with Filters

In this chapter…

- About filters
- Using filters
- Fade command
- Custom and 3rd party filters
- A sub-treasury of filters

ABOUT FILTERS

It seems that everyone loves filters. You can create the most eye-popping special effects with filters and you don't have to look very far to see that the graphic design world is awash in special effects.

Photoshop's plug-in architecture for filters has created a burgeoning industry in third-party filters, some of which are included on the CD with this book. (There are also several other programs, like Fractal's Painter, that can use Photoshop plug-ins.) Even the former Aldus sold filters for Photoshop, and now that Adobe has absorbed Aldus, the Aldus Gallery Effects have been absorbed into Photoshop.

Photoshop 4.0 comes with 97 filters built in. There are indispensable filters like the Unsharp Mask discussed in Chapter 22. You can blur, sharpen, add noise, or remove dust and scratches. You can create lighting effects, 3D effects, and old time effects. There is a new Watermarking filter for copyright protection. There are artistic filters, gee whiz filters, and downright silly filters.

I could write a whole book on Photoshop's filters and all the third-party filters available. You'll notice that Adobe no longer describes every filter in the Photoshop manual. (Just let the editors at MIS:Press know you're interested, and I'll make sure the book gets written!)

Figure 23.1 shows the Filter menu.

Figure 23.1 The Filter menu. Digimarc's 3rd-party plug-in is included with Photoshop, and a demo version of the KPT plug-in is included on the CD with this book.

For the purposes of this book, we will discuss the general workings and application of filters rather than discussing the details of the individual filters themselves.

USING FILTERS

Filters are used to apply effects to image layers, channels, and selections. Filters are accessed from the Filter menu and its associated submenus. There are 13 submenu categories plus the Digimarc submenu which includes the watermarking filter. I'll summarize each a little further on in this chapter.

The process of using filters is completely straightforward.

To apply a filter:

1. Make a selection or choose a target layer or channel.
2. Select a filter from one of the Filter menu's submenus.
3. The effect is either applied immediately, or a dialog allows you to set variables or choose options. Click **OK** in the dialog and the effect is applied.

A few filters, like Blur and Sharpen (Figure 23.2), have a fixed effect. You choose the command from the submenu and the effect is applied to the target layer, channel, or selection.

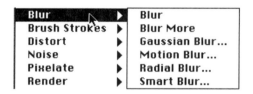

Figure 23.2 The Blur submenu includes two filters, Blur and Blur More, with no options or dialog. The effect of these two is fixed, while the rest of the Blur filters are customizable.

Most filters have variables that are set from dialogs. (You may have noticed that an ellipses after a Filter or command name indicate the presence of a dialog.) It seems that Adobe has worked hard to make sure that Filter categories, names, and variables are sufficiently descriptive that you have some idea what you're using. More helpful are the preview features of most filters.

NOTE Some filters are extremely CPU-intensive and can be slow to redraw a large image. You can test an effect more quickly by applying it to a small representative selection until you find the appropriate settings. Then you can make the overall application without too much fear of needing to undo it.

It's very useful to be able to try out various filter options and settings without waiting for the effects to be applied. For filters with dialogs, there are two preview mechanisms.

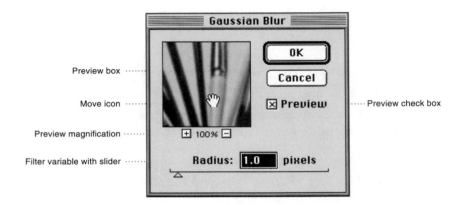

Figure 23.3 This diagram of the Gaussian Blur filter shows both preview mechanisms and a single filter variable.

The first mechanism is the Preview check box.

1. Choose a target layer or channel, or make a selection.
2. Choose a filter from one of the Filter submenus.
3. If the filter dialog has a Preview check box, select the box to preview the image in its window. When you change any of the Filter options or variables, the preview is redrawn. Leave the box unchecked if you want to speed up the process or don't need to preview the effects.

   If a flashing underscore appears under the preview check box, it means that Photoshop is calculating the effect. The flashing stops when the preview is drawn.

The second preview mechanism is the inclusion of a preview box within the filter dialog. Often, this is in addition to the Preview check box. The preview box displays part of the image within the dialog where you can view the effects of the filter at various magnifications.

1. Choose a target layer or channel, or make a selection.
2. Choose a filter from one of the Filter submenus.

   If the filter dialog has a preview box, a preview of the effect on a portion of the layer, channel, or selection will be shown in the preview box. If a flashing underscore appears under the magnification indicator of the preview box, Photoshop is calculating the effect.

3. When you change any of the options or variables in the Filter dialog, the preview box is redrawn.

4. Move the pointer into the preview box. The icon turns into a hand indicating that you can move the image within the preview box by clicking and dragging. Previewing another area causes Photoshop to recalculate and the flashing underscore will appear if it takes more than a second or two.

5. Click on the plus or minus icons under the preview box to change the magnification of the preview. The magnification factor is shown in percent between these two icons.

A Few Filter Shortcuts

It's possible to cancel a filter while it is being applied. Remember, some of them are slow.

- Press **Command-period** (Macintosh) or **Esc** (Windows).

  More often than you may care to believe, an effect is not everything you had hoped for and must be undone.

- The Undo command, **Command-z** (Macintosh) or **Ctrl-z** (Windows) will undo the effects of any single filter.

On the brighter side, you can reuse the most recently applied filter using a command key sequence.

- The top command in the Filter menu lists the name of the last used filter. Select it, **Command/Ctrl-f**, to apply the filter again using the same options and settings.

- To open the dialog of the last used filter and open its dialog, press **Command-Option-F** (Macintosh) or **Ctrl-Alt-F** (Windows).

THE FADE COMMAND

New to Photoshop 4 is a Fade command added to the Filter menu. This is a sort of after effect, because you use it to fade or blend the effects of the last filter you applied. It is also used with the Image Adjustment commands.

1. Apply a filter or Image Adjust command to a layer, channel, or selection.
2. With the same target or selection still active, choose the **Fade** command from the Filter menu, **Shift-Command/Ctrl-F**. The last used command is named in the Fade command (see Figure 23.4).

Figure 23.4 The Fade dialog uses the same Opacity slider and blend modes found in many Options palettes. You can type in a value for the slider, but you can't type a single digit to enter tens of percents.

3. In the Fade dialog, set the opacity from 0%, transparent, to 100%, opaque, which is the default. Pick a blending mode from the Blend drop-down menu. (Blending modes are described in Chapter 3.)

 Color Dodge, Color Burn, Lighten, Darken, Difference, and Exclusion modes are not available with Lab images.

NOTE

4. Select the **Preview** check box to preview the effects of the Fade command.
5. Click **OK** to apply the fade.

 Using the Undo command after executing a Fade also cancels the Filter or Image Adjustment that preceded it, even if the Fade command has been used several times in succession.

NOTE

Custom and Third-Party Filters

Photoshop's plug-in architecture has been extended across most of Adobe's product line and adopted by other software developers as well. So why not write your own custom filters to achieve exactly the effect you've been searching for?

For those of you who believe that there is a programmer buried inside just waiting for the motivational just cause to spring out, take the advice of a former programmer: forget it. The plug-in architecture is an open standard that anyone can write for or use, but it takes total dedication to become sufficiently familiar with all the variables involved to produce a few worthwhile plug-ins.

The Custom Filter

If you're still not convinced, then the Custom filter (Figure 23.5) is for you. This one is down at the bottom of the Filter list in the Other submenu. The Custom filter has a 5 by 5 matrix of blank squares that you type a brightness value into, from -999 to 999. The center square is the current pixel and the squares around it represent the adjacent pixels. Use the Save and Load buttons to save any Custom filters you become enamored of and reuse them with different images.

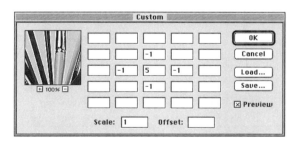

Figure 23.5 The Custom Filter is a useful tool for those dedicated few in need of true customization.

You can certainly make some interesting filters this way, but I find it nearly impossible to predict what the effect is going to be.

Third-Party Filters

If there's really an effect you need that Photoshop does not supply, then there is probably a third-party filter to do the job. There are a number of vendors producing plug-ins to Adobe's specifications. You install them into the Photoshop Plug-ins folder and they work just like any of Photoshop's built in filters. Any folder of filters in the Plug-ins folder are listed at the bottom of the Filter menu.

Creating and Using Watermarks

This third-party filter is supplied by Digimarc and comes with Photoshop 4.0. It makes it possible to affix an electronic watermark to your images so that the likelihood of copyright infringement is somewhat reduced. It seems likely that as the ease of reproducing artwork increases, so will the need for electronic watermarking.

This filter is not documented in the Photoshop manual, and even though the filter is installed with Photoshop, it is not free. You must register your personalized watermark with Digimarc (Figure 23.6) and pay for the service. (There is a three month free trial period.)

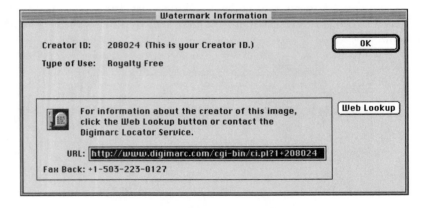

Figure 23.6 Using the Digimarc filter to read a watermark shows the creator ID, and gives you the option of obtaining more information by clicking on the Web Lookup button.

Embedding a watermark adds a hidden identification number to the image and the copyright symbol (©) to the file name (see Figure 23.7). The name change is the only clue to users that a watermark is embedded. The filter is used to read the watermark. You then have the option of connecting to Digimarc's Web site to download the watermark information.

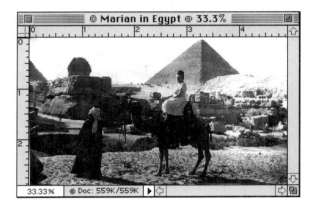

Figure 23.7 The watermark embedded in this image is not discernible except by the copyright symbol prefixing the name and in the file information box along the bottom of the image window.

A SUBTREASURY OF FILTERS

Here is a summary of the categories of filters that come with Photoshop 4.

- **Artistic** filters tend to imitate what has come to be known as "natural" media—anything that existed before digitally produced graphics. You can use these to give your work a less computer-generated look.

- **Blur** filters work the same way as the Blur tool to soften the image, but the filter automatically identify hard transitions before averaging or "blurring" pixels.

- **Brush Strokes** filters imitate a number of different brush effects that can be applied to varying degrees.

- **Distort** filters actually move pixels around to create geometrical distortions and 3D effects.

- **Noise** filters add or remove digital "noise" which is caused by having pixels of randomly distributed color levels. Add Noise is commonly used to hide unwanted effects like banding, while the Dust and Scratches filter can remove the noise-like effect of prints made from dusty negatives.

- **Pixelate** filters make pixels into clumps which can give the effect of various printing or enlarging methods.

- **Render** filters create effects with light like lens flare and lighting effects (which happens to be one of the most variable of all filters). The Clouds filter will turn any image into a cloud-filled sky.

- **Sharpen** filters, like the Blur filters, are the filter equivalent of a tool. Sharpening is achieved by increasing the contrast in adjacent pixels. The filters identify areas where there are significant color changes to apply the sharpening effect. The Unsharp Mask filter, discussed in Chapter 22, is in the Sharpen submenu.

- **Sketch** filters add another group of artistic touches, this time to a hand-drawn effect.

- **Stylize** filters, the antithesis of natural media filters, shift pixels and exaggerate contrasts to bold effect.

- **Texture** filters add texture and pattern-like effects. The Texturizer filter alone includes a number of different textures.

- **Video** filters are used for broadcast-bound images to help images conform to broadcast standards.

- **Other** filters include the already discussed Custom filter, filters that work with masks, create offsets, and emphasize highlights over shadows.

 Some filters require loading image map files to work. Create the image or texture map and save it as a standard Photoshop file, then use the **Load** button in the Filter dialog to load the file and apply the map.

Lesson 23: A Filter in Time

There is no better way to make something of nothing than with the gross application of a few filters. To be sure, filters can be used to achieve very subtle effects. We won't bother being subtle here.

ART IN THE SPOTLIGHT

1. Open the file **BRUSH_CU.TIF** from the Lesson23 folder on the CD. This file comes from PhotoDisc's Object Series. It's a nice picture, but static.

2. Open the Paths Palette. All the images in the Object Series come with clipping paths. Hold down the **Command** key (Macintosh) or **Ctrl** key (Windows) and click on the **Outline Path** in the Paths palette (Figure 23.8) to load the cup and brushes selection.

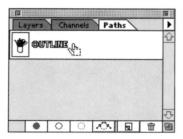

Figure 23.8 Loading a path as a selection marquee to limit the effects of a filter command.

3. Choose **Inverse** from the Select menu, **Shift-Command/Ctrl-I**, to select everything but the cup.

4. Choose the **Add Noise** filter (Figure 23.9) from the Noise submenu in the Filter menu. We'll put some texture into the background so that we have something to work with.

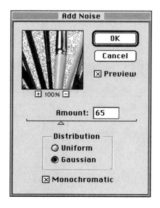

Figure 23.9 The Add Noise dialog with the settings used in this lesson.

5. In the Add Noise dialog, set the Amount to 65, click the **Gaussian** radio button, and select the **Monochromatic** check box. (The choice of Gaussian over Uniform is purely aesthetic; I prefer it. I also prefer adding monochromatic noise, because it creates a sharper contrast with the cup and brushes.) Click **OK**. See Figure 23.10 for the results.

Figure 23.10 The image after adding Gaussian noise to the background and with the selection marquee visible.

6. Choose the **Radial Blur** filter. This is one of those filters with no preview except for the conceptual Blur Center box, which can be dragged around to change the center point for the radial blur effect. However, you can test out effects fairly quickly by clicking the **Draft Quality** radio button and applying and undoing until you find a pleasing combination of settings. The one I found is a blur Amount of 16, Blur Method of Spin, and drag the Blur Center up and to the right as shown in Figure 23.11. Choose **Quality Best** and click **OK**.

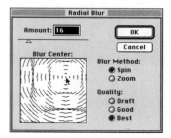

Figure 23.11 The Radial Blur filter with the settings used in this lesson. Instead of a preview box, this filter uses a conceptual preview that is used for one of the settings.

7. We've got a background with something going on (Figure 23.12), so choose **None** from the Select menu, **Command/Ctrl-d**, to drop the selection.

Figure 23.12 The image after application of a radial blur. Notice how the shadows have blurred too, because they were outside the selection.

8. Select **Lighting Effects** (Figure 23.13) from the Render submenu of the filter menu. You could spend a near lifetime trying out the variables in this dialog. You can also create a grayscale texture image as a channel. Fortunately, this is one of the few filters fully described in the Photoshop manual.

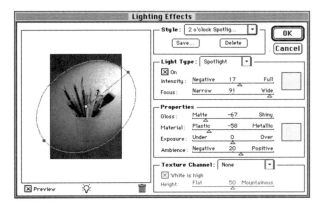

Figure 23.13 The Lighting Effects dialog has a wealth of options that make this both an extremely flexible and frustrating filter to use. Variations encourage experimentation.

9. We'll use one of the many useful presets that come with the Lighting Effects filter. After you've had a chance to enjoy this dialog's options a bit, choose **2 o'clock Spotlight** from the Style dropdown menu, and click **OK**. Figure 23.14 shows the results.

Figure 23.14 The image after adding a dramatic lighting effect.

10. Choose **Fade** from the Filter menu (Figure 23.15), **Shift-Command/Ctrl-F**. We'll use this to soften the overall effect of the lighting filter, but heighten the contrast between foreground and background.

Figure 23.15 The Fade dialog, with nothing that the various Option palettes don't have, allows post-processing to entire operations rather than pre-processing to individual tools.

11. Set the Opacity in the Fade dialog to 80% and choose **Multiply** from the Mode dropdown menu. This leaves the yellow lighting cast on the foreground and removes it from the background without removing the effect itself.

You will find a copy of the completed image saved as **SPIN_DOC.PSD** in the Lesson23 folder on the CD.

Photoshop Inside & Out

In this section...

- File work—input and output
- Making files "Web-ready"
- Printing
- Preferences, Plug-ins, and Performance

Photoshop does not exist in a vacuum. It's designed to work with different operating systems, various storage devices, and an array of output media. Much of what you do in Photoshop will be affected by these variables. Color modes, resolution, image size, file formats—it is important to understand these non-creative aspects of Photoshop so you can do your creative work with the confidence of knowing how things will turn out in the end.

When you start work on a project, you need to know where the output is going. This is common sense. Are you going to be working on a high-resolution color image that will use CMYK color separations, or is this a Web-bound graphic where a resolution of 72 dpi is all you need, but you have to conform to the limited Web color palette? Will the image be used in other programs or with other systems?

Another non-creative issue concerns the efficiency of your system and the way you use Photoshop. Photoshop has a large number of preferences options so you can configure the program to suit the way you like to work. Beyond that are issues of system configuration. There are several things you should know so that you can maximize Photoshop's performance and thus enhance your creativity.

CHAPTER

24

File Work

In this chapter...

- New images
- Opening existing files
- Importing files
- Working with Illustrator files
- Saving files
- Some words about formats
- Exporting files
- File info

Photoshop is a polyglot. It knows so many file formats that it is often used just for its file translation capabilities, and several new Web-specific formats have been added with Version 4.

Photoshop can open, import, or create files from scratch. You can scan images directly into Photoshop or capture frames from video. You can also place images saved in EPS format from Adobe Illustrator or other drawing programs into Photoshop images.

Out the back-end, Photoshop can save images for use by other programs, in other media like film and video, or for the World Wide Web.

NEW IMAGES

As we have already seen, the File New command, **Command-n** (Macintosh) or **Ctrl-n** (Windows), opens a new blank image of the size and resolution you specify. See Figure 24.1.

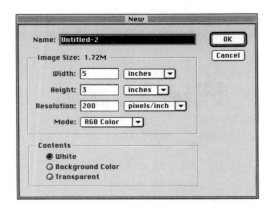

Figure 24.1 The New File dialog.

There are three distinct default settings for the New dialog. You can also type in values instead of using defaults.

To create a new image:

- Choose **File New**. The New dialog opens with default values set to match the contents of the Clipboard.

- Hold down the **Option** key (Macintosh) or **Alt** key (Windows) while choosing **File New**. The New dialog opens with the default values set to match the specifications of the previously opened image.

- With the New dialog open, choose any image from the Window menu and the default values are changed to those of the open image.

You can reset the default New values by entering them into the New dialog and then holding down the Option/Alt key. The Cancel button becomes a Reset button. Click the **Reset** button, the values are reset, and the dialog remains open to be OK'ed or canceled.

There are numerous fields in the New dialog, most with numeric fields.

- **Name**—Type in a name or use the Untitled default.
- **Image Size**—Photoshop calculates the file size for the image dimensions specified. The Image Size specifications are Width, Height, and Resolution, with a dropdown menu to specify color Mode. Type a number into the three dimension fields. Change the units from the dropdown menu next to each—Width and Height can be measured in pixels, inches, centimeters, points, and picas. Width has an additional column, units, which Photoshop calculates from the setting in the Preferences. Resolution can be pixels/inch or pixels/cm. The Modes are Bitmap, Grayscale, RGB Color, CMYK Color, and Lab Color.
- **Contents**—Photoshop needs to know what color to use for the pixels of the new image being created. There are three radio buttons: White fills the contents with White, Background Color uses the currently set Background color (the default is white), and Transparent creates a single image layer with no color values.

NOTE A transparent image has no Background layer and also cannot be saved in any but Photoshop's native format.

Click **OK** to close the New dialog, and an image window is opened to your specifications.

OPENING EXISTING FILES

Photoshop can open images saved in a wide variety of graphics file formats—around two dozen, depending on how you count them. Any of these supported formats can be read by Photoshop and opened directly as a Photoshop image. Some formats are only supported by plug-ins; these are used through the Import command, discussed later in this chapter.

Since the process of opening existing files is as much a function of the operating system as it is of Photoshop, there is a certain amount of variation among the Open dialogs. We won't dwell on operational specifics here, since you should be familiar with the file operations of the system you're using.

Existing files can be opened by double-clicking on the file icon or name (depending on the operating system) or by using the File Open command. The Open dialog will show thumbnail previews of images where available and can be set to display all files or only files in a chosen format. Photoshop can also deal with Windows files with improper extensions.

To open an existing file:

- Choose the **File Open** command and find the file you want in the Open File dialog. The exact configuration of this dialog varies with the operating system you're using.

Importing Files

Some programs force you to use separate Open and Import commands to open files in native format or other formats. Photoshop is more egalitarian and seats all supported file formats at the front of the bus. Photoshop's Import command serves a much more distinct purpose—importing data that requires preprocessing by Photoshop. This includes certain types of files and the use of scanners and frame grabbers. The processing is handled by plug-in modules. Plug-ins are installed in Photoshop's Plug-ins folder, a process that is described in Chapter 26.

To import an image:

- Choose the **Import** command from the File menu, and then choose one of the plug-in modules from the submenu.

The import plug-in modules included with Photoshop are anti-aliased PICT, PICT Resource, Quick Edit, Twain Acquire, and Twain Select. (The two PICT plug-ins are Macintosh only.)

- **Anti-aliased PICT** allows you to open files saved in the PICT format and anti-aliases them upon import.
- **PICT Resource** allows you to open the Resource fork of an application and import the resources. The PICT Resource dialog tells you how many resources the file contains, allows you to click through them in order, and includes a PICT preview to help you find the one you're looking for.
- **Quick Edit** is a shortcut method for opening and editing large files. The Quick Edit dialog allows you to preview the image and select an area of the

image for quick editing. Only the area selected is opened. You can then edit or try out techniques without waiting for the entire image to redraw.

This plug-in is meant for use with files larger than 4mb. It can read Photoshop 2.0 (Macintosh only), Scitex CT, or uncompressed TIFF files. Use the Quick Edit Save option in the File Export submenu to save changes back to the original file.

- **Twain Acquire** works with Twain-compliant scanners and frame-grabbers to create Photoshop images.

- **Twain Select** also works with Twain-compliant scanners and must be used the first time you use your scanner or to switch among multiple Twain-compliant devices.

Most scanners ship with Photoshop plug-ins, which must be copied to Photoshop's plug-ins folder. Photoshop loads these custom scanner plug-ins with the other plug-ins and adds the command to the Import submenu, as shown in Figure 24.2.

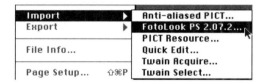

Figure 24.2 The Import submenu showing the five import plug-in modules, plus one additional plug-in for my Agfa StudioScan scanner.

WORKING WITH ILLUSTRATOR FILES

As you might have expected, Adobe has created a special relationship between Photoshop and Illustrator. Photoshop understands the Illustrator file format and can open files directly, or place or paste Illustrator artwork into open Photoshop images.

To open Illustrator artwork as a new Photoshop image:

1. Choose **File Open** and select the Illustrator artwork from the File dialog. If the file isn't listed, click **Show All Files** (Macintosh) or choose **All Formats** from the Windows File Types dropdown menu.

2. The Rasterize Generic EPS Format dialog comes up (Figure 24.3). This is similar to the New File dialog in that you can specify the size, resolution, and mode of the image. Instead of choosing background pixel color, you can select the Anti-aliased or Constrain Proportions check boxes. The former will anti-alias the imported artwork, while the latter keeps the Width and Height dimensions proportional. If you change one, the other is changed proportionally.

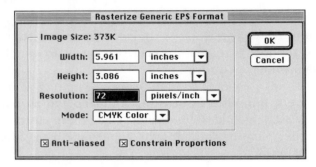

Figure 24.3 The Rasterize Generic EPS Format dialog lets you set the image size for converted Illustrator documents.

3. Click **OK** and Photoshop's built in rasterizer converts the Illustrator vectors into Photoshop pixels.

To place Illustrator artwork into a Photoshop image:

1. With a Photoshop image open, choose the **Place** command from the File menu.
2. Choose an Illustrator file and click **Place** in the standard File dialog. There are no options.
3. Photoshop rasterizes the artwork and places it as an active bounding box at the center of the image. The aspect ratio of the placed image is preserved.
4. Adjust the bounding box, if you wish. Drag the bounding box around in the image, pull or push on the border handles (hold down the **Shift** key to constrain the proportions), or rotate the box by moving the pointer outside the box and dragging in a circular motion. You can also delete the placed image at this point by hitting the **Delete** or **Esc** key.

The bounding box is the only thing that can be edited while it is active.

5. Press the **Return** key (Macintosh) or **Enter** key (Windows) to remove the bounding box. The artwork is placed as a new layer and can be edited like any Photoshop layer.

SAVING FILES

Photoshop includes three variations on the Save command in the File menu for saving your files on disk.

- **Save** saves the file in its current file format. There is no dialog unless the image is untitled and unsaved, in which case the Save As dialog is used.

- **Save As** lets you save an alternate copy of the image. The Save As dialog lets you change the name and format of the file. Choose a format from the Format dropdown menu.

You can only choose formats that support the current image features, like layers, channels, paths, grids, guides, and color mode.

- **Save a Copy** is very similar to the Save As command with the addition of two check boxes at the bottom of the dialog. Check the **Flatten Image** box to save the image without any layers. Check the **Don't Include Alpha Channels** to save only the color channels with the image. Because these two options are available, there are often fewer grayed-out formats when choosing Save a Copy instead of Save As.

Some Words about Formats

Of the many file formats supported by Photoshop (see Figure 24.4), only Photoshop's native format supports all the features of Photoshop 4.0. Other formats support some features, but for most you need to flatten the image before saving. (Table 4.1 lists file formats that support Photoshop's features. All other features require completely flattened images.) In this case, it's often wise to save a copy of the image first in Photoshop format as a backup before flattening and saving in the format you need.

Figure 24.4 The list of file format options in the Save dialog.

Table 24.1 File formats that support Photoshop's features.

File Format	Supported Features
Photoshop	Layers, Alpha channels, Paths
EPS	Clipping paths
JPEG	Paths
PICT	1 alpha channel with 32-bit option
Targa	1 alpha channel with 32-bit option
TIFF	Alpha channels
Raw	Alpha channels
Pixar	1 alpha channel
PNG	Alpha channels

Many of the formats that Photoshop recognizes and uses are platform- or application-specific; we won't discuss those here. There are several standard formats used throughout the industry and each has its own options. Web-specific formats are discussed later in this chapter.

EPS Format Options

The Encapsulated PostScript format (EPS) is an important industry standard supported by most desktop publishing and graphics programs. EPS files are easily transportable and can be used to make high-quality color separations, although this is only available for CMYK images. See Figure 24.5.

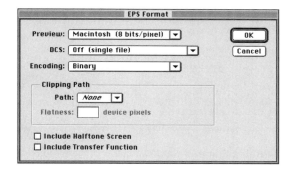

Figure 24.5 The EPS Format save dialog for a CMYK includes DCS options for Desktop Color Separations.

To save a file in EPS format, choose **Photoshop EPS** from the Format dropdown menu in the Save As or Save a Copy dialog. Click **OK** to bring up the EPS Format dialog. There are three dropdown menus for options (four for CMYK images) and two check boxes.

- **Preview**—EPS format images can be saved with a preview that can be displayed quickly in file dialogs and when the image is placed in a page layout or word processing program.

- Choose **None** from the dropdown menu if you don't want any preview. Use this if you need to save space.

- Choose one of the TIFF options, 1-bit for a black-and-white preview or 8-bit for 256 shades of color or gray, if the preview will be used with Windows.

- Choose Macintosh **1-bit**, **8-bit**, or **JPEG** (for compressed 24-bit color previews) for Macintosh-only previews. See Figure 24.6.

QuickTime must be installed to use JPEG previews.

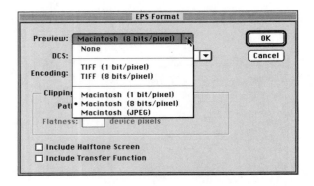

Figure 24.6 The Preview dropdown menu in the EPS Format dialog.

- **DCS**—The Desktop Color Separations format developed by Quark assures high-quality color separations by saving images as five separate files—one for each CMYK channel and a fifth master file for the composite channel. This option is only available for CMYK images.

- Off (single file) is the default.

- On (no composite PostScript) can be used if you are going directly to film from Photoshop without proofing or exporting to another program. This saves space by eliminating the fifth composite file.

- On (72 pixel/inch grayscale) saves the fifth composite file in 8-bit grayscale suitable for low-resolution proofing.

- On (72 pixel/inch color) saves a full-color composite file that can substantially increase file size, but allows accurate color proofing. See Figure 24.7.

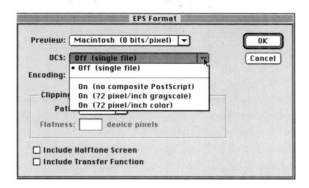

Figure 24.7 The DCS dropdown menu in the EPS Format dialog.

- **Encoding**—Photoshop supports three encoding schemes that affect the efficiency with which the image is stored, but not the image itself.
- ASCII is the most generic encoding, but it creates the largest files. It is the only encoding available for Windows.
- Binary creates more compact files that save both disk space and time when downloading an image to a printer or uploading it to the Internet.
- JPEG is an industry-standard compressed encoding that causes some image loss. The amount of image loss is inversely proportional to the resulting file size. Choose the JPEG quality level (low, medium, high, or maximum) with this in mind. Choose maximum quality if you intend to print the file. See Figure 24.8.

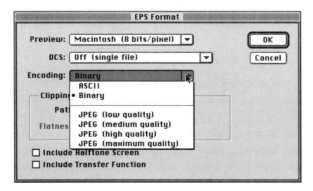

Figure 24.8 The Encoding dropdown menu in the EPS Format dialog.

NOTE

JPEG encoded files can only be printed on PostScript Level 2 printers and do not produce reliable separations.

- **Clipping Path**—Choose a path from the dropdown menu if you intend to use clipping paths with another program. Clipping paths and Flatness settings are described in Chapter 16. This option is grayed when there are no paths defined.

- **Include Halftone Screen** and **Transfer functions**—Clicking these check boxes includes any halftone or transfer function information you've defined in Photoshop for the image. These are both described in Chapter 26.

JPEG Format Options

As mentioned above, the JPEG standard can achieve remarkable image compression, but at the cost of some image loss. The greater the compression ratio, the greater the image loss or the lower the image quality. JPEG has become an important, widely-supported standard for storing Web images, where load times are often more crucial than image detail. See Figure 24.9.

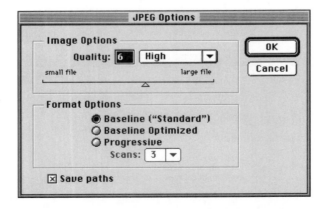

Figure 24.9 The JPEG Options dialog allows you to set the compression/quality ratio and choose a format option.

- **Image Options** gives you three ways to set the compression/quality of the image. For Quality, type in a number (0 is lowest quality, 10 highest), or pick one of four quality levels from the dropdown box. Drag the slider between small file (lowest quality/greatest compression) and large file (highest quality/poorest compression). All three settings change together.

- **Format Options** gives you three choices for the JPEG storage format. Baseline ("Standard") is the default. Choose **Baseline Optimized** for best color quality. Progressive is a Web format that allows JPEG images to load as successive overlays in Web pages. The advantage is that a rough representation of the entire image is visible before the entire image has downloaded. You can set the number of overlays as 3, 4, or 5 from the Scans dropdown box. Not all browsers support Progressive JPEG.

- **Save paths**—select this check box to save paths with the image.

TIFF Format Options

TIFF, Tag Image File Format, is perhaps the most widespread graphics file format. It generally produces more compact files than EPS format, but is considered less reliable for producing high-quality color separations. You can choose to save for IBM PC or Macintosh. (Macintoshes can read and save both formats.) You can also choose LZW compression, which compresses files without any data loss. See Figure 24.10.

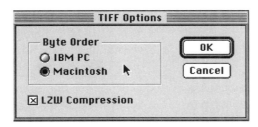

Figure 24.10 The TIFF Options dialog needs only very limited choices pertaining to platform and compression.

Portable Document Format

Adobe's Portable Document Format (PDF) allows you save electronic information, including images, as portable documents that can be viewed on any platform with the Adobe Acrobat Reader. Since Adobe makes the reader available as freeware, this is an effective way to share information without worrying about platforms and compatibility. There are no options when saving in PDF format.

Adobe is also working to make PDF a standard for Web distribution. This is discussed later in this chapter.

EXPORTING FILES

Like the Import submenu, the Export submenu contains plug-ins that allow Photoshop to post-process files upon saving. Perhaps the most important is the new GIF89a Export filter that supplements the Compuserve GIF format available in the File Save dialog's Format dropdown menu. There are only three export plug-ins, as shown in Figure 24.11.

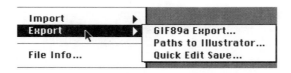

Figure 24.11 The three export plug-ins of Photoshop 4.0's File Export submenu.

- **Quick Edit Save**—The companion to the Quick Edit Open command discussed above, Quick Edit Save is used to save changes made using Quick Edit back to the original file. Even though this command is always available, it only works if you use it with a file opened in Quick Edit mode.

- **Paths to Illustrator**—Any path you define in a Photoshop image can be saved as a file in Illustrator format. The path can be used in Illustrator to create traps for placed images or as a guide for text to be placed back into Photoshop.

  The Paths to Illustrator plug-in adds a single option to the standard save file dialog, Write, and automatically appends ".ai" to the file name. The write dropdown menu lists all paths and also provides a Document Bounds option which exports the path's bounds without the path itself.

  Open the save path as a new document in Illustrator. Crop marks appear with the path to indicate the dimensions of the original image in

Photoshop and the position of the path within that image. This makes it easy to export any changes you make in Illustrator back to Photoshop, as long as you don't edit the crop marks or change the position of the path in Illustrator.

- **GIF89a Export**—Compuserve's Graphic Image Format (GIF) has become the most widely accepted graphics format on the Web. All browsers that read graphics understand GIF. It is a format that compresses without image loss, and although it was developed by Compuserve to speed the transfer of large image files over telephone lines, it is an open standard that works well for any network data transfers, including the Internet and World Wide Web.

  The GIF89a Export plug-in only works with RGB Color and Indexed Color images and it works slightly differently with each. You can also use the Compuserve GIF format in the Save dialog to convert Indexed Color images for Web use. All of these are discussed in detail in Chapter 25.

Publish/Subscribe & Object Linking and Embedding (OLE)

There are competing, platform-specific standards for copying and pasting files from one application to another with "live links." The Macintosh supports Publish and Subscribe, which requires the use of intermediate files saved using the Create Publisher command in the Edit menu. Microsoft's OLE standard is meant to be a cross-platform standard, but Photoshop only supports it in Windows. It requires that applications be OLE-compliant, both on the server and container.

In either case, by using one of these methods, you can embed a file into another application's file by creating a dynamic link. This means that as you update the shared file in the source application, it is automatically updated in the target application.

Since this is an operating system issue, we won't discuss the details of either method here. It is a useful way to place Photoshop files into word processing or page layout applications, but it does require a certain amount of processing overhead. Neither provides a particularly elegant solution. Check your system manual if you need help creating dynamic file links.

We can only hope that the availability of OpenDoc, the cross-platform, vendor-independent standard from Component Integration Laboratories, will solve the problem soon.

ADDING FILE INFORMATION

Photoshop supports the joint standard developed for use by newspapers and the international press to identify transmitted text and images.

To add file information, choose the **Info** command from the File menu. A series of dialogs allows you to specify captions, keywords, categories, credits, origination, copyright and Web address information. You can page through the File Info dialogs using the **Prev** and **Next** buttons, or select one of the dialogs from the Section dropdown menu. Each section has fields that can be filled out to identify the image completely (see Figure 24.12).

NOTE The Caption can be printed by choosing **Page Setup** from the File menu, selecting **Caption**, and printing as usual. Captions can also be used by the GIF89a Export plug-in to create a comment in the GIF header.

The information is stored with the file. Any Macintosh file format can store file information, while only Photoshop, TIFF, and JPEG formats will store file information with Windows files.

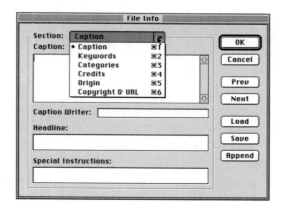

Figure 24.12 The File Info dialog showing the Caption section and the section dropdown menu.

CHAPTER 25

Making Files Web-Ready

In this chapter...

- The limitations of Web-bound graphics
- Indexed color
- GIF89a file format & export
- JPEG file format
- PNG file format
- Acrobat PDF file format

Without even trying, Photoshop has become the preeminent tool for the creation of Web graphics. Adobe didn't really have to change anything to make this happen. It just did. HTML, the language of the Web, only understands pixel-based images and Photoshop is a pixel-based program. Web browsers understand only a few file formats, and since Photoshop is built to deal with lots of file formats, it hasn't been difficult for Adobe to add the formats that were needed.

The file saving capabilities have been extended in Photoshop 4.0 to take advantage of a broader range of Web options, but the program itself was Web-ready before the Web was even invented.

THE LIMITATIONS OF WEB-BOUND GRAPHICS

Aside from the issue of file formats, which will be fully discussed later in this chapter, there are two issues to bear in mind when creating Web-bound graphics.

One is that most Web browsers (that is the people, not the programs) have systems that only support 256 colors. But since the Macintosh and Windows System palettes don't match exactly, there are only 217 colors you can be sure will display correctly on all systems. All other colors are dithered (shown as combinations of other colors) when displayed on screen.

Photoshop provides the Index Color mode so that you can limit the number of colors in an image. This not only reduces the file size, especially for larger images, but assures the accuracy of your images as they are displayed with your Web page. (Color modes are discussed in Chapter 2.)

Second, the effectiveness of a Web site is limited by bandwidth. In other words, if your graphics are too big and take too long to download, you've lost your audience. The various file compression formats available help, but limiting file size is a key design consideration.

Outside of color and file size limitations, any background or image you want to use on your Web site can be created directly in or filtered through Photoshop for proper file formatting.

There are four distinct file formats that Photoshop uses for Web-bound files:

- **GIF** is the most commonly used and supported, but provides the fewest options and features.
- **JPEG** can provide much better compression than GIF, but at the cost of some data loss.
- **PNG** is likely to become the replacement for GIF, but it is not yet fully supported.
- **PDF** provides an alternative format for images that do not conform to HTML and would be difficult to convert.

Each of these formats is described below after a discussion of Photoshop's Index Color mode.

INDEXED COLOR

The color palette of any RGB image can be reduced by using the **Indexed Color** command from the Mode submenu of the Image menu. The Indexed

Color dialog (Figure 25.1) has three options that let you control the way the color palette is reduced and the new color palette is applied to existing pixels.

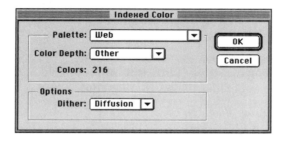

Figure 25.1 The Indexed Color dialog lets you select a color palette and direct its application on the image.

- **Palette**—Choose a palette system from the dropdown menu.
- **Exact** uses only the colors in the image for the palette and can only be used if there are already fewer than 256 colors.
- **System** (Macintosh) and **System** (Windows) use the system palette for those platforms.
- **Web** uses the 216 colors that are common to the Macintosh and Windows System palettes.
- **Uniform** uses a uniform sampling of the color spectrum to create an evenly distributed color palette.
- **Adaptive** samples the colors in the image to create a representative palette of the image colors. You can choose an area of the image to sample by making a selection.
- The **Custom** palette option brings up a dialog that lets you custom arrange the 256 colors to create your own palette. Custom palettes can be saved and loaded so that you can create many images with the same custom palette.
- **Previous** returns the palette to the previous choice and can be used to set multiple images to the same custom or adaptive palette.

While all other palettes force the image to a color system, the adaptive palette finds the 256 colors that best represent the image. However, if you try to display two images simultaneously with different adaptive palettes, an 8-bit display system won't be able to display all the colors of both palettes. Also, if the image is meant for Web use, only the 216 colors in the Web palette won't be dithered.

- **Color Depth**—Choosing one of the Palette options automatically sets the color depth to 8 bits/pixel (216 colors for Web and custom for Exact). By using the Color Depth dropdown menu with Uniform or Adaptive palettes, you can further reduce the size of the image to any setting from 8 to 3 bits per pixels.

- **Dithering**—Reducing the number of colors in an image requires color substitution or dithering. Dithering mixes pixels of available colors to simulate missing colors. There are three dithering choices:

- **None** substitutes available colors for pixels.

- **Diffusion** is the standard dithering algorithm.

- **Pattern** is only available on Macintosh systems. It adds random pixels in patterns to achieve a more even dithering in some images.

NOTE

Avoid dithering GIF images because it interferes with the GIF compression scheme.

Some Notes on Custom Color Palettes

Custom color palettes are not fixed. If you use any of the Image Adjust commands, the palette is adjusted as it would be for any image. You can use this to adjust a custom color palette and then save the palette for use with other images.

You can also edit custom color palettes directly by choosing the **Color Table** command from the Mode submenu of the Image menu. This brings up the Color Table dialog which is identical to the Custom Palette dialog. There are 256 color swatches that you can click on and edit one by one using the Photoshop color picker. You can also choose a predefined palette from the Table drop down menu. More importantly, you can Save and Load custom palettes using the buttons in the dialog (see Figure 25.2).

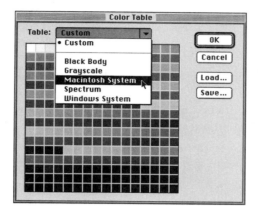

Figure 25.2 The Color Table dialog can be opened either by using the Custom Palette option in the Indexed Color dialog or by selecting the Color Table command from the Image Mode submenu.

GIF89A FILE FORMAT AND EXPORT

GIF is the most common graphics format used on the Web, and Photoshop supports the GIF89a file format in two ways. The Format option for the Save As and Save a Copy dialogs, discussed in Chapter 24, is the old method. Photoshop 4 includes a new export plug-in (Figure 25.3) that gives you additional control when saving to GIF89a format.

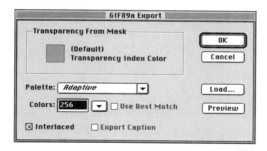

Figure 25.3 The GIF89a Export plug-in can be used to convert RGB and Index Color images for Web use. This figure shows the dialog for RGB conversion.

To Export an RGB image to GIF:

1. Choose the **GIF89a** plug-in from the Export submenu of the File menu.

2. Set the Transparency Index Color by clicking on the color square in the Transparency From Mask option. The default color is "Netscape gray." This color is used when displaying the image to simulate transparency, but is not used by browsers.

3. Choose a color palette from the dropdown menu. The choices are Exact, Adaptive, and System. These options are described above in the section on Indexed Color.

 You can also load a custom palette by clicking on the **Load** button and choosing the palette file from the file dialog.

N O T E

4. You can reduce the number of colors using the Colors dropdown arrow. This can help reduce file size, but is only significant with larger images.

5. Select the Interlaced check box to have your image load in Web browsers in successive passes.

6. If your image includes File Info, discussed in Chapter 24, select the **Export Caption** check box to have the caption information included as a comment with the GIF header.

7. To see how the image will appear in a Web browser, click on the **Preview** button. The Preview window includes Hand and Zoom tools so you can examine the image in whatever detail you wish. The window also displays the color palette in use. See Figure 25.4.

8. Click **OK** to convert and save the file.

Exporting an Indexed Color Image to GIF

The process of converting Indexed and RGB images to GIF is the same, but the dialogs and options are different. With Indexed Color images, the dialog takes the form of a preview window. It has an additional Eyedropper tool that lets you select transparency colors by sampling. (Toggle between plus-Eyedropper and minus-Eyedropper by clicking on the icon while holding down the **Option/Alt** key.)

If the image has alpha channels defined, you can select these from the Transparency From dropdown menu to be used as a transparent background. (Hold down the **Option/Alt** key to invert the transparency selection when choosing Transparency From.) See Figure 25.5.

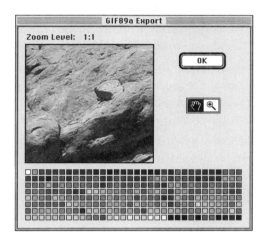

Figure 25.4 The GIF89a Export dialog preview window shows what the converted image will look like in a Web browser.

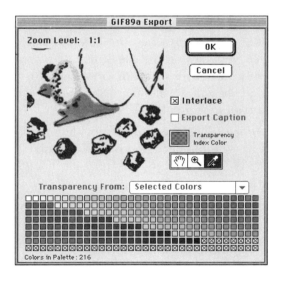

Figure 25.5 The GIF89a Export dialog for Index Color images is a preview window with an Eyedropper tool to let you sample the transparency color.

JPEG FILE FORMAT

The JPEG format has been adopted for Web use because it provides maximum compression and color fidelity. Originally supported by only a few browsers, it is now in fairly general use. (The JPEG save format is discussed in Chapter 24.) Even though JPEG achieves its impressive compression ratios at the cost of data loss, the loss is hardly noticeable at Web resolutions except at the highest compression levels.

By first converting an image to Index Color before saving in JPEG format, you can indirectly control the quality of JPEG color and reduce dithering by reducing the number of colors in an image. For continuous tone images, adaptive color provides the best color results.

While Photoshop cannot add transparency to JPEG images, several applications are available to do this, including Adobe SiteMill.

PNG FILE FORMAT

The W^3 Consortium, the official regulating body of the World Wide Web, has developed a replacement for the GIF format known as Portable Network Graphics or PNG, pronounced "ping." PNG, like GIF, compresses without data loss, but is more efficient. It also provides full grayscale alpha channel support instead of simple transparency.

PNG has been in the works for several years, but it has yet to receive widespread implementation. However, when the UNISYS corporation announced its intention to collect royalties on the use of its GIF patents, PNG received a big boost and is likely to become a major component in the palette of Web designers. If you want the full details, the PNG home page address as of this writing is **http://quest.jpl.nasa.gov/PNG/**.

It's nice to see Adobe taking the lead by providing PNG support before the format has been fully implemented across all popular Web applications. Photoshop supports PNG as one of its Save formats. The PNG Options dialog is shown in Figure 25.6.

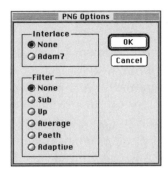

Figure 25.6 The PNG Options dialog allows you to set interlacing and choose a filtering algorithm to improve compression.

Choose **PNG** from the Format dropdown menu in the File Save As or File Save a Copy dialog. There are two options.

- **Interlace**—Like other formats, PNG images can be interlaced or not. However, the interlacing algorithm for PNG is different from all others and is known as Adam7. It provides a more meaningful interlacing that emphasizes the center pixels first, de-emphasizing edge pixels which are completed in the final drawing passes.

- **Filter**—All PNG images are compressed without data loss, but you can filter a file first to improve compression. Choose one of five filters or none. (I have no information on the advantage or disadvantage of any of these filters at this time, except that it's fine to use None.)

Netscape Version 3 does not support PNG directly, but there are many plug-ins available.

N O T E

ACROBAT PDF FILE FORMAT

Adobe developed the Portable Document Format (PDF) as a way to share complex documents across platforms without using the original application. The PDF paradigm has been extended for Web use so that you can not only upload and download PDF files, but you can also view them within your browser.

The PDF format is especially useful when you have images, text, or complex layouts that would be difficult or impossible to convert to HTML, the language of the Web. Adobe's Acrobat family of products are used to create and read PDF files, and Adobe has made the Acrobat reader free. The Acrobat plug-in available for or built into various browsers is also free.

You can save Photoshop images directly to PDF using the PDF Format in the Save As and Save a Copy dialogs, but more often you will be incorporating Photoshop images into more complex documents for saving in PDF format.

Printing

In this chapter…

- Printing in general
- Printing options
- Color separations—CMYK, duotones, etc.
- Trapping
- Spot colors

PRINTING IN GENERAL

Printing is easy. You just choose **Print** from the File menu and whatever you have on the screen comes out on the printer. Alas, the WYSIWYG (What You See Is What You Get) revolution of the '80s has not translated into WYSIWYG color printing. The reality of physics has gotten in the way. In Chapter 2, the theory of color was discussed, and it was pointed out that the process of projecting color onto monitors with light is a different kettle of fish from printing color with ink or pigments.

There are other variables to contend with as well. If the final print is coming directly off a printer connected to your computer (or at least on the same network), you've got it easy. In this case, you're most likely printing low-resolution work or proofs for higher-resolution work. If the former, go ahead and blast away. If the printed color resembles the screen color at all, you've probably done enough. In the latter case, you'll want to calibrate the printer and monitor before starting.

But Photoshop is designed to handle everything from grayscale images on simple inkjet printers to high-end color separations directly in Photoshop and even compensate for printing anomalies like dot gain and transfer functions. Still, the best policy is to work with pre-press houses and printers that keep their machines well-calibrated and clean.

There are numerous printing options, but they vary depending on the system you use and the printer you are sending the image to. There are some Photoshop-specific printing habits to keep in mind.

- Photoshop always prints images in the middle of the page. If you don't want this, paste the image into a page layout program and print from there.

- Photoshop prints faster in portrait than in landscape mode. This is a function of PostScript. To speed up printing, rotate landscape image 90° counterclockwise using the **Image Rotate Canvas** command before printing.

- Photoshop only prints visible layers and channels. You can hide/show layers and channels to change the output. If you want everything to print, use the Layers and Channels palettes to make sure nothing is hidden. Layers are discussed in Chapter 15 and channels in Chapter 17.

- You can print part of an image by first making a selection using the Rectangular Marquee tool (m) before choosing the Print command. In the Print dialog, click on the check box in the Print Range options.

PRINTING OPTIONS

There are two print-related commands in Photoshop's File menu. The Print command, **Command-p** (Macintosh) or **Ctrl-p** (Windows), brings up the print dialog that is part of your system software. We won't discuss the details of this. The other is the Page Setup command. This too varies, but the variety reflects the different capabilities of different printers. We'll discuss the options that work with most printers.

- Select the **Page Setup** command from the File menu to open the Page Setup dialog (Figure 26.1) and set printing options.

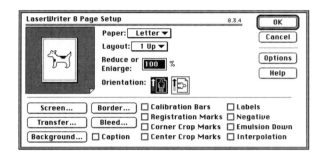

Figure 26.1 The Page Setup dialog varies depending on platform and printer. This Macintosh dialog for Laserwriters includes all standard options.

The top half of the Page Setup dialog lets you choose the paper size, layout, magnification factor, and paper orientation. This is no different from the printing functions available for any application. There is also a preview window that shows the paper orientation and printable area.

- Click on the preview area. The page preview allows you to changethe paper size and printable margins in inches. Click again to see the same information in centimeters. Click again to return to preview mode.

The bottom half of the Page Setup dialog includes additional dialogs and options.

Halftones

Click on the **Screen** button to specify the halftone screen. This brings up the Halftone Screens dialog discussed in Chapter2, and shown in Figure 26.2. Deselect the **Use Printer's Default Screen** check box, then set the screen frequency for each ink color, angle in degrees, and shape of the halftone dot. You can Save and Load settings for specific printers or types of work you use frequently. Use the **Auto** button to enter a printer resolution and halftone frequency and let Photoshop set the angles to avoid rosettes and moirés. If you're printing to a PostScript Level 2 device, select the **Use Accurate Screens** check box.

Figure 26.2 The Halftone Screens dialog with custom screen settings to match the capabilities of the printing press and the demands of the job.

Unless you are printing to a dye sublimation printer, everything you print will be composed of halftone dots. In many cases, the default halftone values work fine, especially with lower-resolution devices. For four-color process printing, your printer (the person, not the machine) may recommend halftone settings for the particular press.

 Best results are usually achieved when the image resolution is twice the halftone screen frequency. If the resolution is more than 2.5 times the frequency, Photoshop displays an annoying alert to warn of this condition.

Transfer Functions

Setting the transfer function allows you to compensate for dot gain anomalies in your imagesetter or printer. *Dot gain* is a measure of ink spread, the amount a dot of ink spreads on the paper it is applied to. See Figure 26.3.

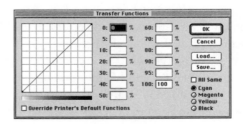

Figure 26.3 The Transfer Functions dialog is used to compensate for uneven dot gains in the printer or imagesetter.

Click the **Transfer** button in the Page Setup dialog to bring up the Transfer Functions dialog. You can adjust dot gain from -100 to +100% for every 5% of gray value in each color plate. You can also save and load transfer functions. This is a good basic way to calibrate a printer to a computer.

Background

There are situations when you don't want the area around your printed image to be white or, in the case of slides, transparent.

Click on the **Background** button in the Page Setup dialog. This brings up the Photoshop Color Picker. You can pick any color, but you probably want to make sure the color you pick is within the printable gamut. (See Chapter 14 for information on color gamuts.) The color you select will fill the remaining printable area beyond the borders of your image.

Border

You can add a black border around your image in any width you specify between 0.00 and 10.00 points. The image is unaffected by selecting this option. Figure 26.4 shows the Border dialog.

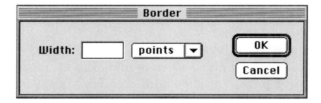

Figure 26.4 The Border dialog adds a black border around any printed image.

Click on the **Border** button. In the Border dialog, specify a width and choose the units from the dropdown bar: inches, millimeters, or points.

Bleed

The bleed dialog affects the placement of crop marks and not the image itself. See Figure 26.5.

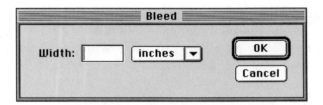

Figure 26.5 The Bleed dialog lets you set trim marks in from the outside edge of the image to create a bleed.

Click on the **Bleed** button. In the Bleed dialog, specify a Width and choose the units from the dropdown bar: inches, millimeters, or points. The Width determines the distance in from the edge of the image crop marks will be printed—the width of the bleed. You can only specify a uniform bleed of 0.00 to 0.125 inches.

Check Boxes

There are a number of different check boxes that can be selected to print various information in the borders of the printed page or that affect the way printing is executed.

- **Caption**—Check this box to print a File Info caption (see Chapter 24) with the image. Captions are printed in 9-point Helvetica and there are no options.

- **Calibration Bars**—Check this box to print an 11-step grayscale strip down the side of the page. When printing CMYK separations, a gradient tint bar is printed on the left of each CMY plate and a progressive color bar is printed on the right.

- **Registration Marks**—Check this box to print both bull's-eye and star target marks on each separation. These marks are used to align plates for printing.

- **Corner Crop Marks**—Check this box to print trim guides at the corners of the image. (Change the position of corner crop marks using the Bleed dialog as described above.)

- **Center Crop Marks**—Check this box to print centerline guides for page alignment.

- **Labels**—Check this box to print the file and channel name on the page.

- **Negative**—Check this box to print the image as a negative. This is useful when using negative film in an imagesetter. This option converts only the output and does not affect the image.

- **Emulsion Down**—Check this box when printing to an imagesetter that uses the emulsion side of the film or paper down instead of the more usual up.

- **Interpolation**—PostScript Level 2 devices can automatically resample images up to higher resolutions. This reduces the jagged appearance of some low-resolution images. This check box has no effect on Level 1 printers, but one assumes that it will work with soon-to-be-released Level 3 devices.

Figure 26.6 shows many of the check box options.

Figure 26.6 A printed page showing calibration bars, registration marks, crop marks, and label. (Carl is a good friend, so don't make fun of his nose.)

Click the **Options/Properties** button to set any additional options that may be available for your printer.

COLOR SEPARATIONS—CMYK, DUOTONE, ETC.

As discussed in Chapter 2, most color printers use the four process color inks, Cyan, Magenta, Yellow, and Black. Even color printers (as opposed to process color printing presses) usually use the CMYK process to create color output. You needn't create separations to use these printers, the composite is printed automatically.

When you send a color job to be printed on a color press, you need to create four color plates, one for each process color of ink. It's the only way a printing press can print in color. There are several ways to do this, but it all boils down to telling Photoshop to print separations as four separate pages, instead of a single-page composite image.

To create color separations, click on the **Print Separations** check box in the bottom-right corner of the Print dialog. Photoshop prints four color separations according to the options you set in the Print and Page Setup dialogs. This check box only appears when you print a CMYK image. See Figure 26.7.

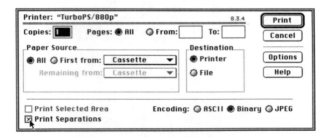

Figure 26.7 Choosing the **Print Separations** check box in the lower-right corner of the Print dialog tells Photoshop to print color separations.

You can proof separations by printing them to any printer. You don't need to print to an imagesetter or make color test prints to proof the separations themselves. However, you do need to use some sort of color proofing device to check fidelity and accuracy.

Duotones and Their Ilk

Not all separations are for color work; they are also used to print duotones, tritones, and quadtones, known collectively and confusingly as duotones. Even though it's possible to manipulate 256 shades of gray in a grayscale image, printing presses can reproduce only about 50 shades. As discussed in Chapter 2, using grayscale separations with different gray or shades of ink provides a means to increase the shading subtleties.

NOTE   Monotone images do not use separations, because they use a single ink color in place of black ink when printing.

To convert an image to a duotone:

1. Choose **Duotone** from the Mode submenu in the Image menu. The Duotone Options dialog appears, as shown in Figure 26.8.

Figure 26.8 The Duotone Options dialog lets you choose the type of duotone, set the ink color, curves, and overprint order for the duotone image.

2. Choose a type (Monotone, Duotone, Tritone, or Quadtone) from the Type dropdown menu.

3. Choose an ink color by clicking on the color square next to each ink.

4. Click on the **Curves** button next to each ink to set the adjustment curve for that ink. These are set exactly the same as the Curves in the Image Adjust submenu, discussed in Chapter 22.

5. Set the order of overprint colors by clicking on the **Overprint Colors** button. This lets you set the order in which colors are printed on the press. This can have a profound effect on the appearance of the final image.

   You can also save and load duotone settings using the Save and Load buttons in the dialog.

6. Click **OK**.

It's important that the halftone settings for duotones be set properly. Use the setting method described above. To print duotone separations, make sure the **Print Separations** check box is selected in the Print dialog.

TRAPPING

Trapping is necessary because slight misalignments in printing plates can cause a gap between inks, allowing the paper color to show through. Such misalignments can also cause inks to overlap where they shouldn't. Photoshop provides a basic trapping algorithm that follows the standard trapping rules as succinctly outlined in the *User Guide*:

- All colors spread under black.
- Lighter colors spread under darker colors.
- Yellow spreads under cyan, magenta, and black.
- Pure cyan and pure magenta spread under each other equally.

The amount of trapping can only be determined by checking with your printer (the person). Set the amount using the Trap command. Choose **Trap** from the Image menu. In the Trap dialog, set the amount of trap and choose the units: pixels, points, or mm. See Figure 26.9.

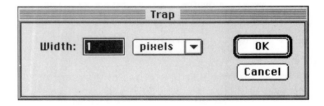

Figure 26.9 The Trap dialog lets you set the amount of trapping to apply to the image.

Trapping is used to compensate for misalignment in solid tints of CMYK. Applying trapping to continuous tone images can create unwanted side effects, like keylines and crosshairs.

N O T E

SPOT COLORS

Spot or custom colors can be used to achieve vivid printed effects. Nowhere is it written that thou shalt use only cyan, magenta, and yellow. One of the most striking things about spot color inks is that they can be out of the standard printable gamut for process colors. You can even use metallic inks.

Photoshop does not support spot colors directly, but there are two ways to use them. The simplest is to create a duotone and specify the custom color inks you wish to use. This applies the inks generally across the entire image.

To use spot colors for specific areas within an image, convert a grayscale image to CMYK and use the C, M, or Y channels for the custom ink selections. When you print separations, tell the printer which separation should be printed with which custom ink.

Preferences, Plug-ins, and Performance

In this chapter...

- Preferences
- Plug-ins
- Performance
- Color settings

PREFERENCES

The Preferences submenu in the File menu allows you to customize Photoshop through eight dialog boxes. Any change you make to preferences is stored in a file when you exit Photoshop and used every time you reopen it.

To revert to the default preferences:

- (Macintosh) Open the Preference folder in the System Folder and drag the file called **Adobe Photoshop 4.0 Prefs** file to the Trash.
- (Windows) Delete the **PHOTOS40.PSP** file in the Prefs subdirectory inside the Photoshop directory.

Photoshop creates a new preferences file the next time you start.

To view and edit the Preferences dialogs:

- Select **Preferences** from the File menu and hold down the mouse button, **Command-k** (Macintosh) or **Ctrl-k** (Windows). A list of the eight dialogs pops up. Slide the mouse over the preference dialog you wish to select and release the mouse button.
- With any Preferences dialog open, select the topmost dropdown menu and hold down the mouse button. Choose a dialog from the list and release the mouse button.
- With any Preferences dialog open, click on the **Next** or **Prev** button to step through the dialogs in order.
- With any Preferences dialog open, use **Command/Ctrl-1** through **8** to switch preference dialogs.

General Preferences

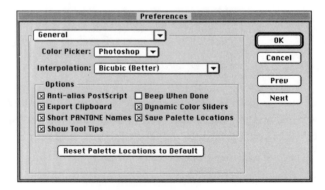

Figure 27.1 The General Preferences dialog.

Dropdown menus:

- **Color Picker**—Choose Photoshop, your System palette, or any other palette you may have installed on your system.
- **Interpolation**—This affects the way Photoshop resamples images. Nearest Neighbor is the fastest but lowest quality, Bilinear is in the middle, and Bicubic is the best but slowest. Bicubic is the default.

Options:

- **Anti-alias PostScript**—Choose this option to anti-alias PostScript files automatically as they are imported.
- **Export Clipboard**—Choose this option to have PostScript convert the contents of the Clipboard when you switch applications. If you switch frequently, this can be a time-consuming process.
- **Short PANTONE Names**—Choose this option to have Photoshop list PANTONE colors by their abbreviated names in the Custom Color dialog.
- **Show Tool Tips**—Tool tips are the helpful one-liners that pop-up when you let the pointer linger over a tool or palette for more than about a second. Deselect this box if you find the reminders annoying.
- **Beep When Done**—Select this option to have your system beep every time Photoshop completes an operation.
- **Dynamic Color Sliders**—Choose this option to have colors update dynamically as you adjust sliders.
- **Save Palette Locations**—Choose this option to have palette locations "remembered" between sessions. Deselect this option to have palettes return to the Photoshop defaults every time you restart the program.

Buttons:

- **Reset Palette Locations to Default**—Click on this button to reset the palette locations to Photoshop's defaults immediately.

Saving Files Preferences

Preferences

Saving Files ▼

Image Previews: [Always Save ▼]

     ☒ Icon
     ☒ Thumbnail
     ☐ Full Size

Append File Extension: [Never ▼]

Options
☒ 2.5 Compatibility   ☐ Save Metric Color Tags

OK   Cancel   Prev   Next

Figure 27.2   Saving Files Preferences dialog.

Dropdown menus:

- **Image Previews**—There are three types of image previews:
- Icons are the preview images created for display as desktop file icons.
- **Thumbnails** are used as image previews in file dialogs.
- **Full size previews** are 72 dpi copies of the image, and are used when importing Photoshop images into certain other applications.

Choose one of these three options from the dropdown menu. The choice applies to all previews:

- **Never Save** never makes image previews.
- **Always Save** saves the previews whose check boxes are selected.
- **Ask When Saving** presents a dialog to let you choose which previews you want saved.

NOTE

You can only save thumbnail previews for Windows, while you can also generate file icons for Windows NT 4.0 and Windows 95.

- Append File Extensions—This allows Macintosh users to generate Windows three-letter file name extensions, like .jpg for JPEG files automatically.

- **Never** does not generate extensions.

- **Always** appends extensions to every file saved.

- **Ask** lets you choose on a file-by-file basis to add extensions.

Options:

- **2.5 Compatibility**—When this option is selected, Photoshop saves additional information with the file so that it can be opened on a Macintosh using Photoshop version 2.5. Unless you know someone stuck with this antiquated version of Photoshop, better to save space and turn this option off.

- **Save Metric Color Tags**—Check this option to use EfiColor separation information for exporting images to QuarkXPress.

Display & Cursors Preferences

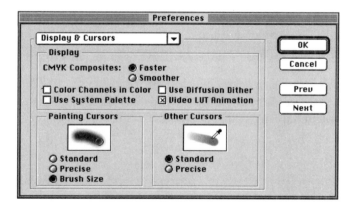

Figure 27.3 Display and Cursors Preferences dialog.

Display options (Note that none of these options affects the saved or printed image, only the display):

- **CMYK Composites**—Choose **Faster** to speed up the display of CMYK images. Choose **Smoother** to improve the display quality of CMYK images.

- **Color Channels in Color**—Check this option to display color channels in their color rather than in grayscale.

- **Use System Palette**—Check this option with displays set to less than 24-bit color to maintain color consistency between windows. When this option is not checked, Photoshop displays each image using an adaptive color scheme that can make the display background and other inactive windows appear odd.

- **Use Diffusion Dither**—Photoshop uses pattern dither by default to draw images on displays set to less than 24-bit color. Pattern dither can result in unwanted patterning effects. Diffusion dithering avoids this effect, but can cause anomalies when the screen redraws. Choose your poison.

- **Video LUT Animation**—Choose this option to allow the sliders in the various Image Adjust dialogs to update the image dynamically. This doesn't work with many Windows displays.

Cursor options:

- **Painting Cursors**—There are three cursor shapes for use with the painting tools. Click on one of the radio buttons to make a selection.

- **Standard** uses the tool icon as the cursor shape. This is the default.

- **Precise** uses a crosshairs cursor. This makes the active point more evident.

- **Brush Size** uses an outline of the brush as the cursor shape. This shows exactly where paint will be brushed.

- **Other Cursors**—All other cursors can use the standard icon-shaped cursor or the precise crosshairs cursor.

By depressing the **Caps-Lock** key, the cursor will toggle to the Precise crosshairs shape.

N O T E

Transparency and Gamut Preferences

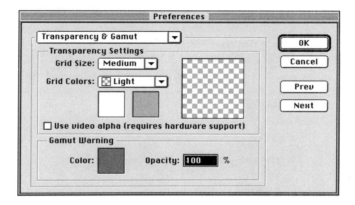

Figure 27.4 Transparency and Gamut Preferences dialog.

Transparency Setting

These **settings** affect the transparency grid that is displayed when an area of an image has no pixels:

- **Grid Size**—Choose **Small**, **Medium** (the default), **Large**, or **None** from the dropdown box. When None is chosen, no other transparency settings are available.
- **Grid Colors**—Choose **Light** (the default), **Medium**, or **Dark** gray, one of five light color tints, or **Custom** from the dropdown box. To create a custom grid, click on the color squares under the dropdown box and select colors from the color picker.
- **Use video alpha**—Check this box to use the alpha setting from your video equipment as the transparency indicator.

Gamut Warnings

- **Color**—Click on the color square to choose a color for the gamut warning from the color picker.
- **Opacity**—Set the opacity of the gamut warning color from 0-100%.

Units & Rulers Preferences

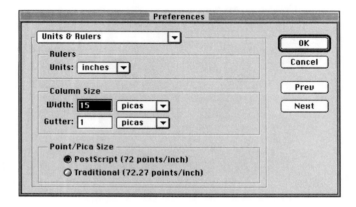

Figure 27.5 Units and Rulers Preferences dialog.

Rulers

- **Units**—From the dropdown menu choose pixels, inches, cm, points, or picas as the unit of measurement for rulers.

Column Size

This is a measurement used by some page layout programs to determine how an image spreads across columns. In Photoshop, column size is used in conjunction with the Image Size and Canvas Size commands (see Chapter 21). You can set the Width and Gutter size for columns in inches, cm, points, or picas.

Point/Pica Size

- Choose the electronic standard of 72 points to the inch or the old printers standard of 72.27 points to the inch.

Double-clicking on a ruler in any image window also opens the Units & Rulers Preferences dialog.

N O T E

Guides and Grids Preferences

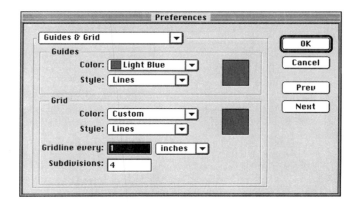

Figure 27.6 Guides and Grids Preferences dialog.

Guides

- **Color**—From the dropdown box, choose one of seven colors, light gray, black, or custom for the color of the guide lines. To set a custom color, click on the color square next to the dropdown box and choose a color from the color picker.
- **Style**—Choose **Lines** or **Dashed Lines** from the dropdown box.

Grid

- **Color**—From the dropdown box, choose one of seven colors, light gray, black, or custom for the color of the grid lines. To set a custom color, click on the color square next to the dropdown box and choose a color from the color picker.
- **Style**—Choose **Lines**, **Dashed Lines**, or **Dots** from the dropdown box.
- **Gridline every**—Set the dimension for major gridlines by pixels, inches, cm, points, or picas.
- **Subdivisions**—Set the number of subdivisions per major gridline.

Plug-ins and Scratch-Disk Preferences

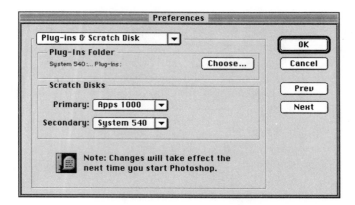

Figure 27.7 Plug-ins and Scratch Disk Preferences dialog.

Plug-In Preferences

- **Choose**—Click on this button to set the location of the Plug-ins folder. Choose your Plug-ins folder from the file dialog and Photoshop will load plug-ins from that location every time it starts.

You need to choose a location only if you move the Plug-ins folder out of Photoshop's default location.

Scratch-Disk Preferences

Photoshop uses disk space when it runs out of RAM. You can choose two disk drives for Photoshop to use. Just select one of your attached drives from the Primary and/or Secondary dropdown menus. The default is your system drive.

Unlike most preferences, these preferences do not take effect until you relaunch Photoshop.

Image Cache Preferences

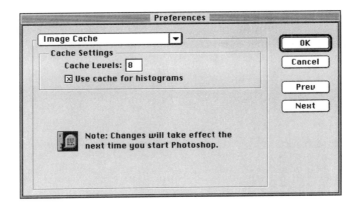

Figure 27.8 Image Cache Preferences dialog.

- **Cache Settings**—Photoshop 4 has implemented an image caching scheme to improve the redraw speed of high-resolution images. By using lower resolution versions to display the results of basic operations, such as compositing, layering, and image adjustments, redraw times are reduced. Select a Cache Level from 1-8 (4 is the default). More cache levels results in better performance, but use more memory.

- **Use cache for histograms**—Check this box to speed up the drawing of histograms.

Unlike most preferences, these preferences do not take effect until you relaunch Photoshop.

PLUG-INS

Adobe has extended the capabilities of Photoshop by providing plug-in modules and by cooperating with third-party vendors who develop additional plug-ins. Plug-ins are small programs that work with Photoshop to enhance or add specific functionality.

All plug-ins (Photoshop and third-party) are stored in the Plug-ins folder. You can change the location of this folder as described above or leave it in the default Photoshop folder. All plug-ins are loaded when you launch Photoshop, so you might want to consider creating a storage location for Plug-ins you don't use very often. This can speed the launching process slightly.

You can change the plug-in folder location by holding down the **Command-Option** keys when launching Photoshop on a Macintosh.

Once installed, plug-ins automatically appear in the correct Photoshop menu or dialog—Import, Export, Open, Save As, Save a Copy, and Filters.

PERFORMANCE

Two variables affect the performance of Photoshop more than any others: processor speed and quantity of RAM. You can buy the fastest PowerMac or Silicon Graphics machine and still not achieve blazing performance if you have insufficient RAM. Here's how to get the most out of any Photoshop platform.

RAM

As discussed in Chapter 2, Photoshop is a RAM-hungry application. First of all, 24-bit high-resolution images get big fast. Start adding layers, channels, and buffers, and you're talking about serious memory requirements. In addition to the memory it takes to store an image, Photoshop needs additional memory to manipulate the image. Some commands require two to three times the image memory to execute. Adobe recommends allotting three to five times the image size in RAM, plus 10 megabytes for application overhead. It's not unusual to see Photoshop running on machines with 128mb or more of RAM, and now you know why.

It's easy to calculate how much free RAM you'll need to achieve peak Photoshop performance. First figure out how large the images you're working on are going to be. Multiply by five and add 10 to figure your optimum RAM amount: 110mb for 20mb images, 60mb for 10mb images, 35mb for 5mb, and with 2mb images you can get away with a paltry 20mb. You'll need an additional 8-16mb of RAM for your system (more for Windows95, less for System 7), and then you need to add the memory requirements for any other applications you want to run at the same time as Photoshop.

Once you've purchased all the RAM you can afford, you need to allocate sufficient memory to Photoshop. (You can only set application partition size on Macs. Photoshop grabs 75% of available RAM on Windows machines, so you're never quite sure what partition is left over for Photoshop.)

To set application partition size (Macintosh only):

1. When Photoshop is not running, select the Photoshop application icon in the Finder.

2. Choose **Get Info** from the File menu (see Figure 27.9).

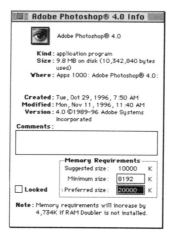

Figure 27.9 The File Info dialog (Macintosh) can be used to change the application memory allocation.

3. In the Info dialog, change the Preferred Size to the number you calculated above or to as much as you can spare for Photoshop.

4. Click the **close** box and the partition is changed.

Scratch Disks

As mentioned earlier in this chapter, when Photoshop needs to use more memory than RAM allows, it use space on disk for virtual memory. This allows Photoshop to work with larger images than you might think possible when you have memory restrictions. While Photoshop's virtual memory algorithms are relatively efficient, you will notice a big performance difference when you need to access information from disk. This is why you want to have as much RAM as possible.

You can set two scratch disks in the Scratch Disk Preferences dialog. The Primary disk should be your fastest and the secondary is available as backup if you fill the first. Since Photoshop stores information for all open images on the scratch disks, it's easy to use up lots of disk space. Adobe recommends buying a disk just to use for scratch purposes, but your investment would be better spent buying more RAM.

Even if you have enough RAM, the amount of free scratch space available must be equal to or greater than your Photoshop memory allocation. This is because Photoshop caches the contents of RAM to the scratch disk during idle time to assure good performance. It will work with less, but here again, more is better.

Keeping your drives defragmented improves their performance for all applications, especially Photoshop.

N O T E

More Virtual Memory

In addition to Photoshop's built-in virtual memory, both System 7 and Windows have their own virtual memory schemes. It's recommended that you use the Memory Control Panel in System 7 to turn off virtual memory when using Photoshop. At the same time, make sure that the Modern Memory Manager is turned on.

If you need additional memory in the form of virtual memory, use RAM Doubler from Connectix. This will improve Photoshop's performance when running with other applications. However, Photoshop's memory allocation must not exceed physical RAM.

N O T E

Virtual Memory in Windows will not affect Photoshop performance unless you have insufficient total RAM. Increasing Windows' virtual memory will help Windows operations, including printing.

Checking Efficiency

The file info box in the lower-left corner of every image window has several viewing options for checking file sizes and execution performance. The default display shows the number of bits that will be sent to a printer if you print the image, and the total file size including layers and channels. File size on disk is affected by a number of system-specific variables and is not quite the same as the print size.

Hold down the arrow next to the file size display and choose **Scratch Size**, **Efficiency**, or **Timing**.

- **Scratch Size** shows the memory required in scratch space for all open images and buffers and the total RAM available to Photoshop.
- **Efficiency** is a measure of how much processing Photoshop is doing in RAM and in virtual memory. As this number drops from 100%, (all processing in RAM) more disk-based processing is occuring.
- **Timing** is a measure of the amount of time it took Photoshop to execute the last instruction.

Additional Performance Tips

The most obvious way to improve performance is to keep your images as small as possible. Don't convert images to CMYK until you are done editing (CMYK images are about 33% larger than RGB images). Don't use extra layers or channels when you don't need them. Work at the final image size and resolution. Using the QuickEdit command can significantly increase efficiency when working with files larger than 4mb.

Experiment with a low-resolution copy of the image. By testing effects like adjustments and filters on a smaller copy, you can find exactly the combination of commands you need to execute and then repeat them on the full-size original.

Using drag and drop to make copies instead of the Cut, Copy, and Paste commands is not only faster, but it doesn't use Clipboard memory. If you need to use the Clipboard or other buffers, you can use the Purge command afterwards to free up additional RAM for image processing.

COLOR SETTINGS

In addition to the Preferences dialogs, Photoshop includes four Color Settings dialogs. These are used to set your color environment so that the color you see on screen matches the color you get from the printer. The variables in this formula include your monitor, your physical workspace, the separation type, the printing press, and the inks used by the printer.

I'll summarize the Color Settings dialogs here, because the discussion of color settings in the Photoshop *User Guide* is quite complete. I recommend reading it carefully to avoid unpleasant printing surprises.

Monitor Setup dialog

1. Choose **Monitor Setup** (see Figure 27.10) from the Color Settings submenu in the File menu. This dialog is used to tell Photoshop the Gamma, White Point, Phosphor type, and lighting conditions of your monitor.

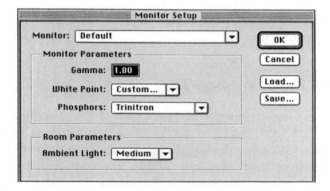

Figure 27.10: The Monitor Setup dialog.

2. Photoshop includes the parameters for most color monitors available. Choose your monitor from the Monitor dropdown menu, and the parameters are automatically set. You can customize these if you wish. Contact your manufacturer for the correct settings if your Monitor isn't listed.

3. Set the Room Parameters by choosing **Low**, **Medium**, or **High** from the Ambient Light dropdown menu. If the room lighting is brighter than the monitor, choose **High**, about the same, choose **Medium**, and if it is dimmer

than the monitor, choose **Low**.

Note that information in the Monitor Setup dialog is used by Photoshop in converting images from RGB to CMYK.

Printing Inks Setup dialog

1. Choose **Printing Inks Setup** (see Figgure 27.11) from the Color Settings submenu in the File menu. This dialog is used to set dot gain and gray balance.

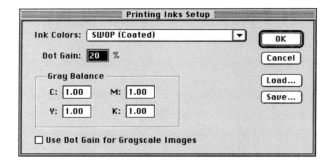

Figure 27.11: The Printing Inks Setup dialog

2. Choose one of the printers or ink types from the Ink Colors dropdown menu. Photoshop uses this choice to set a default dot gain. Test this setting by running a proof.

    Note that while ink characteristics do not vary within printer types, the dot gain can be affected by a number of variables, including paper choice. If you find that the default dot gain set by Photoshop does not match the characteristics of your printer, type in the correct dot gain in the Printing Inks Setup dialog.

3. Choose the **Use Dot Gain for Grayscale Images** check box if you want PhotoshopÕs on-screen display to reflect the dot gain setting.

Separation Setup dialog

1. Choose **Separation Setup** (see Figure 27.12) from the Color Settings submenu in the File menu. The graph in this dialog is used to calculate

the amount of ink needed to produce neutral colors in separations. In other words, given a gray level, you can see how much ink Photoshop will use in each separation to assure a neutral color. (You can see evidence of this in Lesson 14.)

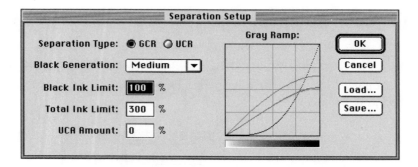

Figure 27.12: The Separation Setup dialog is interesting, but you may never need to change it.

2. GCR is the default separation type. If your printer uses UnderCover Removal, check the UCR radio button.
3. You can customize the settings, but the defaults work best in most cases.

Separation Tables dialog

1. Choose **Separation Tables** (see Figure 27.13) from the Color Settings submenu in the File menu. This dialog is used to create a color separation table or file specific to a printer. You can save and load this file for sending print jobs to different printers or presses or when using different papers or inks.

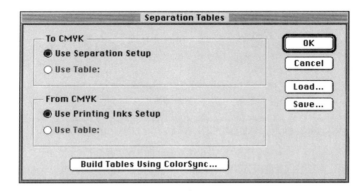

Figure 27.13: The Separation Tables dialog lets you combine the Separation and Printing Inks setups as a single file.

2   Once you have made settings in the Printer Inks and Separation Setup dialogs, you can save them using the Save button and then specify a file name and location. If you wish to reuse a previous setting, click on the **Load** button and choose the file from the file dialog.

3. If you are using a Macintosh and Apple's ColorSync Manager, you can build custom tables by clicking on the **Build Tables Using ColorSync** button.

INDEX

About the CD-ROM

About the CD-ROM

The *Hands-On Photoshop 4* CD-ROM contains sample images and demo software.

FULL-COLOR IMAGES FROM THE BOOK

All the images used in the Lesson sections of the book are located in the Lessons folder, within the Hands-On folder, on the CD. The images are saved in the PSD (Photoshop), TIFF, and EPS formats, and can be accessed by Macintosh, Windows 95, and Windows 3.1 users. Copy these files onto your hard disk and use them to practice what you learn.

Many of the images from the Chapters are also on the CD and are located in the Chapters folder, within the Hands-On folder.

A LIBRARY OF STOCK IMAGES AND PHOTOS

A wide array of stock photos and images from Digital Stock, ImageClub, MetaTools, PhotoDisc, and International Typeface Corporation.

DEMO SOFTWARE AND FILTERS

A demonstration filter from Alien Skin Software and demo software from MetaTools (Macintosh and Windows 95 only), Xaos (Macintosh only), Extensis (Macintosh and Windows 95 only), and Kudo (Macintosh and Windows 95 only).

For installation instructions, see the *ReadMe* files on the CD-ROM.